GARDENS FOR GHOSTS

The Art, Ritual, and Magick of Planting for the Dead

Christina Wilke-Burbach, PhD

Identifiers: ISBN: 979-8-9999971-2-8 (paperback)
                         979-8-9999971-4-2 (eBook)

GRAY HOUSE
PUBLISHING

grayhousepub.com

This book is dedicated to the ghost of my grandpa Joe. You inspired my passion for plants. My fondest memories of you were tending the garden, hunting for mushrooms in the woods, and beekeeping. I was present when you died, and now I caretake your grave.

Finis vitae sed non amoris.

The end of life, but not of love.

Memento Vivere, quia Memento Mori.

Remember to live, because remember you die.

In Flanders Fields
by John McCrae

In Flanders fields the poppies blow
Between the crosses, row on row,
That mark our place; and in the sky
The larks, still bravely singing, fly
Scarce heard amid the guns below.

We are the Dead. Short days ago
We lived, felt dawn, saw sunset glow,
Loved and were loved, and now we lie,
In Flanders fields.

Take up our quarrel with the foe:
To you from failing hands we throw
The torch; be yours to hold it high.
If ye break faith with us who die
We shall not sleep, though poppies grow
In Flanders fields.

Table of Contents

Introduction:
Grief is Grown. Sorrow is Sown.

The use of plants, flowers, trees, and herbs for grief, mourning, symbolism, reverence, remembrance, and commemorating the dead has been a significant practice across various cultures throughout human history. These plants are not just ornamental and for decoration. They carry stories, beliefs, energies, and emotions that help people process loss and keep memories alive. Rooted in the earth yet touched by spirit, these plants carry whispered messages across the veil. These plants serve as sacred messengers, weaving pathways between realms, bridging the land of the living and the mysteries of the dead.

In Ancient Egypt, the lotus flower symbolized the promise of rebirth; its ability to bloom from the murky and muddy waters of the Nile River made it a powerful emblem of the soul's journey into the afterlife. The Greeks and Romans planted cypress trees in cemeteries and used them during funerals—trees that, once cut, do not regenerate; thus, they are poignant symbols of loss and the finality of death. In Victorian England, the language of flowers, known as floriography, allowed mourners to communicate complex emotions through bouquets: lilies for sympathy and peace, rosemary for remembrance, and violets for faithfulness. In Japan and China, white chrysanthemums are essential to funerals and memorials, as white is the color of mourning in many East Asian cultures. This contrasts sharply with Western World associations of black as the color of mourning and grief. Across Latin America, particularly in Mexico's Día de los Muertos traditions, marigolds, "cempasúchil" are thought to guide the spirits of the dead back to their loved ones, their golden blooms and rich scent forming a vibrant bridge between worlds. After World War I, red poppies grew on the battlefields of Flanders and came to symbolize collective mourning in Europe and North America; proof that even fragile blossoms can bear the weight of a world's grief. These botanicals are embedded with spiritual meaning, cultural memory, and an enduring hope that life somehow continues, even in death.

Plants are indispensable to life on Earth, serving as the foundation of food chains and providing a rich source of both nutrition and medicinal compounds. Their aromatic and flavorful properties elevate our culinary experiences, while through photosynthesis, they continuously replenish the planet's oxygen supply. Root systems bind soil particles, preventing erosion, and their presence slows wind movement, helping to cool the atmosphere. Beyond these functions, plants create habitats and resources that support diverse wildlife and complex ecosystems, and their natural beauty enhances our surroundings, uplifting human well-being.

Plants transcend their status as mere living organisms to become vessels of energy, memory, and healing. They resonate with subtle vibrations you can feel in your hands, store echoes of past seasons in their tissues, and forge sacred connections between our inner world and the living Earth. Across cultures and eras, people have turned to plants as teachers, healers, and silent companions on the journey toward inner stillness.

At their core, plants offer a spectrum of healing properties: emotionally they calm anxiety, uplift the spirit, and soothe grief; physically they bolster immunity, aid digestion, and relieve respiratory distress; spiritually they deepen meditation, fortify faith, and clear energy blocks; magically they serve in rites of protection, purification, and intention-setting; and energetically each plant carries a unique vibration, taste profile, elemental quality (hot or cold, moist or dry), astrological association, chakra resonance, and even a masculine or feminine archetype.

This vibrational life can be measured and used. Every plant emits an electromagnetic biofield—visible in Kirlian photographs and biophoton readings—as its sap pulses through xylem and phloem. Sound experiments show that certain musical frequencies, such as 432 Hz or 528 Hz, can boost germination and growth, while gardeners report that tuned bells or wind chimes enliven foliage by mechanically stimulating cells. Flower essences—pioneered by Dr. Edward Bach—capture a plant's oscillation in water, allowing a drop of rock rose to retune our own biofields and shift mood. In vibrational healing, rose oil might be used for the heart chakra at around 528 Hz, cedarwood for the root at 256 Hz, and lavender for the crown at 963 Hz. Smudging with sage or palo santo bathes the aura in that plant's signature frequency, clearing stagnant energy. To sense these vibrations yourself, simply cradle a leaf in your palms, breathe into your hands, and feel the subtle warmth or tingling where plant energy meets your own.

Different parts of the plant bring distinct energetics: roots and rhizomes ground us and nourish the first chakra of survival; tree resins link us to ancient spiritual rites and repair emotional wounds like sacred scabs; seeds and pods spark creativity and personal power; fruits cleanse, uplift, and support lymphatic health while sweeping away limbic stagnation; flowers open the heart to unconditional love and restore emotional balance; leaves, needles, and twigs clear breath and energy channels; and trunks and heartwoods mirror our skeletal core—grounding us yet lifting our gaze skyward.

Ancient wisdom's Doctrine of Signatures teaches that a plant's form, color, or texture "signs" its use. For example, Eyebright (*Euphrasia officinalis*) has small, pale blossoms that feature a dark stripe that resembles an eye, so herbalists traditionally used it to treat eye infections. Bloodroot (*Sanguinaria canadensis*) has vivid red sap that looks like blood, which led to its use for circulatory and blood-related conditions. Mandrake (*Mandragora officinarum*) has forked, humanoid-shaped roots that suggest fertility and strength, so it was long prized as a potency tonic.

Ultimately, the spiritual essence of plants is found in their life cycle—growth, decay, and rebirth—which mirrors our own rhythms. They act as sacred messengers, offering clarity, protection, and awakening. Additionally, plants bring energetic balance to our spaces and anchor rituals of remembrance, from wildflower offerings to memorial trees. Each leaf, bloom, and drop of resin invites us into a deeper conversation with nature and the landscapes of our own souls. It is no wonder that flowers and plants have played a significant role in human health, wellness, spirituality, and ritual throughout history. They also have thousands of years of association with death and dying.

No other idea is as closely linked to death as that of a ghost. The concept of a ghost taps into deep human emotions regarding mortality, memory, and the possibility of an existence beyond death, shaping various cultural beliefs and practices surrounding death and the afterlife. A ghost is typically understood as the spirit or soul of a deceased person that has not moved on to an afterlife or has returned to the living world for some reason. Ghosts are often depicted as ethereal or shadowy figures, and their appearances can vary widely depending on cultural beliefs and individual experiences. Ghosts are often described as having a human-like appearance, though they may be translucent or shadowy or an apparition. Some cultures depict them in a more traditional form, while others view them as more abstract energies. Across cultures and spiritual traditions, the dead are not always a single category. Ghosts may be the most commonly envisioned, but they are just one thread in the tapestry of the departed.

Our beloved dead, or ancestors, are the people from whom you are descended, typically those more distant than your grandparents. Think great-grandparents, great-great-grandparents, and so on, stretching back through generations. They're your biological or cultural predecessors, and in many traditions, they're more than just names on a family tree or a link in your Ancestry DNA or 23andMe. In evolutionary terms, the word can also refer to early forms of life from which modern species evolved.

Ancestors are the roots of your lineage and cultural heritage. They're woven into your identity, carrying a spiritual and cultural essence passed down through generations, like a kind of soul-level DNA. Ancestors can include your biological forebears—distant relatives and elders, your blood and bone as well as individuals from your broader cultural and regional background with whom you share a deep connection. They are the wise ones, the keepers of memory, often seen as elders watching over their lineage.

Spiritually, ancestors can serve as guides, protectors, and sources of insight. While similar to spirit guides, ancestors differ in that they've walked the earth before you—they share your bloodline or have been bonded into your family through sacred ties. Because of this earthly experience, they often feel closer, more grounded, and intimately attuned to the human journey.

For those who are adopted or don't have direct access to their birth lineage, it's still very possible to connect with ancestors on a spiritual level. If you know your birth heritage, you can attune to the energy of those ancestral roots. But even if that information is unknown, your adoptive family can be a powerful source of ancestral connection. Being welcomed into a family, loved and raised within that lineage, is its own sacred bond.

Adoptive ancestors, or chosen family, are just as valid and meaningful. You've been brought into their fold, and that spiritual acceptance allows you to honor and work with them just as deeply as with blood relatives. Ancestors, whether biological or adoptive, recognize the sincerity of your respect, and that's the foundation for a powerful and ongoing relationship.

In many cultures, ancestors are deeply revered. They're believed to guide, protect, or influence the lives of their descendants. This reverence shows up in practices like ancestor veneration, where people honor the dead through rituals, offerings, or storytelling.

Deities are supernatural, divine beings that are worshipped or honored in various religions and mythologies around the world. They're often believed to have control or dominion over certain aspects—like the weather, love, war, or the afterlife—and are central figures in many cultural stories, folklore, and rituals. Some believe that these deities were once alive and used to be our ancestors. Different cultures have their own pantheons—collections of deities—each with unique personalities, powers, and stories. Some religions are polytheistic (believing in many gods), while others are monotheistic (believing in one supreme deity). Some of the more well-known pantheons include:

Greek Pantheon: The Olympians, led by Zeus, ruled from Mount Olympus. This pantheon includes gods like Athena (wisdom), Apollo (sun and music), and Poseidon (sea). Their myths are full of drama, love, betrayal, and epic quests.

Norse Pantheon: Centered in Asgard, the Norse gods include Odin (wisdom and war), Thor (thunder), Loki (trickster), and Freyja (love and fertility). Their stories are gritty and heroic, often ending in Ragnarok—the prophesied end of the world.

Egyptian Pantheon: Egyptian deities like Ra (sun), Osiris (afterlife), and Isis (magic and motherhood) were deeply tied to nature and the afterlife. Their gods often had animal features and were central to elaborate rituals and beliefs about death.

Celtic Pantheon: The Celtic pantheon is a rich and mysterious tapestry of deities, spirits, and mythic figures that reflect the natural world, human emotions, and the spiritual beliefs of the ancient Celtic peoples. Unlike the more centralized pantheons of Greece or Rome, the Celtic gods and goddesses varied by region, spanning Ireland, Scotland, Wales, and parts of continental Europe like Gaul. Celtic mythology is deeply tied to the land and seasons. Many deities are linked to rivers, forests, and sacred hills. The Celts also believed in the Otherworld—a mystical realm of eternal youth and beauty, accessible through burial mounds or misty lakes. Because the Celts passed down their stories orally, much of what we know comes from later Christian scribes, who sometimes altered or reinterpreted the myths.

The Tuatha Dé Danann (Ireland) are the most famous group of Celtic deities, often portrayed as powerful, semi-divine beings who came from the Otherworld. They include:

The Dagda: A father-figure and god of abundance, magic, and wisdom. He wielded a cauldron that never emptied and a harp that could control emotions.

Brigid: Goddess of healing, poetry, and smithcraft. She was so beloved that she was later syncretized into Saint Brigid in Christian tradition.

Lugh: A warrior and master of all arts, associated with oaths, kingship, and the sun.

The Morrigan: A fierce goddess of war, fate, and sovereignty, often appearing as a crow on the battlefield.

Danu: The mother goddess and namesake of the Tuatha Dé Danann.

Epona: A Gaulish goddess of horses, later adopted by the Romans.

Cernunnos: A horned god associated with nature, fertility, and animals—often depicted seated cross-legged with antlers.

Hindu Pantheon: One of the most complex and still widely practiced, it includes Brahma (creator), Vishnu (preserver), and Shiva (destroyer), along with countless other deities like Lakshmi, Saraswati, and Ganesha. Each represents cosmic principles and human qualities.

Roman Pantheon: Heavily influenced by the Greeks, Roman gods like Jupiter, Mars, and Venus mirrored their Greek counterparts but were woven into Roman civic life and politics.

Chinese Pantheon: A blend of Taoist, Buddhist, and folk traditions, this pantheon includes deities like the Jade Emperor, Guanyin (compassion), and the Eight Immortals, each with unique powers and stories.

Yoruba Pantheon (West Africa): One of the most well-known collections of African deities is the Orisha pantheon of the Yoruba people in Nigeria and neighboring countries. These deities, called Orishas, represent natural forces and human traits. These deities are still venerated today, not only in Africa but also in the Americas through religions like Santería. Some key figures include:

Eshu: The trickster and divine messenger, often compared to Hermes. He governs communication and crossroads.

Ogun: God of iron, war, and craftsmanship—patron of blacksmiths and warriors.

Shango: God of thunder and lightning, known for his fiery temper and power.

Yemoja: Mother of all Orishas, associated with rivers and fertility.

Gardens for Ghosts places the presence of deities within the domains of the dead, reflecting on how these divine figures are our ancestors and inhabit these spiritual landscapes, such as the underworld and otherworld.

There are a few other types of the dead that are not ancestors or deities. The Forgotten Dead (those lost to memory, without name or tribute, who still dwell in the liminal spaces) and The Mighty Dead (awakened and enlightened souls who mastered their paths and attained spiritual sovereignty). In general, they are influential historical and spiritual figures. Called by many names in various traditions—Saints, Bodhisattvas, Ascended Masters, and Heroes, they are great figures from the past and serve a unified role: nurturing the spiritual evolution of humanity through mystery and initiation. The concept of the mighty dead is found in various contexts. Then there are unquiet spirits—those who died violently, accidentally, unjustly, or prematurely. In many cultures, they're believed to linger due to unresolved emotions or tasks. Rituals and offerings are made to help guide them to peace. Revenants or undead beings appear in folklore as physical manifestations of the dead—often cautionary tales about improper burial rites or moral transgressions. In shamanic and animistic beliefs, there are land-bound dead—spirits tied not to families, but to places: ancient burial grounds, battlefields, or even specific trees or rivers.

Whether the dead are our ancestors, a spirit, or a deity, *Gardens for Ghosts* explores how botanical and garden design can embody our relationships with the dead, transforming grief into living, growing landscapes. Taking our sorrow and sowing it into magnificent vistas and terrains. Planting for the dead embodies the eternal rhythm of life and loss—an offering to the earth that honors the truth that we, too, belong to nature and will return to nature at our end. It is an act of remembrance and renewal, recognizing that the departed return to the soil from which all life springs....ashes to ashes, dust to dust. In each seed laid, there is both goodbye and genesis, death and rebirth.

Gardens for Ghosts presents the art of creating a garden for a loved one as a ritual. A ritual is a deliberate sequence of actions, words, and symbols performed with focused intention to mark transitions, invoke unseen forces, and transform consciousness. By bringing together a clear purpose, tangible symbols and tools—such as flowers, landscape design, and macabre accessories—a defined structure of repeated gestures, spoken invocations that call on deities or archetypal energies, and a formal closure to ground or release energy, it elevates ordinary activities into a sacred context. In doing so, rituals commemorate life's passages from birth to death, guide practitioners through psychological transformations like grief and healing, reinforce communal bonds, direct magical energies to enact change, and bridge the gap between mundane reality and the spiritual or ancestral realms.

Nothing illustrates the cycle of life and death better than plants, the seasons, and the circle of the sun. Things sprout and begin to grow and are reborn (spring). They fire up and bloom (summer) and reach completeness (late summer). They begin to wither and die (autumn). They rest (winter). Then they are reborn again in spring. These "phases" include an inherent understanding that the cycle continues endlessly, with each period of rest or winter followed by new growth, or spring. This cycle of life and death is perpetual in nature. *Gardens for Ghosts* are outdoor gardens and indoor gardens (cemetarium) for ancestor worship/veneration, for grief and loss, for spirit communication and necromancy, for offerings to underworld/chthonic deities, and for underworld deity worship. Join me on a spiritual botanical journey, where petals and leaves become conduits to the beyond, and gardens whisper the names of the dead. Together, we'll explore how the sacred language of plants can help us honor, remember, and reconnect with those who have passed.

This book offers a comprehensive journey through the rites, flora, and design of mourning landscapes, beginning with a concise history of funeral flowers and Gothic cemetery gardening born of Victorian Spiritualism. It delves into Underworld and chthonic deities from diverse cultures, then profiles the flowers, herbs, and other plants tied to death, the departed, graveyards, spirits, and deities—including those prized for their black blooms and dark foliage that define the Gothic aesthetic. You'll discover how to plan both outdoor gardens for the dead (from simple plots to elaborate park-style cemeteries), create indoor cemetariums, learn to incorporate death witchcraft and sacred earth into your plantings, and master the harvest and use of these botanicals in magick. The book also provides suggested spellwork and rituals for creating these gardens, brought to life with modern examples. This book is my legacy as a gothic gardener, a testament to the alchemy of life and death—where darkness and decay entwine with growth and renewal, crafting landscapes that mourn the past even as they celebrate life's relentless emergence.

Flowers and The Dead: Funerals and Burials

The association between flowers and the dead is at least 60,000 years old and reaches back to the time of the Neanderthals. In the 1950s, Smithsonian anthropologist Ralph Solecki and a team from Columbia University excavated a cave in Iraq known as the Shanidar cave. They unearthed the fossilized bones of eight adult and two infant Neanderthal skeletons—spanning burials from 65,000 to 35,000 years ago. Through soil testing near the burial sites, the researchers found pollen in one of the Shanidar graves and hypothesized that flowers had been buried with the Neanderthal dead. The theory is that mourners had placed flowers around each of the graves, not necessarily to honor the deceased, but most likely to mask the unpleasant scent associated with death and decay.

Embalming and preserving the body have been an evolving art and science since at least 6000 BC. Our ancestors have experimented with herbs, cedar oils, basil leaves, tree-derived resins, cinnabar, incense, tree gums, tar, potash, alcohol, and honey to preserve bodies (and most likely cover the smell as these are all highly aromatic substances). Embalming during the Middle Ages included evisceration, immersion of the body in alcohol, insertion of preservative herbs into incisions previously made in the fleshy parts of the body, and wrapping the body in tarred or waxed sheets.

Modern embalming for funeral purposes is believed to have begun in 1861 in the US Civil War, mainly due to sentimental motives; grieving families wanted their fallen soldiers returned home intact. The essential purposes of this type of embalming are the preservation of the body to permit burial after family and friends have had time to gather, mourn, and pay respects at a natural pace. Embalming also prevents the spread of infection both before and after burial. Blood is drained from the body and replaced with formaldehyde. Gases are released from the body, and internal organs are sterilized and preserved. These methods dramatically reduce unpleasant smells. Before modern embalming techniques, flowers served a purely practical purpose: masking the odors of decay and decomposition. A famous example is President Andrew Jackson. He was 78 years old when he passed away in 1845. By the time his funeral arrived, only 2 days later, his body had already begun to decompose. The odor from the sealed coffin was so overpowering that the undertaker piled a vast mound of fresh flowers on top of it, their heady perfume just strong enough to mask the smell and allow mourners to attend the service without flinching. Contemporary accounts don't record exactly which blossoms were used at his funeral. However, Victorian-era funeral florists typically used strongly scented, slow-wilting blooms such as roses, lilies, chrysanthemums, carnations, and violets. That single act underscored the vital role flowers play in funerals—not just as symbols of beauty, but as nature's own fragrant remedy. As our ancestors discovered ways to preserve the bodies of their dead, the giving of funeral flowers evolved into a way to symbolize the cycle of birth and death and to bestow a parting gift to a loved one. Even today, embalming can't completely eliminate the natural odor of a body. Generous casket sprays of fragrant blooms grew out of an age-old practice of masking that subtle smell. While surrounding floral displays now serve more decorative than practical purposes, the grand arrangement atop the coffin still honors a tradition born of both beauty and function. The common placement of flowers on top of the casket, known as a casket spray, is used both practically to mask the odor of death and sentimentally as a final tribute of love.

It's interesting to note that the origin of wedding bouquets also had to do with masking odor. Brides have carried fragrant herbs and small posies since antiquity and through the Middle Ages. In the Middle Ages, personal hygiene was still crude, and plagues were very common. The fully fledged wedding bouquet became a widespread, decorative wedding staple in the Victorian era (late 1800s to early 1900s). In Victorian Britain—especially in booming cities like London—people still had poor personal hygiene. Bathing facilities were scarce, sewage systems often non-existent or overflowing into the streets, and water supplies frequently contaminated, fueling outbreaks of cholera, typhoid, and other "filth" diseases. Many working-class homes lacked private washrooms, so people relied on chamber pots and public washhouses (the first Baths and Washhouses Acts weren't passed until 1846–47). Streets ran thick with horse dung and raw waste in open gutters until the Public Health Act of 1848 began to install proper sewers. And since the miasma theory held that foul air—rather than microbes—caused illness, efforts focused more on masking odors than on truly disinfecting water or surfaces. Flowers and bouquets helped cover body odors. So flowers with big, bold, heady aromas are perfect in gardens for ghosts!

Funeral flower arrangements vary depending on personal preferences or cultural beliefs. These are some common funeral flower arrangements:

Casket Sprays: Large, lush arrangements that rest on the casket lid.

- Styles

    - Full-couch: covers the entire closed lid

    - Half-couch: spans the lower half when the lid is open

    - Inside-lid inserts: heart-, pillow- or custom-shaped pieces tucked under the open portion

- Flowers and Greenery

    - Blooms: roses, lilies, chrysanthemums, carnations, orchids

    - Foliage: eucalyptus, ferns, salal

- Color and Symbolism

    - Pastels for gentleness

    - Reds for passion

    - Whites for peace

- Purpose: A final family tribute conveying deep respect and love

Wreaths: Circular displays on easels or laid flat by the casket or gravesite.

- Symbolism: The unbroken loop of life, death, and renewal

- Construction: Seasonal blooms (dahlias, hydrangeas, roses) woven into pine, boxwood, or ivy bases

- Custom Touch: Ribbons inscribed with a name or sentiment ("Beloved Mother," "Grandma," "Forever in Our Hearts")

Crosses: Floral shapes of the Christian cross, usually all-white (roses, chrysanthemums, gladioli).

- Symbolism: Faith, resurrection, hope in eternal life

- Variations

    - Spray-style: full coverage of blooms

    - Open-work: flowers outline the cross, leaving a negative-space interior

Sympathy Bouquets and Arrangements: Smaller hand-tied bouquets or vase designs sent to the family home.

- Purpose: A personal gesture of comfort beyond the service

- Design Tips:

    - Calming blooms like lavender, white roses, or blue delphinium

    - Include a handwritten note for extra warmth

Condolence Baskets: Wicker or painted-wood baskets delivered to the funeral home or family residence.

- Symbolism: Support from those who can't attend in person

- Typical Contents: White lilies or roses, baby's breath, greenery, sometimes a potted plant or orchid

Floral Cremation Wreaths: Wreaths or sprays designed to surround an urn at a memorial or at home.

- Placement: Around the urn's pedestal, hung behind it, or laid flat at its base

- Design Ideas:

    - Mini-wreaths (8–12") for mantles or tables

    - Rings of succulents and dried blooms for a modern, long-lasting tribute

Understanding the Meaning Behind Funeral Flowers

Red flowers are the greatest testament to love. Their bold color mirrors the intensity of feelings we hold for those we've lost, making them an ideal choice for commemorating someone who meant a lot to us. When incorporated into funeral arrangements, red roses, carnations, and geraniums powerfully convey the heartfelt love and deep respect we have for the departed.

Blue flowers emanate a sense of peace and calm. Their tranquil shades provide comfort amidst the grief, bringing solace to those in mourning. Including blue blooms, like hydrangeas, delphinium, irises, or forget-me-nots, in a funeral setting expresses our heartfelt desire for serenity and comfort for both the departed's spirit and their grieving loved ones.

The warmth of orange flowers exudes energy and strength. They symbolize the vibrant spirit of the deceased or the solid bonds we shared. By choosing orange flowers such as marigolds, gerbera daisies, or lilies for a funeral bouquet, we honor the lasting impact the individual had on our lives.

With its rich hues, purple flowers convey dignity, respect, and admiration. They resonate with sentiments of honor, reflecting a life well-lived. Funeral arrangements featuring purple flowers like irises, lavender, or lilacs serve as a tribute to the deep respect and esteem we held for the deceased.

Known for symbolizing friendship and warmth, yellow flowers bring a sense of brightness and positivity even in sorrowful times. By incorporating sunflowers, yellow roses, or daffodils in funeral arrangements, we remind ourselves of the joy the departed brought into our lives and the cherished moments we shared.

Pink flowers are all about grace, gentleness, and love. Their soft shades evoke tender feelings, making them a moving way to express our affection for those we've lost. Using pink blooms like roses, carnations, or cherry blossoms in a funeral bouquet conveys the love and gentle influence the person had on our hearts.

Green flowers embody renewal, life, and hope. They offer a soothing presence in times of grief, reminding us of life's continuous cycle. Including green flowers or foliage like Bells of Ireland, Green Chrysanthemums, Zinnias, Green Hydrangeas, Lady's Mantle, Green Orchids, and Green Hellebores (Lenten Rose) in a funeral arrangement expresses a belief in eternal life and conveys hopeful wishes for the departed's soul.

Symbolizing purity, innocence, and peace, white flowers are a common choice for funerals. Their elegant appearance embodies the peace we wish for the departed. Arrangements featuring white blooms such as lilies, roses, daisies, baby's breath, or chrysanthemums deliver messages of tranquility and sincere intentions.

Symbolism and Meaning of Common Funeral Flowers

The following flowers are commonly used in funeral flower arrangements at the time of this writing.

Daisies are synonymous with innocence and purity. Their uncomplicated beauty is particularly fitting when recalling someone who led a life of honesty and simplicity. In a funeral setting, daisies symbolize the purity of the deceased's soul, serving as a comforting reminder of their innate goodness.

Representing strength and resilience, snapdragons can symbolize the lasting spirit of the deceased or the strong bonds we shared. Including snapdragons in a funeral bouquet allows us to celebrate the person's strength and the enduring impact they left on our lives.

Tulips are often tied to love and renewal. Their vibrant colors and graceful shape make them a lovely tribute to a lost loved one. In funeral arrangements, tulips symbolize our enduring love for the deceased and our faith in life's renewal.

With their elegant beauty and lasting blooms, orchids symbolize love, beauty, and strength. Including orchids in a funeral bouquet conveys profound love and admiration for the departed's inner strength and beauty.

Gladiolus flowers reflect strength, integrity, and sincerity. Their striking presence is particularly fitting for someone who led a life marked by honor. In a funeral arrangement, gladiolus can symbolize respect for the character of the deceased and sincere condolences.

Frequently associated with purity and rebirth, calla lilies are renowned for their elegance. Their graceful appearance makes them a favored choice for funerals.

Including calla lilies in a bouquet symbolizes our wish for the deceased to find peace and renewal.

Lilies are a traditional funeral flower, symbolizing the restored innocence of the deceased's soul. Their fragrant blooms offer comfort and solace to grieving hearts, reinforcing our belief in the purity of their spirit and our desire for their eternal peace.

The iris stands for hope and faith. With their vibrant colors and intricate shapes, they make a beautiful tribute to loved ones lost. Including irises in a funeral bouquet conveys our hopeful wishes for their journey and our faith in the afterlife.

Roses

- Including red roses in a funeral arrangement expresses profound love and esteem for the departed.
- Pink roses symbolize grace, gentleness, and love.
- White roses are a staple at funerals. Their pristine color embodies the peace we wish for the departed. Arrangements featuring white roses convey tranquility, peace, and reflect our pure intentions.
- Though less commonly used, black roses signify death, farewell, and rebirth. They can strongly articulate feelings of grief and represent a symbolic farewell. Using black roses in an arrangement conveys deep sorrow and acknowledges the cycle of life and death.

After the funeral, many of these flowers are then placed at the final resting space, whether it is a grave, niche, cremation garden, or crypt. As discussed, this practice most likely began to cover up odor but has now morphed into offerings and gifts for the dead. Placing flowers on graves remains a central gesture of respect for the fallen. Tracing its roots to the dawn of civilization, the ritual of placing flowers on graves is an age-old gesture of reverence and remembrance. In ancient Greece, this tender act held a deeper meaning—flowers were laid upon resting places as symbols of peace, with the hope that blooms might spring forth if the departed had truly found peace. In Athens, the most formal occasion for grave-decorating was the annual Genesia festival. Held in the autumn, Genesia was devoted entirely to the dead: families cleaned and swept the tomb site, poured libations of wine and oil into the earth, shared a modest meal at the graveside, and placed wreaths of wild celery, parsley, or coriander atop the monument. As they placed those garlands, mourners would speak the names of the departed and offer prayers, believing that the aroma and ritual nourished the soul in its journey through Hades. Every year, the Greeks would return to ancestral plots to renew those wreaths and keep the bond between the living and the dead alive. Across ancient Egypt, water lilies were delicately laid upon tombs, embodying the soul's journey toward the afterlife. In Japan and China, chrysanthemums have long stood as quiet tributes to ancestors, blooming with reverence and remembrance. Among many Indigenous cultures in North America, wildflowers are gathered and offered in sacred connection to the spirit world. And throughout the Pacific islands—from Hawaii to Tahiti—vibrant blossoms like hibiscus and plumeria continue to grace resting places, a joyful celebration of lives once lived and still cherished.

Flowers become a visual and tangible representation of grief and a symbolic offering of love, respect, and remembrance. The short lifespan of cut fresh flowers mirrors human mortality, reminding visitors both of loss and life's renewal. People leave flowers after funerals, on death anniversaries, on birthdays, during major holidays or simply after a quiet graveside visit—anytime they wish to renew their tribute and solidify their bond to the dead. In America, the tradition of placing flowers on graves began after the Civil War, inspired by the grief over Abraham Lincoln's death, leading to the establishment of Decoration Day on May 30th. Decoration Day was set for May 30 partly because it didn't fall on any specific battle anniversary and came during the height of spring bloom, ensuring an abundance of fresh flowers for the tribute. From the start, ceremonies took on deep symbolic weight: volunteers cleaned headstones, laid roses and garlands on graves, and led solemn processions to cemeteries—each blossom expressing collective gratitude, personal remembrance, and the reaffirmation that freedom is secured through sacrifice. By the late 19th century, every Northern state observed Decoration Day, while Southern states held parallel commemorations for their Confederate dead. After World War I, the holiday expanded to honor all Americans who died in military service, and as "Memorial Day" gradually supplanted "Decoration Day" in common usage during the 1960s, Congress officially designated Memorial Day a federal holiday on the last Monday in May in 1971.

Decoration Day institutionalized the simple act of strewing fresh flowers on graves into a powerful, annual ritual. As the observance broadened after World War I and became Memorial Day, the floral custom outgrew its military origins, embedding itself in everyday mourning: from wreaths on Veterans Day to bouquets left on birthdays and anniversaries to the blossoms lovingly left after a regular graveside visit. Today's global practice of leaving flowers at a loved one's grave traces directly back to the Decoration Day tradition of honoring sacrifice with fresh blooms. At the cemeteries where I work, May is by far the busiest month of the year for visiting fallen loved ones and decorating graves. It begins with the week of Mother's Day and ends with Memorial Day weekend. I sell more flower placements during the month of May than at any other time during the rest of the year. Flowers at gravesites trace a route from prehistoric ritual to our modern acts of remembrance; the enduring human need to honor those we've loved and lost.

Gardens and the Dead: The Victorian Era

The inspiration for this book is the Victorian Era. I think it's really important to understand the Victorian Era, death culture, and the relationship between gardens and the dead that emerged during this time frame to comprehend gardening *for* the dead. The Victorian Era refers to the period of Queen Victoria's reign in England from 1837 to 1901. During the late 1800s, Victorian society was deeply preoccupied with death to the point of obsession. This fixation was largely influenced by Queen Victoria, who mourned her husband, Prince Albert, for over 40 years. It is uncommon to find a photograph of the Queen where she is not dressed in full black mourning attire. Just as Parisian fashion influenced trends in America, Queen Victoria's mourning practices set a global standard for proper etiquette during this time. I like to think that Queen Victoria was the original "goth." Her grief and sorrow became fashionable.

Queen Victoria was born Princess Alexandrina Victoria on May 24, 1819, at Kensington Palace and became queen at just 18 on June 20, 1837. Prince Albert of Saxe-Coburg and Gotha was born on August 26, 1819, at Schloss Rosenau in Germany. Queen Victoria and Prince Albert were first cousins: Victoria's mother, Princess Victoria of Saxe-Coburg-Saalfeld, was the sister of Albert's father, Ernest I, Duke of Saxe-Coburg and Gotha.

Victoria and Albert were first cousins (it was not uncommon for royals to marry relatives). Victoria was physically attracted to Albert and noted in her diary that Albert was "extremely handsome," with large blue eyes, fine teeth, and a "delightful" expression. Their attraction to each other, as well as their shared family ties, led her to propose to him in October 1839. Her proposal was an extraordinary step for a reigning monarch. In early-Victorian Britain, social and royal protocol dictated that marriage proposals be addressed to the monarch, never initiated by them. Queen Victoria chose to sidestep these conventions.

The couple had nine children—four sons and five daughters—many of whom married into Europe's royal houses, earning Victoria the nickname "the Grandmother of Europe." After falling ill for 2 weeks, Prince Albert died of typhoid fever on December 14, 1861. Devastated, Queen Victoria entered a prolonged mourning, wore black for the rest of her life, and secluded herself from public duties for years. Based on both of Victoria's and Albert's writings and journal entries, they deeply, profoundly, and authentically loved each other. Their reciprocal, passionate bond was uncommon in royal marriages. Their love endured long past his death and defined her entire reign. Her mourning practices and profound grief came to define the deathcare industry as we know it today. Many modern funeral practices, as well as Occult traditions, began during the Victoria Era as a direct response to the Queen's sorrow and the frequent death rates of this era.

Mourning Culture

During the Victorian era, modern medicine was virtually nonexistent. The absence of modern medical practices led to frequent deaths and high mortality rates, and frequent outbreaks of famine and infectious diseases such as tuberculosis, pneumonia, bronchitis, smallpox, measles, and whooping cough. Stillbirths were common, and the average lifespan was significantly shorter than today. The average lifespan during the Victorian era was 40 to 45 years. Hospitals were often unhygienic environments where patients were left to die. Death usually occurred at home, where families witnessed the grim process firsthand. Since death was a frequent visitor during the Victorian era, people began planning for it while they were young. Dying was an open and ongoing conversation. As death approached, there was no ambiguity as to what the person wanted or what was expected of the family. The family knew in advance what type of coffin the dying wanted, where they wanted to be buried, and what they wanted to wear. Women frequently made their own shrouds and would even include them in their wedding dowries.

This ever-present death spawned elaborate mourning customs: families wore specific attire to signal grief, held ornate and expensive funerals, created memento mori, erected grave monuments, engaged in photography of the dead, and practiced customs driven by superstition. Victorians also tried to keep as much as they could from the deceased to remember them by, even going to the extent of taking photos of the dead and wearing lockets made from the deceased's hair.

The death practices of the Victorian era were among the most intricate in the Western world. Mourning attire served as a family's outward expression of inner grief, while funerals became elaborate ceremonies reflecting social status and norms. There is a massive list of rules and regulations regarding death, burials, and mourning in this era. Disregarding the rules implied that the offender was immoral or had dishonored the deceased. This was so important that it did not matter if it presented a financial hardship for the poor.

The Victorians recognized three distinct stages of mourning:

Full Mourning: This was the most intense phase and was worn for the closest relatives, including husbands, parents, children, and siblings. It typically lasted for one year and one day after the death of a close relative. During this period, women wore heavy black crepe dresses, often layered over crinoline petticoats, accompanied by a long black crepe veil that covered their faces. Jewelry was strictly prohibited, and social activities were significantly limited. Men maintained a simpler mourning code, donning black suits, gloves, and a black hatband. Children sometimes wore dark clothing for the same duration.

Second Mourning: Following full mourning, this phase lasted about nine months. Women began to reintroduce black silk instead of crepe and were allowed to wear minimal jewelry, typically made from jet or onyx. The weeping veil was lifted to the back of the head, and minor embellishments, such as black ribbons, became permissible. Men's clothing remained largely unchanged from the full mourning phase, continuing to wear dark suits and accessories.

Half Mourning: The final stage, half mourning, lasted roughly three months. During this time, widows and other close mourners could incorporate muted colors, like gray, lavender, and mauve, into their attire. Fabrics became lighter, and ornamentation gradually reemerged, although black remained the predominant color. At the end of this period, mourners were considered free from formal mourning restrictions, though many continued to wear simple black clothing for a while as a personal mark of respect.

Mourning attire launched a mass-market industry. The development of coal-based synthetic dyes made true black fabrics affordable, leading to department stores stocking specialized mourning garments and accessories. London's department stores—Harrods, Whiteleys, and Marshall and Snelgrove—dedicated entire sections to mourning attire. Customers could choose ready-made black gowns, capes, veils, ribbons, and jet jewelry under one roof. Mail-order catalogs further extended this reach into the countryside, standardizing mourning fashion across

Britain. Synthetic black dyes cut costs, allowing every social class the affordability of fashionable black mourning attire.

Victorian funerals were grand public spectacles that both evoked solemn respect and broadcast a family's social standing, from the ornate hearses—richly carved, draped in heavy black crepe, and topped with plumed horses—to the long, measured processions of mourners in full black attire accompanied by hired professional mourners. Working-class families often joined burial clubs—mutual aid societies that collected small weekly contributions—to cover coffin, hearse, and grave fees so even the poorest could have a proper burial. Deaths were announced with black-bordered cards and newspaper obituaries, while invitations on mourning stationery detailed service times and etiquette, ensuring friends and neighbors joined the public ritual. At the graveside, clergy led prayers as mourners laid lilies or wreaths inscribed "Rest in Peace," sometimes burying personal tokens with the deceased, and concluded the ceremony with a solemn scattering of earth or chalk to symbolize final closure. Elaborate floral displays spelling out sentiments such as "At Rest" or "Gone But Not Forgotten" were also common.

During the Victorian era, headstones also evolved from simple markers into elaborate memorials reflecting the era's sentimentality and fascination with death. Gravestones turned into upright monuments and grew larger and more ornate, often bearing heartfelt inscriptions and detailed carvings that celebrated the lives of the departed rather than simply marking their graves. By the late 19th century, granite became popular in headstones and monuments for its durability and range of colors, replacing marble and other softer stones. The Gothic Revival of this time introduced pointed arches, trefoil cutouts, and spired finials.

During mourning, social activities—balls, theatre visits, and even parties—were strictly forbidden. Mourners were expected to be isolated and often withdrew from public life until at least the second or half-mourning phases. Victorians also engaged in behaviors driven by superstitions. Victorian society viewed death not as a private sorrow but as a gateway between the living and the spirit world, prompting a host of rituals to protect the bereaved and guide the departed. At the moment of passing, clocks stopped to memorialize the transition and ward off misfortune, while all wild bird feathers were removed from pillows and mattresses to prevent the spirit from lingering. Coffins were carried feet first out of the home so the deceased could not look back and summon another soul, and mirrors were shrouded in dark cloth to keep wandering spirits from becoming trapped indoors. Families even held a formal "telling of the bees," draping hives in black and offering funeral tea to honor the colony's shared soul, while coins placed over the eyes of the dead and family photographs turned face-down until mourning concluded served as final safeguards against spirit intrusion.

Some unique Victorian death customs and mourning etiquette include funerary dolls, postmortem photography, and death jewelry. During the Victorian era, it was common for families to photograph their recently deceased loved ones. Post-mortem photography gained particular popularity in Britain between 1860 and 1910. Photographers aimed to create portraits that depicted the deceased as they had been in life, so they often attempted to make them appear alive. For instance, some photographs, particularly those of children, portrayed them as if they were simply sleeping, while others were posed sitting up, sometimes with their eyes open.

In a time when many families faced the loss of loved ones before they reached adulthood, post-mortem photographs served as de facto family portraits. These images provided comfort by offering a sense of control over death and creating a tangible keepsake during periods of mourning. They were often displayed in parlors or kept in albums, reinforcing connections across the boundary between life and death.

Photography was a relatively new medium at this time, and by the 1850s, the duration of portrait sittings had been reduced from minutes to seconds. These technical advances made it possible to capture images of the recently deceased in posed arrangements, leading to dedicated deathbed and post-mortem sittings. For many Victorians, a post-mortem portrait might be their first experience with photography, allowing them to retain a lasting image of relatives who had never been photographed while alive.

The rise of photography in the mid-19th century coincided with high mortality rates—particularly among infants and children—due to epidemics and limited medical care. Families turned to post-mortem portraits as one of the few ways to preserve a lasting image of loved ones they might never have had the opportunity to photograph when they were alive.

To simulate lifelike appearances, photographers often posed corpses with wire stands or clamps to prevent blurring from even slight movements. In some cases, family members or photographers would paint the eyelids or gently open the deceased's eyes to enhance the lifelike appearance. Props such as chairs, pillows, and the hands of family members were used to support fragile bodies in seated or reclining poses. Today, Victorian death photographs are viewed as haunting artifacts that some may see as disturbing and macabre. But they are a very important window into the past in understanding how cultures coped with loss, memorialize the gone, and confront their own mortality.

Another aspect of Victorian Death Culture that some might find chilling is the custom of funerary dolls. This may definitely be the inspiration for haunted dolls in Hollywood Horror movies. Mourning dolls were modeled after an infant or young child who had passed away. They were life-sized effigies sculpted from wax or porcelain, with bodies filled with sand to mimic the weight of a corpse. Their serene, closed-eye faces were framed with the deceased child's actual hair and clothing.

Families displayed these dolls during wakes alongside—or sometimes in place of—the deceased infant, treating them as tangible stand-ins. Families would then lay the dolls on their graves following their burial. In certain instances, after the funeral service, some families took the dolls home. Owners often cared for them much like living children—changing their clothes, putting them in the infant's crib, and brushing their hair as a way to preserve a connection to their loved one.

Besides postmortem photography and funerary dolls, mourning jewelry was another way to remember the dead. Queen Victoria inspired the trend of wearing mourning accessories, also known as hair jewelry. Victorian mourning jewelry became popular in the late 1800s as a tribute or memento to honor the memory of a deceased loved one. Common materials used included jet, onyx, pearls, dark tortoiseshell, and natural rubber. The designs of rings, lockets, earrings, and brooches often incorporated the deceased's hair and teeth. White enamel was used to signify the death of an unmarried female, while children were sometimes remembered with pearls, symbolizing tears. Turquoise was associated with the sentiment of "thinking of you." Wealthier families would enhance mourning jewelry with precious stones to commemorate their loved ones.

Human hair was commonly braided, woven, or encased under glass in these pieces. Although less common, some rings included the teeth of the deceased. Certain pieces also contained scraps of cloth or fabric that belonged to the deceased, while others featured tintype portraits or miniature paintings. Lockets often held a portrait or photo on one side and a lock of hair on the other. Mourning brooches frequently included a compartment for a lock of hair or featured symbolic designs.

The Evolution of the Deathcare Industry

During this time, there was a significant growth in funeral-related businesses, including coffin makers, embalmers, and gravediggers. The modern funeral industry has its origins in the Victorian Era. In early Victorian Britain and America, coffin-making and body care were often side businesses for carpenters and cabinetmakers. As funerals became more elaborate, these tradespeople honed their skills, adopted the title of "undertaker," and by the end of the century, transformed into full-time, professional "funeral directors" who operated dedicated funeral homes, rather than ad-hoc parlors or private residences.

Mid-19th-century advancements, particularly those spurred by the American Civil War, helped standardize arterial embalming. This practice allowed bodies to be preserved for longer periods, enabling formal wakes and public viewings in funeral establishments. What initially began as a wartime necessity quickly evolved into a civilian custom, embedding embalming as a core service offered by funeral homes.

Before the 1870s, most funerals were conducted entirely at home. The deceased was laid out in the family parlor, draped in black crepe and surrounded by lilies or funeral wreaths, with mourners visiting over several days. Victorian death-care entrepreneurs began converting spare rooms into showrooms and entire houses into funeral homes, complete with viewing parlors, selection salons, and carriage services. This laid the foundation for today's funeral-home layout and operations.

Funeral directors capitalized on the emerging market by offering comprehensive packages that included coffin selections, corpse preparation, floral arrangements, printed stationery, and procession logistics. This standardization transformed what had once been deeply personal and variable rites.

Contemporary funeral homes still reflect Victorian models, featuring:

- Specialized facilities (viewing rooms, arrangement rooms, chapels, prep rooms)
- Standard service tiers and add-ons (embalming, limousines, lead cars)
- Professional funeral directors overseeing every detail

These enduring structures and offerings trace directly back to the innovations of the 19th century and the era's preoccupation with ritualized mourning.

Although the first obituaries (simple death notices) were published in ancient Rome around 59 B.C.E. in papyrus newspapers known as Acta Diurna (Daily Events), the Victorian Era elevated these death notices to a new level. Death was regarded as a natural part of life, and obituaries became a form of public mourning. Prior to the Victorian Era, obituaries were literally just notices that someone had died. The Victorian obituaries were often lengthy and detailed, focusing on the character and virtues of the deceased. During this period, obituaries began to include personal details, such as family relationships and hobbies, creating a more complete picture of the individuals' lives. This trend continues in many obituaries today, as they aim to celebrate a person's life and capture their personality rather than simply announce their death.

The Rise of Spiritualism

The Victorians also ignited a marked surge in mysticism and fascination with the supernatural. The religion of Spiritualism gained popularity between 1840 and 1920. Victorians also turned to the occult to help them cope with their losses.

Long before it became an organized movement, the idea that the souls of the departed could interact with the living existed in shamanistic and animistic traditions around the world. In Europe, the term "spiritualism" was first recorded in 1796 by Emanuel Swedenborg, who wrote about spirits and an afterlife realm accessible through visions and inner experiences.

Spiritualism emerged as a new religious movement in the 1900s in Europe and America, based on the belief that the spirits of the dead exist and have both the ability and inclination to communicate with the living through a medium. A medium can be an actual person (psychic medium) or a tool, such as a spirit board or a spirit trumpet.

Spiritualism also involves a metaphysical belief that the world consists of both matter and spirit. Spiritualists maintain that continued existence after death is possible, and that communication with the spirit world can and does occur.

The afterlife, known as the "spirit world," is viewed by spiritualists not as a static place, but as a realm in which spirits continue to evolve. These two beliefs—that contact with spirits is possible and that spirits are more advanced than humans—lead spiritualists to a third belief: that spirits can provide valuable knowledge about moral and ethical issues, as well as spiritual truths. Spiritualism reached its peak growth in membership from the 1840s to the 1920s, particularly in English-speaking countries. By 1897, it was estimated that spiritualism had more than eight million followers in the United States and Europe, mostly from the middle and upper classes.

The practice of spiritualism as we know it today, or communicating with the dead, began with the Fox sisters in Hydesville, New York, in March 1848. The Fox family moved into a new house in December 1847, and sisters Kate and Margaret Fox started hearing unexplained "rappings" on the walls and furniture. These rappings and tappings were believed to be a spirit in the house. The sisters began communicating with the spirit through tapping. Neighbors were invited to witness the events, and they asked intimate questions that only the deceased could know. The spirit responded correctly with a series of raps corresponding to the letters of the alphabet. This made headlines and sparked public fascination. These Hydesville rappings are widely regarded as the founding incident of modern spiritualism.

Ghosts have existed in some form throughout history, but for many, the events presided over by the Fox sisters served as proof that consciousness exists after death on another plane. This phenomenon spurred the formation of Spiritualism as a full-fledged religion, complete with séances, psychic mediums, ectoplasm, and ghost photography. There was even a school of Spiritualism in rural Wisconsin where students could learn grammar, mathematics, and how to channel the dead. This school still exists at the time of this writing; it is located in Wonewoc, Wisconsin. I used to live nearby, and locals referred to it as "Spooky Hill."

Core beliefs in Spiritualism propose that the universe consists of at least two fundamental substances: matter and spirit. Within this framework, spiritual entities such as souls, an afterlife, the spirits of the deceased, and deities are recognized as integral components of existence. A central tenet is the survival of the soul after physical death. A psychic medium is an individual who possesses the ability to connect with the spirit world and the unseen energies that surround us. By utilizing psychic abilities such as clairvoyance and clairaudience, they can perceive information from the spirit world and communicate with those who have passed on. Many spiritualist-trained mediums are "evidential" and are able to provide evidence related to the spirit's life on Earth. Mediums utilize this ability to communicate with the deceased and deliver their messages to the living. They serve as a channel or bridge between our world and the spirit realm, which suggests the existence of parallel worlds that remain invisible and inaccessible to us in our current state. Psychics and mediums serve as vital links between these realms. Furthermore, evidence of spirit contact is validated through various physical phenomena, including raps, taps, levitation, and manifestations of "ectoplasm."

Not to be confused with post-mortem photography, spirit photography also proved to the spiritualists that ghosts and spirits were real. Spirit photography emerged in the 1860s during the rise of Spiritualism. The introduction of modern photography played a significant role in blurring the lines between spirit photography and reality for many people in the 19th century. As a relatively new invention at that time, photography became a powerful tool for those seeking to provide "proof" of the spiritual realm. This phenomenon coincided with high mortality rates and the Spiritualism Movement, creating a perfect environment for spirit photography to flourish.

The inception of spirit photography is attributed to William H. Mumler, a Boston engraver who, in the early 1860s, discovered a ghostly figure in one of his self-portraits. Upon closer inspection, he identified the apparition as his deceased cousin. This accidental discovery led Mumler to pursue spirit photography as a profession. His work tapped into public grief and fascination, quickly transforming photography from a mere likeness-maker into a claimed portal to the afterlife. By capturing images of the departed alongside the living, spirit photography provided tangible "proof" of the afterlife to a society grappling with grief and the mysteries of death.

The ghostly images in spirit photographs were primarily achieved through double exposure, a technique where two images are superimposed onto a single photographic plate. Spirit photographers combined two negatives on one plate, creating a faint "ghost" image alongside the living subject. They exposed the same glass plate twice—once with the living subject and once with a pre-existing spirit image—to create apparitions that appeared to float above or behind the main portrait. This method allowed them to insert faint images of "spirits" next to the primary subject. Some photographers used small dolls or mannequins rigged to thin wires, positioning them just out of frame to drift into the shot during a long exposure. When combined with dark backgrounds and careful lighting, these props enhanced the impression of independent, floating spirits. Other techniques included the use of pre-prepared glass plates with existing images and careful manipulation of lighting and shadows to create spectral effects. Some practitioners, like Mumler, claimed these effects were accidental or spiritually guided, while others were found to be intentionally deceptive.

Despite skepticism and many photographers facing accusations and convictions for fraud, spirit photography resonated deeply with Victorian society, which was grappling with high mortality rates and a fascination with the afterlife. The images served as both mementos and perceived evidence of continued existence beyond death.

Séances became very popular during the Victorian era. Many people at that time sought to communicate with deceased loved ones, driven by high mortality rates and widespread grief. Séances offered comfort, entertainment, and, in some cases, exploitation. Because the church deemed speaking to the dead a sin, many séances were held in private homes.

Queen Victoria and Prince Albert showed a keen interest in Spiritualism, participating in séances as early as 1846. Instead of attending public gatherings, they hosted small, private events at Windsor Castle, inviting trusted mediums to facilitate their contact with the spirit world. Following Prince Albert's death in 1861, Queen Victoria's grief led her to engage even more deeply with séance practices. Her discreet involvement added an element of respectability to Spiritualism, encouraging interest among the upper class without overtly endorsing the movement.

Typical Victorian séances were held in dimly lit parlors or dedicated studios. Participants would sit around a circular table, often holding hands, with candles burning nearby. Personal items, such as photographs, jewelry, or letters belonging to the deceased, were placed at the center of the table to strengthen the connection with the spirits. The séance was usually led by a medium, who was most often a woman. Various tools, including spirit trumpets, planchettes, and spirit boards, became popular for these gatherings.

Spirit trumpets, which emerged in the late 19th century, were designed to amplify the faint whispers attributed to spirits during séances. Mediums and participants discovered that these cone-shaped devices transformed barely audible sounds into recognizable voices. Early versions of the trumpets were homemade from cardboard or metal, measuring about two feet long with a four-inch bell end, and were primarily intended to channel spirit "voices." By the 1890s, manufacturers began producing sleeker models made of aluminum or tin.

During the séance, participants would place the trumpet at the center of a darkened room, sometimes suspending it so it appeared to "float" under psychic influence. While sitting at the table, people held hands, and the medium entered a trance or acted as a "voice box," channeling the spirits through the trumpet's mouthpiece. This method of direct-voice mediumship accelerated communication with the spirit world compared to earlier techniques, such as table rapping or spelling out letters of the alphabet.

Spirit Boards became very popular during the Victorian Era. Attendees at séances often grew frustrated with how long it took for spirits to tap out messages on the wall. The planchette, a small plank, was first used in France in 1853. It was designed as a flat wooden board equipped with two brass casters and a downward-pointing pencil aperture. Users would lightly place their fingers on the top surface, allowing involuntary movements—believed to be driven by spirits—to spell out messages on the paper beneath.

As Spiritualism gained popularity in Victorian parlors, numerous manufacturers began producing planchettes in various shapes—such as heart, shield, and triangular—and materials, ranging from hardwoods to rubber and glass. The spirit board, also known as the Ouija board, evolved from the planchette. In 1886, Spiritualist camps in Ohio reported widespread usage of proto–Ouija boards to facilitate faster communication with spirits. A Ouija board is a flat board printed with the letters A–Z, the numbers 0–9, and words like "yes," "no," "hello," and "goodbye." Participants place their fingers lightly on a small, heart-shaped indicator called a planchette, which moves across the board to spell out messages allegedly from the spirit world.

Spirit Boards, including Ouija boards, are often misunderstood as a form of divination. Today, we may view Ouija boards with suspicion and fear, questioning why one would want to open a channel to the spirit world and risk inviting disaster. However, the Victorians did not share these fears; for them, communicating with the dead was simply a form of conversation with those who had passed.

Investigations by scientists and magicians gradually uncovered the tricks behind many "spirit" phenomena, yet the allure of contacting lost loved ones continued well into the 20th century and persists today. If you're reading this book, it's likely because you have had experiences with mediums and mediumship, or at least have a curiosity about it. If you enjoy séances, Ouija boards, and mediums, you have our Victorian ancestors to thank!

Gothic Revival

The Victorian era witnessed transformative breakthroughs across all branches of science, including communication, transportation, medicine, chemistry, and natural history. Driven by the Industrial Revolution and the expansion of empirical research, these developments reshaped daily life, public health, and Britain's global influence. Charles Darwin's theory of natural selection revolutionized biology, while inventions such as the telephone, steam locomotives, the light bulb, and the sewing machine transformed technology and industry. However, these advances also elicited a mix of emotions among Victorians. As rapid technological evolution challenged traditional beliefs and religious views, many clung to superstitions and established doctrines, leading to widespread anxieties that permeated every aspect of Victorian life. Some of these themes were explored through literature and storytelling.

The Victorian period gave birth to Gothic literature. This era saw the emergence of ghost stories, vampires, and monstrous figures, exploring themes of wonder, morbidity, terror, and the macabre. Notable writers included Mary Shelley, Edgar

Allan Poe, and Bram Stoker. The idea that there might be something beyond that which is immediately in front of us titillated the Victorians.

Mary Shelley (1797–1851) is often credited as the creatrix of modern science fiction and Gothic romance through her novel *Frankenstein* (1818). This groundbreaking work explores the ethics of creation, scientific hubris, and profound isolation. Edgar Allan Poe (1809–1849) mastered the short story and poetic fragment, delving into themes of madness, obsession, and the supernatural in works like *The Tell-Tale Heart* and *The Fall of the House of Usher*. He even laid the foundation for detective fiction with *The Murders in the Rue Morgue*. Bram Stoker (1847–1912) immortalized the vampire myth in his novel *Dracula* (1897), weaving together folklore and themes of foreign invasion, sexuality, and Victorian anxieties about science and faith.

Each of these authors confronts mortality in unique ways: Shelley through reanimated corpses, Poe with eerie encounters with the dead, and Stoker through undead predators. Their protagonists often spiral into loneliness and psychological collapse, reflecting broader societal fears—Victor Frankenstein's unbridled ambition, Poe's blurring of reason and irrationality, and Van Helsing's reliance on ancient lore to confront modern medical challenges.

Other notable Gothic authors and their works include Emily and Charlotte Brontë, who excelled in creating brooding atmospheres—Emily with the storm-tossed passion of *Wuthering Heights* and Charlotte in the Gothic romance of *Jane Eyre.* Charles Dickens infused chilling tension into *Bleak House* and *Great Expectations*. Robert Louis Stevenson explored humanity's dark duality in *Strange Case of Dr. Jekyll and Mr. Hyde*, while Oscar Wilde layered dread over *The Picture of Dorian Gray*. Additionally, Gaston Leroux captivated readers with the haunting romance of *The Phantom of the Opera.* So many groundbreaking, pivotal works of literature were created during the late 1800s. It's interesting to think that these common themes emerged at the same time, before mass communication and the internet and social media disseminated info.

Besides Gothic literature, the Victorians also loved Gothic architecture. During the Victorian era, the Gothic Revival—or Victorian Gothic—reimagined medieval architectural motifs such as pointed arches, ribbed vaults, tracery, finials, and hood moulds/drip moulds. This romantic medievalism, evident in churches, university halls, train stations, and private homes, promised a return to moral and spiritual authenticity. Many supporters were drawn from the High Church and Anglo-Catholic revival, viewing Gothic design as a principled alternative to the secular classicism of their day.

Advances in iron and, later, steel construction empowered architects to achieve soaring vaults and intricate ornamentation that far exceeded medieval precedents. By the 1850s through the 1870s, Gothic Revival had become the dominant style across Britain and its empire, before gradually giving way to the Arts and Crafts movement and emerging modernist trends in the 1880s and 1890s.

The Gothic Revival extended beyond buildings into the decorative arts, from furniture and textiles to wallpaper—most famously through William Morris and his Arts and Crafts workshop. Victorian designers even translated Gothic sensibilities into garden layouts, blending slender vertical forms, statues, and stonework with lush, organic plantings. By embracing detailed ornament and rich color, today's landscape designers can evoke the mystery and serenity of medieval cloisters without veering into the macabre.

Victorian Gardens and Gothic Gardens

The Victorian era saw a whirlwind of horticultural innovation—new methods for studying, cultivating, and exhibiting plants emerged almost daily, just as gardening itself exploded into a national craze. Public botanical gardens sprang up to meet this fervor, offering dedicated spaces for research, propagation, and public display. Chief among them was the Royal Botanic Gardens at Kew, which threw open its gates in 1840 and quickly became a global center for plant exploration, hybridization, and the spectacular presentation of exotic flora. If you ever travel to the United Kingdom, definitely check out all the amazing botanical gardens! They are still awe-inspiring to this day.

Gardening became immensely popular in England during the Victorian era. During the mid-Victorian period, often referred to as the "Golden Age of Horticulture," industrial wealth and increased leisure time transformed gardening from a basic necessity into a fashionable pastime. With the rise of social and economic advancements, the British people had more free time than ever before, leading to the emergence of the "Victorian garden."

No longer were beautiful gardens and landscaping just for the wealthy elite; middle-class families also began to create ornamental gardens focused on aesthetics rather than mere food production. Freed from the constant need to grow their own food, these families invested time and resources into gardens that showcased their status and taste.

Horticultural magazines, seed catalogs, and public flower shows fueled enthusiasm for both native and exotic plants. This era saw plant hunters and hybridizers introducing a wealth of new species, including double-flowered roses, bi-colored lilies, Chinese silver grass, and fountain grass. Regular seed catalogs offered not only "rare" specimens but also hearty vegetables and herbs, enabling gardening enthusiasts to blend beauty with utility.

A carefully maintained lawn served as the backdrop for Victorian landscapes, representing elegance and hospitality. The introduction of the lawnmower in the 1870s made it easier to maintain large expanses of grass, which became venues for tea parties, croquet matches, and social gatherings. Lawn enthusiasts took pride in their smooth, green lawns, which beautifully framed flower beds and garden decorations.

Classic Victorian gardens included a vibrant mix of Acacia, Ageratum, Alonsoa, and Amaranthus alongside cheerful Asters, Scarlet Basil, tuberous Begonias, and delicate Bluebells; enrich borders with Caladium, Calendula, Campanula, Chrysanthemum, Cobaea, Cockscomb, and Coleus; add texture with Dianthus, Dusty Miller, ferns, and Fuchsias; scent the air with Geraniums—both standard and scented varieties—and Heliotrope; layer in Impatiens, Lobelia, Marigolds, Moonflowers, Morning Glories, and Nasturtiums; brighten shady spots with Oxalis, Pansies, Periwinkles, Petunias, Portulacas, and Primroses; crown beds with Roses in full and miniature forms; and finish with the vertical accents of Snapdragons, the sweet clusters of Alyssum, the climbers Thunbergia, and the vivid blooms of Verbena and Zinnia.

Fencing was a vital component of Victorian gardens. It served not only to define property boundaries but also to showcase one's economic status through the type of fencing chosen. Cast iron was the preferred material for affluent households, and the more impressive the home, the more ornate the garden fencing. Those who could not afford cast iron often opted for rustic wooden fencing, as long as it wasn't a traditional wood picket fence, which was deemed outdated. If a picket fence was used, it typically needed to be concealed or softened with vines or shrubs.

There were several types of English gardens during the Victorian Era:

1. Traditional English Garden: Characterized by an abundance of roses, diverse plant varieties, neatly trimmed hedges, clean straight lines, lush greenery, seating areas, and decorative gates.

2. Cottage Garden: These gardens seamlessly blend colors, textures, forms, and fragrances. There is no concern for spacing or planting in odd numbers, nor is there a focus on variations in plant height. The charm of a cottage garden lies in its seemingly random design, creating a natural and relaxed atmosphere.

3. Gothic Garden: Popular during the Victorian era, these gardens were reminiscent of a theme park, filled with carefully orchestrated effects and morbid reflections on death. They attracted crowds for the same reasons that horror movies captivate us today—a thrilling scare. The enclosed gardens offered a respite from the daily struggles of life. The color palette for Gothic Garden flowers included Victorian mourning colors such as black, white, gray, purple, lavender, and scarlet, with black being the color most associated with mourning attire.

Victorian Gothic gardens were dark and romantic, reflecting the era's fascination with death, medieval architecture, and lush, mysterious plantings. They created outdoor spaces that felt both eerie and enchanting. These gardens featured dramatic hardscape elements, including pointed stone arches, ornate wrought-iron gates, cast-iron borders, and dark reflecting pools, evoking images of crumbling cloisters and forgotten graveyards. Winding gravel paths led to secluded "rooms," each framed by weathered statues or moss-covered columns, instilling a sense of suspense and discovery.

The plant selections in Gothic Gardens supported the somber mood, featuring near-black or deep-hued blooms—such as petunias, tulips, and bachelor's buttons—in shades of onyx, burgundy, and midnight purple, contrasted by ghostly white sweet alyssum or silver-leafed ferns. Foliage plants like black coleus and dark-leaved coral bells filled gaps throughout the year, ensuring the garden's brooding atmosphere remained intact even when flowers faded.

Soft, lantern-style lighting and the strategic placement of shadow-casting elements enhanced the nocturnal romance of these gardens, transforming them into settings for Victorian-inspired ghost stories and moonlit strolls. By merging Gothic architectural motifs with moody horticulture, these gardens offered the Victorians an outdoor retreat that balanced beauty, mystery, and a touch of the macabre.

Victorians, constantly surrounded by loss and fascination with mortality, came to view death as an ordinary—and even beautiful—part of life. They memorialized the departed with elaborate mourning rites and sought a bittersweet glimpse of the afterlife through spirit communication, séances, and spirit photography. This intricate culture of death arose both as an unconscious response to the era's high mortality and as a reflection of Queen Victoria's own grief and spiritual interests.

Now it should come as no surprise that the Victorians created the most gothic of gardens...Gardens of the Dead. Due to high mortality rates, burials were moved to large parks and gardens in the countryside, as cities no longer had the space for graveyards, cemeteries, and churchyards. They had simply run out of room. The disposal of the dead was a significant issue in 19th-century London, where burial was the norm and cremation was uncommon and unheard of. The challenge lay in accommodating an ever-increasing number of corpses, as the capital's large population filled its small churchyards, burial grounds, and vaults.

For the middle and upper classes, one solution was to relocate their deceased loved ones to landscaped burial grounds—spacious parks located in the semi-rural suburbs outside urban centers. Between 1832 and 1841, seven major "garden cemeteries," including Kensal Green and Highgate in London, were established as pastoral parks surrounded by trees, meandering paths, ornamental plantings, and medieval-inspired architecture. These designs reflected both sanitary concerns and the Romantic appreciation for nature.

Within these garden cemeteries, families and horticultural enthusiasts transformed individual graves into miniature gardens. They created cradle graves—bed-like enclosures framed by headstones and footstones—planting them with seasonal flowers, shrubs, and climbing plants drawn from fashionable Victorian floras. These living memorials blended mourning and horticulture, allowing the deceased to rest among blooms and sculpted greenery. By the 1860s, garden cemeteries surrounded London on all sides.

A few years ago my family did DNA testing and found out we were related to Queen Victoria. I have always been very drawn to the Victoria Era and all the facets of this time frame. My heartfelt gratitude to the Victorian culture for laying the foundation of both my gardening and spiritual practice.

Thank you, Victorian pioneers of mourning and mystery, for teaching us that grief can be shaped into art, plants, ritual, and solace. You draped your black crepe and crafted delicate jet beads not to hide sorrow but to honor it; you laid out garden cemeteries where the dead could sleep among roses and yew, turning loss into living landscapes; you channeled longing through séances, spirit photography, and spirit boards, revealing that hope and heartache walk hand in hand. In your elaborate funerals and whispered prayers to the beyond, you found a bittersweet beauty in the final farewell—reminding us that remembering, like love, need not fade with the last breath. Thank you for forging a culture that met death not with silence, but with ceremony, compassion, and an unquenchable wonder at what lies just out of sight.

As we move forward, please ask yourself: *Who do you want to create a garden of the dead for? Why? What is your intent?* Then you will choose your type of garden, flowers for your garden, design your garden, choose accessories, gather the tools for your garden, create your garden, activate it with spellwork, and dedicate your garden.

Join me now, as we dive deep into creating various gardens for the dead, inspired by the macabre, haunting beauty, eerie elegance, and gothic allure of the Victorian Era.

Flowers for the Dead

There are approximately 400,000 known species of plants worldwide. While the plants I am about to suggest may seem like an overwhelming number, it's important to remember that this is a tiny fraction of the plants that exist. I highly recommend the following plant finders online to help you visualize what the plant looks like, as well as see special recommendations for successfully growing that plant.

The National Gardening Association's Plants Database is exceptional:
www.garden.org/plants

The Missouri Botanical Garden Plant Finder:
www.missouribotanicalgarden.org/plantfinder/plantfindersearch.aspx

The U.S. National Arboretum Plant Finder:
www.usna.usda.gov/discover/plant-finder

World Flora Online (An Online Flora of All Known Plants):
www.worldfloraonline.org

Floriography is the language of flowers, where each type and color of flower carries its own unique meaning, symbolism, and sentiment. Even the combinations of flowers, the number of stems, and the way a bloom is presented are meaningful. Flowers have been used to convey coded, secret messages. For instance, flower dictionaries like Madame Charlotte de la Tour's *Le Langage des Fleurs* (1819) provide "translations" of blooms into words. While floriography existed before the Victorian Era, it gained popularity during this time, allowing people to communicate without speaking, using intentional combinations of flowers. The practice was influenced by the complex social etiquette and heightened emotions of the era. Below are examples of flowers and their primary meanings in floriography, particularly those that may be appropriate for a garden dedicated to a lost loved one.

Below are common flowers paired with their botanical names and their traditional meanings according to Floriography:

Rose (*Rosa*): Love, passion
Lily (*Lilium*): Purity, renewal
Carnation (*Dianthus caryophyllus*): Enduring love
Iris (*Iris germanica*): Wisdom, hope, valor
Daffodil (*Narcissus*): New beginnings, rebirth
Daisy (*Bellis perennis*): New beginnings
Marigold (*Tagetes erecta*): Grief, remembrance
Poppy (*Papaver rhoeas*): Remembrance, consolation
Geranium (*Pelargonium*): Comfort, friendship
Zinnia (*Zinnia elegans*): Thoughts of absent friends
Magnolia (*Magnolia grandiflora*): Perseverance
Hydrangea (*Hydrangea macrophylla*): Gratitude, heartfelt emotion
Honeysuckle (*Lonicera japonica*): Devotion, bonds of love

The doctrine of signatures is an ancient concept that predates Floriography. This belief holds that the appearance, shape, color, or other characteristics of plants and natural objects indicate their medicinal uses. This idea can be traced back to Hippocratic medicine, where it was thought that cures could be found in nature. The Greek physician Dioscorides expanded upon this idea in the first century CE. The actual term "doctrine of signatures" was first introduced by Jakob Böhme in his 1621 work *De Signatura Rerum*. This mystical work explores the notion that every created thing bears an inward "signature" or sign that reveals its divine purpose and hidden properties.

According to the doctrine, if a plant part resembles a body organ, it is believed to treat ailments associated with that organ. The color and nature of the plant, as well as the environment in which it grows, also suggest its uses. For example, succulents, which are known for their moisture retention, imply that they may be used for hydration. Using this concept, here are some classic examples of the doctrine of signatures related to grief, loss, death, and dying:

Bleeding Heart (*Lamprocapnos spectabilis*): The heart-shaped blooms hang on the stem like little pendulums. The tips of the plant drip with crimson-tipped "blood," leading to its use for soothing broken hearts and easing mourning.

Poppy (*Papaver spp.*): The milky or blood-red sap of poppies evokes the image of bleeding; as a result, they have become symbols of consolation and sleep, especially sleeping as a coping skill to escape from sorrow.

Yarrow (*Achillea millefolium*): The tiny, stitch-like clusters of flowers suggest healing powers. Yarrow was commonly planted in funerary gardens to help stop "emotional bleeding."

Rue (*Ruta graveolens*): With its glaucous, tear-shaped leaves and a bitter scent, rue symbolizes repentance and purification, offering comfort and relief during periods of grief.

Bloodroot (*Sanguinaria canadensis*): The vivid red sap from its root is seen as a sign of cleansing the circulatory system, symbolically washing away deep emotional wounds.

Mandrake (*Mandragora officinarum*): This plant features an anthropomorphic root that represents life, death, and transformation. It has been used in rituals to guide souls and ward off malevolent spirits.

Lily-of-the-Valley (*Convallaria majalis*): The delicate, tear-shaped white bells of this flower imply sorrow yet also promise renewal, signaling that grief may eventually give way to hope.

Monkshood (*Aconitum spp.*): Its helmet-shaped blooms were seen as protective helmets for the spirit, used in mourning rites to shield the bereaved from despair.

Skullcap (*Scutellaria spp.*): Tiny flowers resembling miniature skulls. The flowers are believed to quiet restless grief and guide the mind toward peaceful acceptance.

Angel's Trumpet *(Brugmansia)*: The hanging, bell-like blossoms were likened to funeral bells announcing a soul's departure. Its sedative properties further symbolized the transition into eternal rest.

Death Camas (*Toxicoscordion venenosum*): Named for its fatal toxicity, the white, starry flowers were planted at graves to mark the boundary between the world of the living and the underworld.

Crown Imperial (*Fritillaria imperialis*): With its upturned, crown-like clusters, this flower symbolized the soul's coronation in eternity, honoring those deemed heroic in life.

Valerian (*Valeriana officinalis*): The dense, globular blooms and strong sedative aroma made valerian a representation of the departed's peaceful rest and a remedy to soothe insomnia in mourners.

Henbane (*Hyoscyamus niger*): Its dark-seeded pods and poisonous sap were featured in ancient rites to guide souls safely onward, warning of death's gravity through their perilous nature.

Mistletoe (*Viscum album*): The evergreen sprigs dotted with translucent, tear-like berries represent a combination of vitality and mourning, promising that life endures beyond loss.

Poinsettia (*Euphorbia pulcherrima*): The star-shaped red bracts were used in winter funerals to symbolize rebirth during the year's darkest point, with their crimson hue recalling blood and sacrifice.

Yew Tree (*Taxus baccata*): This is a tree and does not flower. However, its dark, needle-like leaves and bright red arils have become a signature of graveyards, symbolizing both eternal life and the finality of death.

Rosemary (*Rosmarinus officinalis*): Its needle-like leaves resemble tears, and its evergreen scent has long been used in remembrance rites to comfort mourners and honor memories.

Weeping Willow (*Salix babylonica*): The tree's drooping branches mimic streams of tears, making it a classic planting in graveyards that embodies collective sorrow.

Foxglove (*Digitalis purpurea*): The pendulous, bell-shaped blossoms resemble falling tears. As a heart tonic, it was believed to soothe both physical and emotional heartache.

Elder (*Sambucus nigra*): With hollow stems and dark berries, it evokes the emptiness and void left by loss. Elder was often woven into funeral garlands to mark the transition between worlds.

Pomegranate (*Punica granatum*): Clusters of blood-red seeds mirror droplets of blood and are linked to Persephone's descent, symbolizing the inevitability of death and the promise of return and rebirth.

Hellebore (*Helleborus niger*): With dark, helmet-shaped blooms, hellebore was planted around burial sites to ward off evil spirits and protect the departed on their journey.

Snowdrop (*Galanthus nivalis*): These delicate, nodding white flowers, often called "tears of snow," offer consolation and hope during winter's darkest days.

Skeleton Flower (*Diphylleia grayi*): In the rain, its petals turn translucent like fragile tears, serving as a living metaphor that beauty and vulnerability can coexist in grief.

Boneset (*Eupatorium perfoliatum*): With jointed, hollow stems resembling a skeleton's bones, it was used to heal both fractures and broken spirits during mourning.

Ivy (*Hedera helix*): This evergreen vine clings persistently, symbolizing eternal bonds and fidelity, reminding the bereaved that love endures beyond death.

Angelica (*Angelica archangelica*): Its umbrella-like flower heads suggest a protective canopy, making it a common choice to plant at burial sites to shield the soul on its journey.

Blackthorn (*Prunus spinosa*): The tree's gnarled, thorny branches symbolize enduring hardship, and its placement in graveyards serves as a living barrier against malevolent forces.

Hemlock (*Conium maculatum*): Known for its spotted, poisonous stems and ominous legacy, hemlock represents the finality of death and is sometimes ritually placed to mark a soul's passage.

Belladonna (*Atropa belladonna*): The glossy, jet-black berries contrast with the plant's pale flowers. Its toxic nature and dark fruit evoke the shadow of mortality and the thin veil between worlds.

Juniper (*Juniperus communis*): The evergreen needles and resinous scent symbolize eternal life and purification. You can burn the sprigs before, during, or after funerals to cleanse the air of grief.

Cypress (*Cupressus sempervirens*): With its tall, columnar form and dark foliage, the cypress tree embodies mournful uprightness and offers hope for resurrection, making it a quintessential cemetery tree.

Columbine (*Aquilegia spp.*): The nodding, spurred blossoms resemble Victorian mourning women's veils, linking this flower to sorrow, the release of grief, and spiritual uplift.

Pincushion Flower *(Scabiosa):* With its tightly clustered center, scabiosa represents poignant remembrance, with each stamen symbolizing a tiny emblem of memory held close.

Thistle (*Cirsium vulgare*): Its spiny armor and purple blooms speak of endured pain while also providing protection. In grave garlands, it stands as a testament to wounded hearts that remain unbroken.

Oleander (*Nerium oleander*): Despite its lush, evergreen appearance, every part of the oleander plant is poisonous. It serves as an elegant reminder of beauty's fragility and the hidden dangers of grief.

Bluebell (*Hyacinthoides non-scripta*): The delicate, downward-facing bells resemble tears shed for the departed, while clusters of bluebells under trees mark pathways where souls might wander.

Meadow Saffron (*Colchicum autumnale*): Blooming in the fall when most flowers fade, its ghostly blossoms symbolize unexpected loss and the quiet promise of renewal beneath the frost.

Coltsfoot (*Tussilago farfara*): One of the first spring flowers, coltsfoot boasts bright yellow heads that herald new life emerging from winter's grief—an emblem of hope after sorrow.

Maidenhair Fern (*Adiantum spp.*): The delicate, drooping fronds resemble streams of tears, and in folklore, the plant was often placed near graves to comfort those who are bereaved.

Milkweed (*Asclepias syriaca*): Its silky floss carries seeds on the wind, symbolizing the gentle release of the soul and its journey from this life.

Sundew (*Drosera spp.*): The dew-like glands on the leaves glisten like fresh tears, marking it as an herb of consolation for heavy spirits.

Spikenard (*Nardostachys jatamansi*): This fragrant root was used in ancient anointing oils during funerals—its rich aroma honors the departed and helps ease collective sorrow.

Witch Hazel (*Hamamelis virginiana*): The fissured bark and spring blossoms were brewed into salves to soothe bruised bodies and, by extension, to heal wounded emotions.

Solomon's Seal (*Polygonatum spp.*): Arching stems with dangling, bell-shaped flowers mirror tears of mourning. The plant's root was brewed as a tonic to bear the burdens of life.

St. John's Wort (*Hypericum perforatum*): Golden blooms dotted with black "tears" were carried to ward off depression, offering light in the darkest times of grief.

Hoary Alumroot (*Heuchera villosa*): Knobby roots and silvery foliage symbolize endurance through hardship and have traditionally been grown on burial mounds to honor lasting remembrance.

Goatsbeard (*Aruncus dioicus*): Its tall, feathery white plumes evoke veils of mourning. The plant's presence in grave gardens represents communal sorrow and support.

Boneset (*Eupatorium perfoliatum*): Its hollow stems look like a skeleton's frame. Historically, it was brewed to "rebuild" broken hearts.

Basil (*Ocimum basilicum*): The tiny hairs on the leaves resemble tears. Europeans once wove basil into funeral wreaths to chase away despair.

Black Cohosh (*Actaea racemosa*): Slender stalks topped with white flower spikes nod under their own weight, signifying the gravity of loss. Roots were used to quiet restless minds.

Peganum (*Peganum harmala*): Clusters of scarlet seeds and ash-white stems featured in Mediterranean rites to cleanse the remnants of grief and mark the passage of souls.

Corpse Flower (*Amorphophallus titanum*): This plant emits a staggering scent of decay, serving as nature's poignant reminder of mortality and the cycle of life and death.

Ghost Pipe (*Monotropa uniflora*): With its translucent, waxy stems that lack chlorophyll, this plant mirrors pallor and stillness, making it a silent companion for the bereaved.

Death Lily (*Amaryllis belladonna*): Its blooms emerge on a leafless stalk, symbolizing beauty arising from emptiness—an emblem of hope springing from the void of grief.

Snake's-Head Fritillary (*Fritillaria meleagris*): The nodding, checker-patterned bells of this flower evoke the veiled garments of mourning, reminiscent of tears hidden behind a sash.

Devil's Claw (*Proboscidea louisianica*): The hooked seedpods resemble piercing claws, speaking to the sharp pain of loss while promising eventual release when the seeds break free.

Widow's Tears (*Pituranthos chloranthus*): Glossy seed capsules ooze a sap likened to mournful weeping, making this plant a symbol of unspoken sorrow.

Black Dahlia (*Dahlia 'Black Beauty'*): Its nearly ebony petals and layered form evoke the weight of grief and the hidden complexity of mourning.

Stinking Iris (*Iris foetidissima*): With dark foliage and foul-scented blooms, this plant marks the boundary between beauty and decay, encapsulating loss's dual nature.

Funeral Mint (*Salvia funerea*): Grown near desert graves, its gray-green leaves and white flowers represent purification and the spirit's journey through barren landscapes.

Evening Primrose (*Oenothera biennis*): Pale yellow blooms that open at dusk suggest the soul's passage into twilight—mourning by moonlight and release in darkness.

Monarch Butterfly Weed (*Asclepias tuberosa*): Bright orange clusters recall flames of remembrance, and as it nourishes migrating butterflies, it symbolizes the soul's onward flight.

Pheasant's Eye (*Adonis aestivalis*): Blood-red flowers with black centers mimic wounds yet herald the return of spring, pairing grief's pain with the promise of renewal.

Funeral Cypress Sprigs (*Cupressus sempervirens*): Even cuttings of this somber, upright foliage were tucked into wreaths, signaling steadfast hope in resurrection.

Poppy of the Dead (*Papaver somniferum*): Richly hued seedpods and soporific latex embody eternal sleep, serving as both a comforting and cautionary symbol.

Snowy Umbrella (*Eryngium yuccifolium*): Its stark white, spiky blooms evoke a funeral canopy, shielding mourners under a sky of stars.

Passionflower (*Passiflora spp.*): The corona filaments radiate like a crown of thorns, while the five stamens and three styles recall Christ's wounds—inviting reflection on sacrifice and resurrection.

Crown of Thorns *(Euphorbia milii)*: Its clustered bracts and vicious spines mirror the martyr's crown, marking it as a living emblem of suffering and steadfast faith beyond death.

Heartsease (*Viola tricolor*): Small, heart-shaped petals in three colors offer comfort for broken hearts, symbolizing emotional healing after the rupture of grief.

Nightshade (*Solanum spp.*): Clusters of glossy black or purple berries suggest forbidden fruit and the shadow of mortality, used in folk rituals to acknowledge death's inevitability.

Briony (*Bryonia dioica*): Twisting vines and jet-black berries evoke loss and entanglement, often woven into funeral garlands to mourn tangled fates and broken bonds.

Boxwood (*Buxus sempervirens*): Dense evergreen foliage stands for immortality; when pruned into funeral wreaths, it promises life beyond the grave.

Elm (*Ulmus spp.*): Classic "mourning trees" in Victorian cemeteries, their broad canopies offered shade and a solemn backdrop for remembrance.

Aspen (*Populus tremula*): Trembling leaves that quiver at the slightest breeze symbolize the soul's departure and the fragility of life.

Usnea (*"Old Man's Beard" lichen*): Draping, silver-gray strands were hung over graves to signify age, memory, and the passage of time.

Dropwort (*Filipendula vulgaris*): Pendent rootlets and white umbels resembling tears make this plant a token of sorrow and the promise that grief will eventually dissolve.

Jimson Weed (*Datura stramonium*): This plant features ghostly, trumpet-shaped flowers and potent, hallucinogenic seeds that were historically used in shamanic rites to gain insight into the soul's journey beyond death.

Devil's-Bit Scabious (*Succisa pratensis*): The root of this plant is known for being "bitten off," symbolizing souls that have been cut short. It was often sown in mourning beds to honor those who left too soon.

Flannel Flower (*Actinotus helianthi*): With its soft, silvery-white bracts resembling burial shrouds, this Australian native flower carries connotations of pallor and solemn remembrance.

Everlasting (*Helichrysum italicum*): The golden, papery blooms of the everlasting flower retain their shape and color, serving as emblems of memory's endurance following a loss.

Lungwort (*Pulmonaria officinalis*): The spotted, lung-shaped leaves and pink-to-blue flowers of lungwort link it to breath and grief, and it has been used to alleviate the metaphorical "suffocation" of sorrow.

Dead Nettle (*Lamium galeobdolon*): This plant has pale, nettle-like foliage and muted blooms, which have led to its association with the departed and the quiet hush of graves.

Hops (*Humulus lupulus):* The drooping cones, dripping with sap, are reminiscent of tears; in some folk traditions, they are used to flavor "mourning ales" served at wakes.

Woodbine (*Lonicera periclymenum*): Its twining, entangled vines symbolize the clinging nature of grief, serving as a living reminder that sorrow can bind the heart.

Night-Blooming Cereus (*Epiphyllum oxypetalum*): This flower blooms only for one night before wilting, serving as a metaphor for life's fleeting beauty and the thin veil between dusk and the afterlife.

Caper Spurge (*Euphorbia lathyris*): With its pungent sap and tall, spiky stature, this plant is often found around burial plots, acting as a guardian plant that protects souls in the darkness.

Stechlin Cypress (*Taxodium distichum*): Its feathery foliage, which turns copper in autumn, mirrors the themes of seasonal death and rebirth, marking the passage of time in graveyards.

Lady's Mantle (*Alchemilla vulgaris*): Dew collects in its cup-shaped leaves like pearly tears, giving the herb a reputation for providing soothing comfort and gentle consolation.

Pansy (*Viola × wittrockiana*): Derived from the French word pensée, meaning "thought", pansies serve as botanical symbols of remembrance, often included in mourning wreaths to convey the message of "thinking of you."

Pasque Flower (*Pulsatilla vulgaris*): Blooming around Easter, its wispy seed heads and fleeting petals reflect themes of death and resurrection, making it a fitting emblem of grief transformed into hope.

Goldenrod (*Solidago spp.*): Tall, feathery plumes rise above fading blooms, symbolizing the soul's ascent and the promise of renewal following loss.

Spider Lily (*Lycoris radiata*): These flowers appear on bare stalks without leaves, representing sudden departure and the fleeting beauty of life.

Bee Orchid (*Ophrys apifera*): With petals that mimic a bee's body, this flower reminds us of life's delicate dance and the bittersweet sting of memories that linger at the edge of grief.

Cotton Grass (*Eriophorum spp.*): Soft, white tufts evoke funeral shrouds and offer tender comfort amidst the stillness of mourning landscapes.

Lady Slipper Orchid (*Cypripedium spp.*): The pouch-like blooms resemble vessels that cradle the soul, prepared for its release from earthly sorrow.

Heather (*Calluna vulgaris*): In Celtic tradition, purple heather honors the departed, providing solitude and the quiet strength needed to endure loss.

Mallow (*Malva spp.*): With its velvety petals and round seed discs resembling soft lips, mallow has been used as an emollient—soothing both the skin and grieving hearts.

Golden Chain Tree (*Laburnum anagyroides*): Cascading yellow blossoms have been interpreted as tears of gold—beauty brought forth from grief, illuminating the path from mourning to memory.

Silphium (*Ferula tingitana*): Although nearly extinct, its tall umbels once symbolized farewell offerings. Resinous stalks were snapped off and left at tombs as tokens of loss.

Butterbur (*Petasites hybridus*): The enormous drooping leaves of this plant resemble bowed heads in mourning. The oil extracted from its flower buds was burned to soothe restless spirits.

Star of Bethlehem (*Ornithogalum umbellatum*): The white, star-shaped blooms of this plant are believed to have guided dying souls like a celestial beacon, offering hope amid grief.

Ghost Gum (*Corymbia papuana*): With its smooth, white bark and leafless limbs against the dusk sky, this tree holds an ethereal presence in burial grounds, symbolizing the soul's pale departure.

Dragon Arum (*Dracunculus vulgaris*): The deep maroon spathe and foul scent mimic decaying flesh, confronting mourners with the realities of mortality and the cycle of life and death.

Blood Lily (*Scadoxus multiflorus*): Spherical clusters of blood-red blooms resemble drops of spilled life force, symbolizing both the pain of loss and the intensity of remembrance.

Spanish Moss (*Tillandsia usneoides*): Draping silvery-grey strands hang like tears from oak trees overhanging a grave, embodying a veil of collective sorrow.

Toad Lily (*Tricyrtis hirta*): Speckled, nodding flowers suggest hidden tears, with their late-season blooms reflecting the beauty and melancholy entwined at life's edge.

Firethorn (*Pyracantha coccinea*): Masses of bright red berries resemble clusters of tears frozen in place, offered as a tribute to undying grief.

Cypress Vine (*Ipomoea quamoclit*): Finely divided, fern-like foliage resembles trailing tears, while its star-shaped red flowers echo blood drops for the departed.

Mountain Ash (*Sorbus americana*): Bright clusters of orange-red berries glimmer like tiny memorial candles in autumn, marking the passage from life into memory.

Mophead Hydrangea (*Hydrangea macrophylla*): Large flower heads that change from vivid to ghostly blue-grey whisper themes of transience and fading remembrance.

Weeping Poplar (*Populus alba 'Pendula'*): Long, drooping branches sway like mourning veils, turning graveyards into living cathedrals of shared lament.

Japanese Weeping Maple *(Acer palmatum 'Dissectum'*): Lace-like, cascading leaves in autumnal crimson embody the tender fragility of human sorrow made visible.

Funeral Palm (*Chamaedorea elegans*): Upright, dark green fronds recall the solemn columns of a mausoleum, standing sentinel over graves and comforting the bereaved.

Black Mondo Grass (*Ophiopogon planiscapus 'Nigrescens'*): Glossy, nearly black blades form a living shroud over borders—an evergreen emblem of grief's enduring shadow.

Crown of Tears (*Plumbago auriculata*): Clusters of powder-blue flowers drip like teardrops; the genus name, "plumbago," hints at lead-heavy sorrow.

Elephant Ear (*Colocasia esculenta*) Giant, pendulous leaves mimic the bowed hoods of mourners, creating a lush canopy of shared grief in remembrance gardens.

Resurrection Plant (*Selaginella lepidophylla*): This plant's fronds curl into a brown ball when dry and unfurl when exposed to water, symbolizing revival and hope rising from grief.

Asphodel (*Asphodelus albus*): In Greek mythology, its pale, starry blooms carpet the underworld. Planting it in memorial gardens signifies the passage into the realm of shades.

Wormwood (*Artemisia absinthium*): With its silver, lacy foliage and intensely bitter taste, wormwood mirrors the sting of sorrow. It is often used to evoke and honor bittersweet memories.

Tansy (*Tanacetum vulgare*): The clusters of button-like yellow flowers were historically strewn over tombs to delay decay, symbolizing immortality beyond the veil of death.

Chamomile (*Matricaria chamomilla*): The small, daisy-like heads resemble consoling tears; infusions of chamomile are known to soothe both physical and emotional anguish.

Stinging Nettle (*Urtica dioica*): Its hairs provoke a burning sting and are thought to purge stagnant grief, encouraging the mourner to seek renewal.

Echinacea *(Echinacea spp.*): The spiky coneflower head resembles a sun drawn inward, interpreted as a symbol of strength to heal broken spirits.

Lobelia (*Lobelia inflata*): The inflated seed pods echo labored breathing; its traditional use as a respiratory tonic has become a metaphor for drawing fresh courage.

Spurge Laurel (*Daphne laureola*): Its glossy leaves and toxic berries hint at the hidden perils of death, reminding observers that beauty can conceal profound sorrow.

Blood Arum (*Arum italicum*): The striking maroon veins on pale spathes evoke the idea of lifeblood. Gardeners have planted it along pathways to guide lost souls.

Safflower (*Carthamus tinctorius*): Petals dotted with red spots were historically used to dye funerary cloths, with each fleck symbolizing a mourner's tear.

Camphor Tree (*Cinnamomum camphora*): Its camphorous scent clears the heaviness of the air, symbolizing the purification of grief's lingering shadows.

Coltsfoot (*Tussilago farfara*): One of the first spring flowers, its sudden yellow heads rising above dead leaves promise comfort and new life after winter's loss.

Guelder-Rose (*Viburnum opulus*): The flat clusters of white blooms followed by red berries represent tears turning to blood, marking the transition from sorrow to remembrance.

Funeral Bellflower (*Campanula medium*): Elegant, nodding bells herald a final toll; planted near headstones, they mark each visitor's step with a silent peal.

Finally, my absolute favorite flower of the dead, according to the Doctrine of Signatures is resurrection lilies. Lilies are my favorite flower hands down, but these gothic beauties are otherworldly. I have them in my own garden, but I did not plant them. They mysteriously showed up one year. Their mystical appearance strengthens my love for them. Resurrection lilies, or "naked ladies," are late-summer Lycoris bulbs whose bare, leafless stalks suddenly sprout pale, white-pink blooms long after their spring foliage has died back—an unmistakable signature of life emerging from apparent death. Their flowers open and fade within days, mirroring the fleeting nature of mortality and the soul's swift transition beyond. The soft, rosy-tinged petals speak of a departed purity and the promise of renewal, while the toxic, alkaloid-rich bulbs serve as a built-in warning of death's hidden dangers. By first shedding their leaves—decaying underground only to rebirth as blooms—these plants enact the cycle of decay followed by resurrection. Planted around graves, naked ladies stand as living symbols of the afterlife and the enduring memory of those who have passed.

These "signatures" deepen the tapestry of botanical symbols for grief, loss, and transition—each plant offering its own quiet counsel to those in mourning. With both floriography and the doctrine of signatures in mind, here are some additional blooms you might plant in a Garden for the Dead.

Flowers in Underworld Mythology

Nearly every culture's cosmology and pantheon include an underworld or netherworld—a realm of the dead that exists beneath or beyond the living world, where the souls of the deceased journey after death. The concept of an underworld may be as ancient as humanity itself. Typically, the underworld is a subterranean space that can be neutral and may contain both pleasant (paradise) and unpleasant (punishment) sections. It's important to keep the concepts of the underworld and hell separate, as they are not the same thing.

Many cultures have further divisions within their underworlds. For example, in Greek mythology, the Underworld is surrounded by five rivers: Styx, Acheron, Cocytus, Phlegethon, and Lethe. It is divided into at least four regions: Tartarus (reserved for punishment), the Elysian Fields (for heroes), the Fields of Mourning (for those who suffered from love), and the Asphodel Meadows (for the majority of ordinary souls).

Christianity describes a three-tiered universe, distinguishing between Heaven, Hell, and Purgatory. In ancient Egypt, souls journey through the Duat toward the Fields of Aaru or the dark Amenti. Norse mythology includes realms such as Hel, Fólkvangr, Valhalla, and Niflhel. In Celtic lore, the afterlife consists of Annwn, Mag Mell, and Dubnos, while the Slavic traditions mention Nav or Vyraj.

If you are interested in learning more about the underworld, I highly recommend exploring various mythologies and spiritual traditions, including Greek, Roman, Norse, Celtic, Egyptian, Chinese, Hindu, Buddhist, African Traditional Religions, Aztec, and Mesopotamian beliefs.

According to Greek mythology, the asphodel flower, known as *Asphodelus albus,* is said to grow in the Fields of Asphodel in Hades, where ordinary souls and shades wander after death. Its white flowers stand for remembrance and the endless afterlife, providing both food and beauty for the spirits of the deceased.

Poppies *(Papaver spp.)* appear often in Greek mythology as symbols of sleep, forgetfulness, and death. Connected to Hypnos, the god of sleep, their soothing petals represent the peaceful rest of the underworld and the oblivion after life's final breath.

In the Greek story of Kore/Persephone, she ate 6 pomegranate seeds while in the underworld. Therefore, pomegranate seeds tie her to Hades for six months each year. The red pomegranate represents the cycle of death and rebirth, fertility, and the necessary descent into the underworld. If you live in a hot, arid climate, a pomegranate tree would be an amazing addition to your Garden for the Dead.

Another flower associated with Persephone is the narcissus (daffodil). According to the myth, she was so captivated by a patch of narcissus flowers that Hades was able to surprise her and abduct her into the underworld.

Aconite, commonly known as Wolf's Bane, is a deadly flower believed to grow from the saliva of Cerberus, the three-headed watchdog of Hades. Cerberus, often referred to as the "hound of Hades," stands guard at the gates of the Underworld to prevent the dead from escaping and the living from entering.

The hyacinth emerged from the earth where Apollo's tears fell after Zephyrus's jealous wind killed his beloved Hyacinthus. Each spring bloom serves as a living memorial to their doomed love.

Red anemones grew from the blood of Adonis, who was loved by both Persephone and Aphrodite. Their bright red petals symbolize sacrifice, new life, and the deep mystery of death.

The cypress tree *(Cupressus semperviren)* is called "the mournful tree" by the ancient Greeks. It is planted at graves and funeral sites, and its dark green form serves as a living reminder of grief, memory, and the soul's journey to the underworld.

Mistletoe has a Norse story connected to the death of Baldur, the god of light and innocence. After Frigg's tears fell on it, the plant became a symbol of both death and hope because Baldur's death and eventual rebirth is linked to its white berries and evergreen leaves.

Cempasúchil, the golden marigold in Aztec tradition, is part of Day of the Dead celebrations. It is thought to guide spirits back home with its bright petals and warm scent, connecting the living with those who have passed.

In Japan, the red spider lily blooms along riverbanks and in graveyards each autumn. Its fiery petals and ghostly fragrance guide lost souls to the next world.

Yew trees are associated with both Celtic and Greek mythology, death, and immortality. Their poisonous seeds and evergreen needles represent danger and the promise of new life, making yews natural protectors at old burial sites.

Flesh-Eating Plants

Carnivorous, creepy, flesh-eating plants are perfect for Garden for the Dead. These plants eat insects and small creatures. They are really unique-looking, too! These plants have evolved to live in bog environments and nutrient-poor soil. Most species thrive in acidic, waterlogged environments, bogs, swamps, and sandy wetlands—where soil nutrients are scarce. They occur on all continents except Antarctica. Surprisingly, there are about 600 carnivorous plants in the world. Carnivorous plants seem to capture people's fascination more than any other plant species. Their unusual ability to lure, trap, and digest prey makes them endlessly intriguing. Here are some suggested flesh-eating plants for your garden:

Venus Flytrap (*Dionaea muscipula*): the iconic snap-trap native to the Carolinas, USA

Pitcher Plants: North American *Sarracenia*, tropical *Nepenthes*, South American *Heliamphora*, and Australian *Cephalotus* follicularis

Sundews (*Drosera spp.*): over one hundred species whose gland-tipped tentacles curl around captured prey

Butterworts (*Pinguicula spp.*): roughly 120 species with mucilage-coated leaves that dissolve insects, found across Europe and the Americas

Bladderworts (*Utricularia spp.*): more than 200 free-floating or terrestrial species using bladder traps in aquatic or damp habitats

Corkscrew Plants (*Genlisea spp.*): about 22 species employing lobster-pot traps in wet, sandy soils

Waterwheel Plant (*Aldrovanda vesiculosa*) – a rootless, free-floating snap-trap that captures aquatic prey underwater

Albany Pitcher Plant (*Cephalotus follicularis*) – the lone species of its family, with hairy pitfall traps and non-carnivorous leaves for photosynthesis

Cobra Lily (*Darlingtonia californica*) – a California/West Coast native whose tubular leaves and "cobra hood" lure insects into a pitfall trap

Dewy Pine (*Drosophyllum lusitanicum*) – the Portuguese sundew, with sticky, gland-tipped leaves that capture and digest insects on dry hillsides

Monkey Cups (*Nepenthes spp.*) – tropical pitcher plants whose large, nectar-lined pitchers can even trap small vertebrates (frogs, lizards, mice, etc.) in Southeast Asia and Madagascar

Sun Pitchers (*Heliamphora spp.*) – South American pitcher plants forming slender, tubular traps on tepui mountaintops

Rainbow Plants (*Byblis spp.*) – Australian flypaper traps whose glistening hairs glitter like morning dew to attract insects

Aquatic Bromeliad (*Catopsis berteroniana*) – a rare tank bromeliad that digests insects drowned in its water reservoirs

Tome: *(Triphyophyllum peltatum)* – a rare tropical plant that can become carnivorous when it lacks nutrients

Flycatcher Bush *(Roridula spp.)* – evergreen shrubs from South Africa with sticky leaves

The flyctacher bush does not digest the bugs, but traps them, so the assassin bug (*Pameridea roridulae*) can eat them. The flycatcher and the assassin bug have a symbiotic relationship, as the bugs then leave their feces behind on the plant, which it then eats. Brutal.

Brazilian Pipewort (*Philcoxia minensis*)– a carnivore with underground sticky leaves that trap worms in sandy soils

Plants That Smell Like Death

No judgment from me if you choose to use these plants that smell like death and decay in your Garden for the Dead. These plants use their foul odors to attract pollinators like flies and beetles that are drawn to the scent of decomposing flesh. Here are some plants notorious for their stink:

The Corpse Flower, *Amorphophallus titanum,* is famous for smelling like rotting flesh

The Stinking Corpse Lily, *Rafflesia arnoldii*, smells like decaying meat

Skunk Cabbage, *Symplocarpus foetidus* emits a foul, skunky

Voodoo Lily, *Dracunculus vulgaris*, smells like a decomposing animal

Dead Horse Arum, *Helicodiceros muscivorus*, that smells like—you guessed it—decaying horse

Trillium erectum, often called Stinking Benjamin, has a meat-like aroma

Helleborus foetidus, the Stinking Hellebore, smells pungent when the leaves are crushed

Iris foetidissima, the Stinking Iris, has a beefy, stale smell

Chenopodium vulvaria, the Stinking Goosefoot, gives off a smell of fishy ammonia.

The female Ginkgo, *Ginkgo biloba*, produces seeds that smell like rancid butter or vomit

Fritillaria imperialis, the Crown Imperial, has a sulfurous, sweaty smell

Stapelia hirsuta, the Starfish Flower, mimics rotting meat

Passiflora foetida, the Stinking Passionflower, smells like wet dog and decaying foliage

The roots of *Valeriana officinalis*, known as Valerian, release a sweaty sock-like aroma. But interestingly, Valerian flowers are incredible smelling and very intoxicating.

Durio zibethinus, better known as Durian, has a complex smell of sewage and gym socks

Holly (*Eryngium maritimum*): Beautiful blue thistle-like flowers, which some say smell like dog feces

Paperwhite Narcissus (*Narcissus papyraceus*): A polarizing scent—some love it, others say it reeks of dirty socks

Montauk Daisy (*Nipponanthemum nipponicum):* Pretty flowers, but the foliage can smell like motor oil

Bradford Pear Tree (*Pyrus calleryana*): the scent is often compared to rotting fish

Boxwood (English variety) (*Buxus sempervirens*): A classic hedge plant that can smell like cat urine in the sun

Pineapple Lily (*Eucomis bicolor*): Striking flowers with a sulfurous, rotten meat smell

Yellow Alyssum (*Aurinia saxatilis*): Its golden blooms come with a cheesy aroma

Flowering Pear Tree (*Pyrus calleryana*): blossoms that smell like vomit due to butyric acid

Lantana *(Lantana camara)*: Colorful and butterfly-friendly, but the leaves smell like gasoline when crushed

White Stopper (*Eugenia axillaris*): Native to Florida, this shrub releases a skunky aroma on warm breezy days

Society Garlic (*Tulbaghia violacea*): True to its name, it smells strongly of garlic

Plants with Unusual Shapes, Names, and Varying Textures

The following plants have unique names and very unique shapes and structures that are excellent in a garden for the dead.

Lady's slipper orchids (genus *Cypripedium*, family *Orchidaceae*) are terrestrial perennials distinguished by a pouch-shaped labellum that resembles a slipper or moccasin, which lures pollinators into their exotic bloom. These are typically woodland plants and are harder to find.

- *Cypripedium acaule* — pink lady's slipper, moccasin flower
- *Cypripedium calceolus* — yellow lady's slipper
- *Cypripedium parviflorum* — small yellow/yellow lady's slipper
- *Paphiopedilum spp.* — tropical Asian slipper orchids

Bat Flower. Its dramatic, wing-like bracts and dangling "whiskers" in deep blackish purple evoke the mystery of twilight and the passing of day into night.

- *Tacca chantrieri* — black bat flower
- *Tacca integrifolia* — white bat flower

Mouse Plant or Mousetail plant (Arum Family, Araceae) *Arisarum proboscideum*, known as the mouse plant or mousetail plant, is a shade-loving perennial in the Araceae family native to the Mediterranean, prized for its quirky, hooded flowers that mimic a tiny mouse's snout and its glossy, heart-shaped foliage.

Bear's Breeches (*Acanthus mollis*) Glossy, deeply lobed leaves topped with white-and-purple hooded flowers add architectural weight and a sense of enduring remembrance beneath taller specimens.

Skeleton Plant (*Diphylleia grayi*) When rain touches its pure white petals, they turn translucent—like nature's own stained glass.

Devil's Backbone (*Pedilanthus tithymaloides*) Zigzag, succulent stems that twist upward, evoking life's unpredictable journey.

Crown of Thorns (*Euphorbia milii*) Thorny stems crowned with bright red or pink bracts, symbolizing both suffering and protection.

Fishbone Cactus (*Epiphyllum anguliger*) Flat, zigzagging pads reminiscent of skeletal fins—adds textural contrast and a subtle aquatic allusion.

String of Hearts (*Ceropegia woodii*) Silvery, heart-shaped leaves that drape like garlands of affection—a gentle reminder that love endures.

Monkey Face Orchid (*Dracula simia*) With patterns that mimic a primate's face, this quirky bloom brings a touch of whimsy to solemn spaces.

Sea Holly (*Eryngium amethystinum*) Spiky, metallic-blue heads on wiry stems lend a steely resilience—perfect for symbolizing steadfast memory amid loss.

Honesty (*Lunaria annua*) Known as the "silver dollar" plant, its translucent seed pods shimmer like coins of remembrance—skins that linger long after petals fall.

Protea (*Protea cynaroides*) With its artichoke-like head and stiff, bristly petals, the King Protea symbolizes courage and change, anchoring memorial gardens with both texture and bold form.

Smoke Bush (*Cotinus coggygria* 'Royal Purple') Feathery, cloud-like clusters of plumes drift above dark foliage, conjuring the ephemeral and guiding thoughts skyward.

Orchid Cattleyas (*Cattleya spp.*) Their waxy, dramatic blooms stand for resilience and exquisite beauty; in muted tones (cream, lavender, smoky mauve) they suit bouquets where orchids offer both shape and longevity.

Coral Bells (*Heuchera spp.*) Compact rosettes in rust, deep burgundy, or shimmering silver add a velvety underlayer—symbolic of the depths beneath our grief and the promise of new growth. I have a number or coral bells in my garden and they make an excellent ground cover. They also come in neon yellow, burnt orange, chartreuse, lime green, lemon yellow, amber, caramel, cinnamon, peach, orange, rosy pink, red, burgundy, plum, purple, lavender, silver, pewter gray, bronze, dark chocolate, and near-black. They look particularly striking when interplanted with black flowers. They are amazing accent plants.

Dragon's Blood Stonecrop (*Sedum spurium*) forms a resilient carpet of succulent leaves that shift from emerald to blazing crimson as autumn approaches, offering a molten burst of color in rockeries and borders.

Dragon's Blood Stonecrop thrives in sun-drenched crevices, its tightly packed rosettes maturing from plum to deep burgundy under strong light, creating a living mosaic of rich, dark hues.

Blood-lies-Bleeding (*Amaranthus cruentus*) drapes pendulous tassels of deep crimson blooms that sway like liquid rubies in the breeze, lending a theatrical elegance to both bouquets and beds.

Love Lies Bleeding (*Amaranthus caudatus*) pours cascades of burgundy catkin-like flowers in trailing ropes, symbolizing unending devotion through its lush, pendulous form.

Bewitched After Midnight (*Ipomoea batatas*) unfurls heart-shaped leaves in inky purple that gleam like polished obsidian, weaving a spell of shadowy sophistication in containers or as groundcover.

Dracula Celosia (*Celosia cristata* 'Dracula') towers with velvety, wine-red plumes that arch like gothic tongues, injecting sumptuous drama and unique texture into floral arrangements or garden borders. This plant absolutely looks like Dracula's cape! I love this plant so much!

Red-veined dock (*Rumex sanguineus*) spreads broad, lime-green leaves laced with scarlet veins, introducing a bold, graphic pattern and vibrant contrast to shaded gardens or cut-leaf displays.

Funeral Tree *(Nuxia floribunda)* Named for its use in traditional funeral rites in Africa, it bears fragrant white clusters ideal for quiet reflection.

Plants that Kill: Poisonous Plants, a.k.a. Baneful Plants, or "The Banes"

Toxic plants, also known as baneful plants, are those rich in both danger and folklore. Throughout history, plants like belladonna, henbane, and mandrake have been central to witchcraft and mythology, known for their powerful properties used in rituals or feared for their mind-altering effects. These plants are filled with chemical compounds that can paralyze, disrupt bodily functions, or even cause death. Many of them provide therapeutic compounds when used in controlled doses; for instance, morphine is derived from the opium poppy, and atropine comes from belladonna. Symbolically, toxic plants often represent transformation, danger, and the mysterious boundary between life and death, enticing us with their beautiful flowers and haunting scents. They embody nature's dark alchemy, reminding us that beauty can sometimes have a perilous edge. The following plants that can kill are perfect for a garden for the dead.

Hellebore (*Helleborus*) is a beautiful flower in the buttercup family that blooms in early spring in the shade.

Hemlock: Hemlock is the common name given to a number of plants in the carrot family, including the aptly named Poison Hemlock (*Conium maculatum*), the water hemlocks (*Cicuta*), and the water dropworts (*Oenanthe*).

Belladonna (*Atropa belladonna*): Atropa belladonna, also known as Deadly Nightshade or simply Nightshade, is a perennial herb with drooping, tubular purple flowers followed by shiny black berries, symbolizing silence or falsehood and serving as a Victorian-era warning of death.

Daturas (*Datura spp.*): Datura, also known as Moonflower and Jimsonweed, bear large hooded, trumpet-shaped flowers in the Solanaceae family, symbolizing purity, hope, and new beginnings in spiritual traditions despite their toxic potency.

Foxglove (*Digitalis purpurea*): Digitalis purpurea produces tall spires of tubular, bell-shaped blooms from late spring to early summer, symbolizing insincerity and reflecting the dual power to heal hearts and harm lives.

Henbane (*Hyoscyamus niger L.*): Hyoscyamus niger bears winged stems with small yellow flowers veined in purple and harbors potent tropane alkaloids, symbolizing delirium and linked to witchcraft, necromancy, and the conjuring of souls in medieval lore.

Common monkshood *(Aconitum napellus L.):* Aconitum napellus is a tuberous-rooted perennial with dense racemes of hooded purplish-blue flowers, symbolizing protection and danger, often used in folklore to ward off evil spirits.

Monkshood genus (*Aconitum spp.*): Aconitum comprises over 250 perennial species with palmate leaves and racemes of helmet-shaped flowers in hues ranging from blue to white, embodying themes of power, peril, and the fine line between healing and poison across cultures.

Elder (European elder, *Sambucus nigra L.*): Sambucus nigra is a multi-stemmed deciduous shrub with clusters of fragrant white flowers and glossy black berries, symbolizing protection and regeneration, traditionally planted to ward off evil spirits.

Elders (*Sambucus spp.*): Sambucus is a genus of 20–30 fast-growing shrubs or small trees bearing pinnate leaves, large umbels of white flowers, and dark berries, symbolizing healing, renewal, and the protective power of folklore against witches and malevolent forces.

Mandrake (*Mandragora officinarum L.*): Mandragora officinarum is a perennial herb with human-shaped, branched roots, bell-shaped flowers, and yellow fruits, symbolizing supernatural potency, fertility, and protection. Its uprooting is fabled to unleash a fatal scream in legendary lore.

European mistletoe (*Viscum album L.*): Viscum album is a hemiparasitic evergreen with dichotomous branches, leathery yellow-green leaves, and sticky white berries, symbolizing peace, love, and the bridging of worlds, prominently featured in ancient rites and modern Christmas customs.

American mistletoe *(Phoradendron leucarpum)*: Phoradendron leucarpum is an evergreen, hemiparasitic shrub with opposite leathery leaves and white berries, symbolizing love and protection as it is commonly sold and hung as Christmas mistletoe in North America.

Wormwood (*Artemisia absinthium*): Artemisia absinthium is a long-lived, fragrant perennial herb with silver-green, feathery foliage and a woody base, symbolizing bitterness and resilience through its historic role in medicinal remedies and the absinthe controversies.

Yew tree (*Taxus baccata*): *Taxus baccata* is an evergreen tree with flat, dark-green needles in two ranks and bright red arils, symbolizing immortality, death, and resurrection, often planted in churchyards to represent the soul's transcendence.

Morning glory (*Ipomoea purpurea*): Ipomoea purpurea is a twining annual vine with heart-shaped leaves and trumpet-shaped purple flowers that open in the morning and close by afternoon, symbolizing fleeting beauty and the passage of time.

Castor/Ricin plant (*Ricinus communis*): Ricinus communis is a tall perennial with palmately lobed glossy leaves and spiny seed capsules, symbolizing duality—life through its beneficial castor oil and death through the ricin toxin it produces. Made famous in the television series, Breaking Bad.

Delphinium/Larkspur (*Delphinium spp.*): Delphinium species form tall spikes of five-petaled, spur-tipped flowers in blues, purples, and pastels, symbolizing lightness, positivity, and caution due to their toxic nature.

Mayapple/American mandrake (*Podophyllum peltatum*): Podophyllum peltatum is a rhizomatous woodland perennial with umbrella-like leaves and nodding white flowers, symbolizing concealment and transformation as its hidden fruit emerges under foliage in spring.

Tobacco *(Nicotiana tabacum*): Nicotiana tabacum is a sticky-haired annual herb with broad, ovate leaves and multibranched panicles of scented tubular flowers, symbolizing both spiritual communion and the perils of addiction through its nicotine content.

Lily of the Valley (*Convallaria majalis*): Convallaria majalis is a perennial groundcover with parallel-veined lanceolate leaves and fragrant, nodding white bell-shaped flowers, symbolizing purity, humility, and the return of happiness despite its high toxicity.

Bitter nightshade (*Solanum dulcamara*): Solanum dulcamara is a climbing nightshade vine with simple, ovate leaves and clusters of purple tubular flowers followed by bright red berries, symbolizing enigma and danger in folktales of hidden perils.

Dogbane (*Apocynum cannabinum*): Apocynum cannabinum is a bushy perennial with opposite lanceolate leaves and milky exudate, symbolizing protection and resourcefulness through its historic use as a fiber for rope and traditional medicine despite its toxicity.

Fleabane (*Erigeron spp.*): Erigeron species are tufted perennials with daisy-like heads of numerous white rays surrounding yellow discs, symbolizing the repulsion of negativity and pests in folklore that touted their flea-driving virtues.

Wormbane/Witchbane (*Ruta graveolens*): Ruta graveolens is a woody perennial with pinnately divided blue-green leaves and clusters of dull yellow flowers, symbolizing protection and purification in magical traditions that used its bitter scent to ward off evil.

Easter Lily/True lilies (*Lilium spp.*): Lilium species are bulbous perennials bearing large, often fragrant, trumpet- to Turk's-cap-shaped flowers in whites, pinks, and reds, symbolizing purity, resurrection, and the Virgin Mary in Christian iconography.

Jessamine/Carolina jessamine (*Gelsemium sempervirens*): Gelsemium sempervirens is an evergreen twining vine with glossy lanceolate leaves and fragrant yellow trumpet flowers in late winter, symbolizing hope and the imminent arrival of spring despite its poisonous sap.

Oleander *(Nerium oleander)*: Nerium oleander is a sub-tropical evergreen shrub with leathery, narrow leaves and clusters of showy pink, purple, or white flowers, symbolizing caution and unyielding love as its beauty conceals deadly toxins in all parts.

Gloriosa (*Gloriosa superba*): Gloriosa superba is a tuberous climber with wavy, reflexed petals in fiery red-yellow hues and tendrilled leaves, symbolizing passionate aspirations and warning of danger due to its colchicine-rich toxicity.

Angel's Trumpet (*Brugmansia spp.*): Brugmansia are woody trees or shrubs with large pendulous, trumpet-shaped flowers in white to pink that release fragrance at dusk, symbolizing spiritual journeys and divine messages while bearing potent hallucinogenic alkaloids. These make an excellent pairing with Datura as Angel Trumpet points downward from the heavens, and Datura points upward from the underworld. The flowers also look similar.

Pokeweed (*Phytolacca americana*): Phytolacca americana is a tall perennial with glossy purple-red stems, lanceolate leaves, and racemes of greenish flowers maturing to dark berries, symbolizing transformation through its traditional use in dyes and poisonous reputation.

Daffodil/Narcissus (*Narcissus spp.*): Narcissus are bulbous perennials bearing white, yellow, or orange barked flowers with central trumpets, symbolizing rebirth and vanity in myth and representing hope and prosperity in various cultural festivities.

False Hellebore (*Veratrum viride*): Veratrum viride is a herbaceous perennial with broad, strap-like, pleated leaves and greenish panicles of saucer-shaped flowers, symbolizing ancient warnings and the perilous boundary between medicine and poison.

Autumn Crocus (*Colchicum autumnale*): Colchicum autumnale is a cormous perennial sending up naked lavender-pink blooms in autumn, followed by spring foliage, symbolizing hidden dangers and the fleeting nature of beauty through its colchicine content.

Lantana (*Lantana camara*): Lantana camara is a frost-tender shrub with clusters of multicolored tubular flowers and fragrant ovate leaves, symbolizing freedom and adaptability yet warning of its invasive, toxic reputation in tropical regions.

Mountain Laurel (*Kalmia latifolia*): Kalmia latifolia is a broadleaf evergreen shrub with gnarled stems, glossy foliage, and rose-to-white cup-shaped flowers in spring, symbolizing caution and sublime beauty in Appalachian folklore, where it grows on rocky slopes.

Chinese Lanterns (*Physalis alkekengi*): Physalis alkekengi is a perennial with ovate leaves and conspicuous orange-red papery calyces enclosing round berries, symbolizing hidden value and transient illumination in autumn displays and dried arrangements.

Stinging Nettle (*Urtica dioica):* Urtica dioica is a herbaceous perennial with opposite, serrated leaves and stinging hairs that inject histamine upon touch, symbolizing resilience and the necessity of confronting challenges directly to avoid harm.

Giant Hogweed (*Heracleum mantegazzianum*): Heracleum mantegazzianum is a tall biennial with massive umbrella-like umbels of white flowers atop grooved, purple-blotched stems, symbolizing both the allure and peril of unchecked growth due to its phototoxic sap.

Yellow Dock (*Rumex crispus*): Rumex crispus is a perennial with a tall flower stalk, wavy-margined basal leaves, and shiny brown seeds encapsulated in papery calyces, symbolizing healing and adaptability as a folk remedy despite its oxalic-acid content.

Rosary Pea (*Abrus precatorius*): Abrus precatorius is a twining perennial vine with pinnate leaves and bright red seeds with black spots, symbolizing protection and the soul's vigilance in Indian traditions despite containing the lethal toxin abrin.

Rhubarb (*Rheum* × *hybridum*): Rheum × hybridum is a clump-forming perennial with large, triangular poisonous leaves and stout edible stalks in red to green, symbolizing the tension between nourishment and toxicity in cottage-garden cuisines. Stalks are edible and the leaves are poisonous.

Wisteria (*Wisteria spp.*): Wisteria sinensis is a vigorous climber with pinnate leaves and pendulous clusters of fragrant violet-blue pea-flowers in spring, symbolizing devotion and longevity, yet caution due to its weight and invasiveness when unsupported.

Dieffenbachia (*Dieffenbachia spp.*): Dieffenbachia is a tropical perennial with large variegated leaves and inconspicuous spadix flowers, symbolizing domestic protection and the hidden perils of its calcium-oxalate crystals when grown as a houseplant.

Hydrangea (*Hydrangea spp.*): Hydrangeas are woody shrubs and climbers with large mophead or lacecap flower clusters that change color based on soil pH, symbolizing heartfelt emotions and gratitude through their seasonal displays of pink, blue, and white hues.

Rhododendron (*Rhododendron spp.*): Rhododendron is a genus of woody evergreens with leathery leaves and clusters of bell-shaped flowers in a rainbow of colors, symbolizing caution and majestic beauty, revered as Nepal's national flower and Washington State's emblem.

Azalea (*Rhododendron subgenera Tsutsusi and Pentanthera*): Azaleas are typically deciduous rhododendrons with funnel-shaped, often fragrant, five-stamen flowers in spring, symbolizing passion and fragile beauty while warning of temperance and delicate emotions.

Poppy *(Papaver somniferum)*: Papaver somniferum is an annual herb with glaucous foliage, stout stems, and large four-petaled flowers in white, mauve, or red, symbolizing sleep, peace, and remembrance while serving as the source of both opiate medicines and narcotics.

Please see the chapter *Handle with Care* to learn how to safely garden with baneful plants.

Death Colored Plants

Necrotic colored plants are perfect for a Garden for the Dead. Choose flower colors that are deep purple, dark scarlet red, grey, and nearly black, as well as plants with dark foliage.

Victorian Mourning Colored Plants: As discussed, there were three distinct mourning periods: full mourning, second mourning, and half-mourning. There were rules of what men and women should wear in each period of mourning as well as colors. Women were expected to wear *black* mourning attire for up to two years or longer depending on the relation of the dead. After a set period of time, they could decrease their mourning by transitioning into *shades of purple, grey, and white* and begin to reenter society.

Striking White Flowers

Here's a selection of standout white blooms known for their bold presence and lasting impact in the garden:

Shasta Daisy *(Leucanthemum × superbum)*: This classic perennial bears large, pure white ray florets surrounding a bright yellow central disk, atop clumps of dark green, lance-shaped foliage and stiff, 2–3 ft flower stems, creating a cheerful, long-blooming summer display.

White Coneflower *(Echinacea purpurea 'White Swan')*: 'White Swan' features slightly drooping, pure white petals encircling a copper-orange central cone, all atop 2–3 ft tall stems with coarse, lanceolate leaves, and remains a reliable, deer- and drought-tolerant summer bloomer.

Snowdrop Anemone (*Anemone sylvestris*): This anemone forms spreading patches of deeply lobed, medium green leaves topped in spring by 1.5–2 in, fragrant, cup-shaped white flowers with prominent yellow stamens, nodding gracefully on 18 in stems.

White Bleeding Heart (*Dicentra spectabilis 'Alba'*): In late spring, this shade-tolerant perennial sends up arching, fern-like foliage from which dangle 4–6 weeks of pristine white, heart-shaped flowers on 2–3 ft stems, before the foliage retreats in summer dormancy.

White Astilbe (*Astilbe × arendsii*): Clump-forming and shade-loving, this hybrid astilbe features feathery, plume-like panicles of pure white, star-shaped blossoms above fern-like, bronze-green foliage from mid to late summer, in moist, humus-rich soil.

White Foxglove (*Digitalis purpurea 'Alba'*): This biennial produces 3–4 ft tall spikes of tubular, pure white, spotted interior foxgloves, each bell tipped with delicate, downward-facing lips above a basal rosette of fuzzy, ovate leaves in partial shade to sun.

White Yarrow (*Achillea millefolium*): A clump-forming perennial with fern-like, aromatic foliage, this yarrow bears flat-topped corymbs of small, creamy-white ray and disc flowers from early summer into fall and tolerates poor soils and drought.

White Columbine (*Aquilegia spp.*): These spring perennials form 1–3 ft mounds of delicate, spurred white flowers likened to doves in flight above 12–18 in, deeply dissected foliage, thriving in partial shade and well-drained, humus-rich soil.

White Coral Bells (*Heuchera spp.*): Evergreen rosettes of rounded, silver-white to deep green leaves are topped by airy sprays of small, bell-shaped white blooms in early summer, valued for shade gardens and attractive to hummingbirds and pollinators.

White Candytuft (*Iberis sempervirens*): This evergreen subshrub forms a 12 in high by 16 in wide mound of glossy, oblong leaves and a billowing display of fragrant, tight clusters of pure white, 4 petaled flowers in spring on dry, sunny slopes.

White Balloon Flower (*Platycodon grandiflorus 'Fuji White'*): Known for its balloon-like buds that pop into 2 in wide, pure white, bell-shaped flowers with five pointed lobes, this 1.5–2 ft perennial sports toothed, ovate leaves and blooms profusely from June to August in sun to part shade.

White Monkshood (*Aconitum napellus 'Album'*): This stately perennial sends up 3–4 ft stalks bearing numerous large, white, hooded flowers above deep-hewn, dark emerald foliage in cool, moist summer conditions. Prized for use in cut arrangements.

White Windflower (*Anemone blanda*): A low-growing bulb with deeply cut, fern-like foliage that naturalizes in drifts and bears 1 in, 9–14 petaled white flowers on 4–8 in stems in early spring before going dormant.

White Iris (*Iris spp.*): Tall or beardless, white iris cultivars (e.g., 'Immortality') feature ruffled, pure white standards and falls atop erect, sword-like foliage, offering elegant spring blooms that reflect light in gardens, moon gardens, and cut arrangements.

Peony (*Paeonia lactiflora 'Festiva Maxima'*): This award-winning herbaceous peony forms 3 ft glossy, divided foliage topped in late spring by large, 5–7 in wide, double, fragrant white blooms occasionally flecked with crimson, perfect for borders and vases.

Plants with Gray Flowers

Iris 'Low Ho Silver' (*Iris × germanica* 'Low Ho Silver'): An intermediate bearded iris standing 12–18 in tall, it sports fragrant, silver-white falls and standards with a pale yellow touch at the hafts on neutral to slightly alkaline soils in full sun.

Lily 'Silver Scheherazade' (*Lilium* 'Scheherazade'): This Oriental lily produces 8–10 in, trumpet-shaped flowers of crimson edged in gold with white-tipped recurved tepals that fade to cream, atop 4–7 ft stems, against arrow-shaped leaves in sun to part shade.

Rose 'Silver Shadows' (*Rosa* 'Silver Shadow'): A repeat-flowering hybrid tea rose with fully double, fragrant blooms in an unusual shade of silver-lilac, set against glossy green foliage and suited to full sun and alkaline soils.

Globe Thistle (*Echinops sphaerocephalus*): This 2–5 ft perennial forms woolly-stemmed, thistle-like gray-green, deeply dissected foliage topped by 1–2 in white spherical flower-heads in full sun and well-drained, acidic soils, prized for drought tolerance and pollinator attraction.

Silver Sage (*Salvia argentea*): A short-lived perennial with a rosette of densely woolly, scalloped silvery leaves to 8 in and erect spikes of hooded, blush-white flowers with silvery calyces in summer, thriving in dry, sunny Mediterranean-style borders.

Dusty Miller (*Senecio cineraria*): This evergreen bedding plant features silvery, lobed, felted foliage up to 2 ft tall and sprinkles of small yellow daisy-like flowers, valued for drought tolerance, full sun resilience, and contrast in summer gardens.

Silver Lace (*Polygonum aubertii*): A fast-growing perennial vine that climbs to 30 ft, with twining stems bearing ovate leaves that emerge reddish-green then mature to bright green, with panicles of fragrant, creamy-white flowers in mid-late summer, ideal for screens and arbors.

Mountain Daisy (*Celmisia semicordata*): A small alpine perennial from New Zealand with billowing mounds of gray-green basal foliage and solitary 1–2 in white flowers in summer, adapted to rocky, high-elevation habitats.

Mouse Ears (*Cerastium spp.*): These low, mat-forming perennials bear soft, gray-green, pinnately divided leaves and clusters of small white, five-lobed flowers with pink anthers in spring, thriving in disturbed, temperate regions worldwide.

Edelweiss (*Leontopodium nivale*): A short alpine perennial with dense, woolly white hairs covering its bracts and leaves, forming a star-shaped flower-head of small yellow florets in high-elevation limestone habitats across Europe.

My favorite gray flowers are hellebores. Hellebores with gray-toned flowers are rare and captivating, often appearing in hybrid cultivars that blend slate, silver, and dusky purple hues. One standout is *Helleborus* 'Dashing Groomsman', a dramatic variety with double slate-gray petals tinged in deep plum. The flowers reach up to 3 in across and bloom in early spring, facing outward to showcase their moody elegance. Their glossy, deep green foliage adds contrast and remains evergreen year-round. Another notable cultivar is *Helleborus* 'New York Night', part of the

Honeymoon series, which features purple-gray to midnight petals with cream-colored stamens. These blooms offer a velvety texture and a sophisticated palette that pairs beautifully with silver-leaved companions like *Brunnera* or *Artemisia*. These gray-flowered hellebores thrive in partial shade, prefer moist, well-drained soil, and are deer-resistant, making them ideal for woodland gardens or shaded borders.

Deep Purple Flowers

Allium spp.: Ornamental alliums produce spherical umbels of vivid violet-purple flowers atop naked scapes rising 2–3 ft above linear, grass-like foliage, thriving in full sun and dry, well-drained soils.

Alpine Betony (*Betonica officinalis*): A clump-forming perennial with narrow, heart-shaped, wrinkled leaves and tall spikes of deep purple-violet, tubular flowers in midsummer, preferring full sun to partial shade and well-drained soils.

Anemone (*Anemone coronaria*): This tuberous-rooted perennial bears single, 2 in, deep purple daisy-like flowers with 9–14 petal-like sepals above dark green foliage in early spring to summer, thriving in sunny to light shade, moist, well-drained soil.

Anise Hyssop (*Agastache foeniculum*): An upright perennial with 2–3 ft spikes of fragrant, deep violet-purple tubular flowers from early summer to fall, set against toothed, aromatic, lanceolate leaves, adaptable to dry, well-drained soils in sun to part shade.

Aster spp.: Late-season perennials like *Symphyotrichum novae-belgii* produce 2–4 ft stems crowned with daisy-like, deep purple-lavender ray and yellow disc flowers from September through frost, preferring full sun and moist, well-drained soil.

Balloon Flower (*Platycodon grandiflorus*): Clump-forming perennials whose buds puff up like balloons before opening into 2–3 in, deep violet-purple star-shaped flowers on 1–2 ft stems, with toothed, blue-green leaves, in sun to part shade, midsummer blooms.

Bee Orchid (*Ophrys apifera*): A terrestrial orchid with 6–20 in stems bearing bee-mimicking, deep purple-brown flowers with velvety labella and green sepals, pollinated by pseudocopulation in Europe's grasslands and wood edges.

Astilbe (*Astilbe × arendsii*): Shade-loving perennials forming 1–3 ft mounds of bronze-green, fern-like foliage topped by 10–15 in plumes of deep purple flowers from late spring to summer in moist, humus soils.

Bear's Breeches (*Acanthus mollis*): Large 3–5 ft perennials with glossy, 2 ft lobed leaves and erect spikes of white flowers hooded by burgundy-purple bracts in late spring to midsummer, in sun to part shade, rich soil.

Clematis 'Arabella' (*Clematis* 'Arabella'): A non-vining, compact perennial with 3.5 in open-faced sepals of deep blue-mauve fading to purple, borne on self-supporting 3–5 ft stems in full sun to part shade from late spring to fall.

Hellebore (*Helleborus spp.*): Winter-blooming perennials with leathery, evergreen foliage and 3–4 in cup-shaped flowers in deep purple-black hues, often with spotted or edged tepals, in shade to part sun in winter–spring.

Iris 'Blue Magic' (*Iris hollandica* 'Blue Magic'): Dutch iris with 22–26 in blade-like leaves and 4–6 in deep royal purple-blue flowers with yellow markings on 2–3 ft stems in late spring, in sun and well-drained soil.

Hyacinth 'Miss Saigon' (*Hyacinthus orientalis* 'Miss Saigon'): Early spring bulbs with 6–8 in flower spikes densely packed with starry, deep violet-purple, highly fragrant florets above 8–12 in strap-like leaves in full sun to part shade.

Pansy 'Celestial Midnight' (*Viola × wittrockiana* 'Celestial Midnight'): Compact, evergreen perennials forming 8 in mounds of dark green leaves, covered from early spring to late fall by 1–2 in dark violet-blotch flowers with bright yellow eyes in part shade to sun.

Salvia 'Amistad' (*Salvia* 'Amistad'): Upright herbaceous perennials reaching 3–5 ft, with 4 in spikes of tubular, midnight violet flowers that attract hummingbirds and butterflies from midsummer to fall, in full sun to part shade in well-drained soils.

Deep Burgundy Flowers

Burgundy Calla Lily (*Zantedeschia spp.*): Upright rhizomatous perennials with 15–20 in tall dark glossy foliage and 6–8 in upright, waxy, trumpet-shaped spathes in deep wine-red atop 15–20 in stems in summer, in well-drained, slightly acidic soil.

Burgundy Dahlia (*Dahlia spp.*): Tuberous perennials offering 1–4 ft mounds of foliage topped by large, fully double to decorative blooms in rich burgundy to wine-red shades from midsummer to fall, in full sun and fertile, well-drained soil.

Burgundy Iceberg Rose (*Rosa* 'Burgundy Iceberg'): A floribunda rose forming 3 ft glossy green bushes adorned from late spring to frost with 4 in clustered, double blossoms of deep burgundy with cream reverse and a mild honey fragrance in full sun and well-drained soil.

Chocolate Cosmos (*Cosmos atrosanguineus*): Tuberous perennials reaching 2–3 ft tall, with dark reddish-brown, 1.5 in chocolate-scented flowers on slender stems from early summer to fall, above pinnate, dark green leaves in full sun and well-drained soil.

Burgundy Red Lily (*Lilium spp.*): Trumpet or Oriental hybrid lilies reaching 3–7 ft tall with 6–10 in downward-facing, velvety burgundy-red blossoms, often with a yellow or green throat and spotted tepals, in sun to part shade with moist, well-drained soil.

Burgundy Carnation (*Dianthus caryophyllus*): Compact perennials or annuals with 8–12 in stems bearing 2–3 in double to semi-double burgundy-red flowers with frilled edges and a spicy clove scent, in full sun and well-drained, slightly alkaline soil.

Holy Grail Hibiscus (*Hibiscus moscheutos* 'Holy Grail'): Upright, 4–5 ft hardy perennials with near-black foliage and 9 in deep burgundy-red rose-mallow flowers opening continuously from midsummer to fall in full sun and moist, well-drained soil.

Hollyhock 'Burgundy Towers' (*Alcea rosea* 'Burgundy Towers'): Biennial or short-lived perennials that form 6–8 ft spires of large, single to semi-double deep burgundy-red blooms from early summer in full sun and fertile, well-drained soil.

Carolina Allspice (*Calycanthus floridus*): A 6–9 ft deciduous shrub with opposite, ovate leaves and solitary 2 in aromatic dark burgundy flowers with a spicy fragrance from spring to summer in sun to part shade and moist soils.

Hellebore 'Burgundy' (*Helleborus* × *hybridus* 'Burgundy'): Clump-forming perennials with evergreen, lobed foliage and 3 in nodding deep burgundy-black rose-shaped flowers from late winter to early spring in shade to part sun and well-drained, humus-rich soil.

Black Magic Rose (*Rosa* 'Black Magic'): Upright hybrid tea roses that reach 5–7 ft, bearing 5 in high-centered, velvety deep red nearly black blooms with a light fruity fragrance from late spring to fall in full sun and well-drained soil.

Merlot Red Scabiosa (*Scabiosa atropurpurea* 'Merlot Red'): Annual pincushion flowers on 2–3 ft stems, producing 2–3 in merlot-red ray florets around a button-like center, in full sun and well-drained soil, reblooming with deadheading.

Black Flowers and Plants

In Western Cultures, black is the color of grief and mourning. Black flowers carry layered symbolism: they embody solemn respect and lasting devotion for those we've lost, channeling deep grief into a quiet tribute; yet they're also harbingers of renewal, appearing in art and literature to signal that closing one chapter makes way for the next; at the same time, they serve as gentle markers of major life transitions—whether the end of a career, a relationship, or another defining era—offering a wordless farewell while quietly inviting hope for what lies ahead.

Please note, there really is no such thing as a black flower in nature. These flowers are really deep burgundy or purple, and the darkest varieties have been bred and selected over time to appear black. But look at a black flower as the sun shines through, and you will see it is not really black.

Black Bat Flower (*Tacca chantrieri*): A tropical perennial distinguished by its large, bat-shaped, deep blackish-purple flowers up to 12 inches across, accented by long, whisker-like bracts and lush lance-shaped green foliage, forming dramatic clumps in shaded, humid conditions.

Black Calla Lily (*Zantedeschia* 'Black Star'): Showcases broad, trumpet-shaped, almost black-maroon spathes surrounding a pale lavender spadix, emerging directly from a thick rhizome into speckled dark green foliage, prized for its striking, long-lasting blooms in full to partial sun.

Black Velvet Petunia (*Petunia* 'Black Velvet'): Features velvety, deep purple-black, trumpet-shaped flowers borne on a dense, low mound of green foliage from mid-spring to mid-fall, creating a rich, textural groundcover that resists deer browsing and thrives in full sun with regular deadheading.

Black Hollyhock (*Alcea rosea* 'Nigra'): A biennial or short-lived perennial with tall, sturdy spikes of funnel-shaped, deep maroon-black flowers up to 3 inches wide, set against lobed green leaves, blooming profusely in mid to late summer and easily naturalizing through self-seeding in full sun and well-drained soil.

Black Pansy (*Viola* 'Sorbet Black Delight'): Produces compact mounds of serrated dark green leaves and masses of black-indigo blooms with yellow eyes and violet streaks, offering winter hardiness, heat tolerance, and a self-seeding habit ideal for containers, borders, and mass plantings in sun to partial shade.

Black Hellebore (*Helleborus niger*): Known as the Christmas rose, it bears winter-blooming, cup-shaped flowers of pure white fading to blush pink atop evergreen, deeply lobed, waxy leaves, thriving in part to full shade on humus-rich, neutral to alkaline soils and valued for its early-season interest and frost tolerance.

Black Iris (*Iris chrysographes*): Forms clumps of glossy, sword-shaped green leaves and erect stems of 30–60 cm bearing striking dark violet-black flowers with golden markings on the falls, blooming in late spring and thriving in moist, fertile, well-drained soil in full sun to partial shade.

Queen of the Night Tulip (*Tulipa 'Queen of Night'*): This single late-flowering tulip bears smooth, cup-shaped blooms in a velvety deep purple so intense they appear almost black atop 24–26″ stems, set against broad, lanceolate green foliage, and it thrives in USDA zones 3–8 with an RHS Award of Garden Merit for outstanding garden performance. Yes, I am weird, but I love to kiss these gorgeous blooms. This is prettiest tulip I have ever seen. Very deserving of its name.

Black Scabiosa (*Scabiosa atropurpurea*): This fast-growing, deciduous perennial forms 2–3′ stems topped by 2″ spherical pincushion flowers in rich burgundy-black punctuated with white "pins," emerging repeatedly from spring to fall above a clump of green foliage, and it excels in full sun with regular water while resisting verticillium wilt and deer browsing.

Black Lily (*Lilium* 'Landini') is an Asiatic hybrid whose erect stems reach 35–39 inches (just over 3 feet), topped in early to mid-summer by large, bowl-shaped, satiny blooms in deep burgundy-black. It pairs effortlessly with annuals and perennials in borders or containers, thriving in full sun to part shade.

Black Rose (*Rosa* 'Black Baccara') is a hybrid tea rose that sends up long, sturdy stems bearing high-centered, velvety dark red-burgundy flowers from spring through fall. Its glossy dark green foliage and repeat blooms make it a prized choice for cut flowers and dramatic garden accents in fertile, well-drained soils.

Black Petunia (*Petunia × atkinsiana*) is the classic garden petunia, born of *P. axillaris* and *P. inflata*. Its single or double blossoms—frilled, barred, or solid—span up to 4 inches across and appear in nearly every color imaginable. It flourishes in sun, well-drained soil, and moderate moisture.

Opium Poppy 'Black Swan' (*Papaver somniferum* 'Black Swan') is an annual whose sturdy 24–36 inch stems support fully double, dark red-black blooms up to 4¾ inches wide. Below a silvery carpet of deeply lobed foliage, decorative seed pods follow the flowers, and the plant prefers full sun and well-drained soil.

Onyx Sempervivum (*Sempervivum* SUPERSEMPS® 'Onyx') Black Hen and Chicks form solitary rosettes 2.8–3.1 inches across in deep plum-purple to black. It thrives in full sun with razor-sharp drainage and is hardy to Zone 4, making it perfect for rock gardens, containers, or striking groundcover.

Black Hyacinth hybrids (*Hyacinthus spp.*), often sold under names like 'Dark Dimension,' produce densely packed spikes of deep purple-black flowers that can appear jet-black in dim light. These mid-spring bloomers stand above fleshy blue-green leaves in sun to partial shade.

Black Fritillaria (Chocolate Lily) (*Fritillaria camschatcensis*) bears nodding, bell-shaped flowers in shades of dark brown to purplish-black atop slender, unbranched stems 8–20 inches tall. It thrives in moist, well-drained soils and cool temperate climates.

Black Violet (*Saintpaulia ionantha*) is a rosette-forming perennial with softly hairy, dark green leaves. Clusters of five-petaled, velvety blooms—ranging from dark purple to nearly black—hover just above the foliage, lighting up shaded windowsills and tabletops.

Black Forest Calla Lily (*Zantedeschia* 'Black Forest') is a rhizomatous perennial with arching glossy leaves 12–24 inches long. From midsummer to fall it produces satiny, purple-black, trumpet-shaped spathes around upright yellow spadices, making a bold statement in moist, shaded spots.

Dracula Orchid (*Dracula vampira*) is an epiphytic, shade-loving orchid with leathery pseudobulbs and slender leaves. Its uncanny, lantern-like flowers are veined in dark purple-black, with elongated sepal tails up to 4¼ inches, swaying like small ghosts under the canopy.

Midnight Ruffles Hellebore (*Helleborus* 'Midnight Ruffles') forms a tidy mound of glossy, deeply lobed evergreen foliage. Each stem is topped in late winter or early spring by a double, ruffled flower about 3 inches across in a near-black hue with pale yellow centers.

Black Magic Rose (*Rosa* 'Black Magic') is a vigorous hybrid tea rose that grows 5–7 feet tall. Its glossy, dark green foliage frames 30–40-petal blooms in velvety deep red to nearly black, appearing from late spring until frost.

Penny Black Nemophila (*Nemophila menziesii* 'Penny Black') is a low-growing annual about 8 inches tall and 12 inches wide. In summer it is studded with 0.8-inch saucer-shaped, deep purple-black flowers edged in crisp white above a mound of gray-green, scalloped foliage.

Chocolate Cosmos (*Cosmos atrosanguineus*) is a tuberous, tender perennial native to Mexico. Its 1½–2-inch, deep crimson to near-black blooms smell of chocolate and are carried on slender, reddish-brown stems 24–36 inches tall from early summer to fall.

Black Tree Aeonium (*Aeonium arboreum* 'Zwartkop') is an evergreen succulent shrub to around 3 feet tall. It bears gray-brown stems crowned by 6–8-inch rosettes of glossy, dark purple-black leaves that intensify under full sun, occasionally topped with conical clusters of small yellow star-shaped flowers in summer.

Black Pearl Loropetalum (*Loropetalum chinense* var. *rubrum* 'Black Pearl') is a semi-evergreen shrub roughly 3½–5 feet tall and wide. Its oval, leathery leaves range from deep purple-brown to nearly black, and in late winter to early spring it bears clusters of fragrant, rose-pink, strap-shaped flowers.

Black Beauty Elderberry (*Sambucus nigra* 'Black Beauty') is a vigorous deciduous shrub 8–15 feet tall. Its finely cut, dark purple pinnate leaves are topped in early summer by flat clusters of lemon-scented pinkish-purple flowers, later followed by glossy black berries that draw birds.

Black Scorpius Tulip (*Tulipa* 'Black Scorpius') bears goblet-shaped blooms in mid-spring atop sturdy 16–20-inch stems. The velvety, deep burgundy-black flowers make a dramatic focal point in beds and containers.

Black Charm Lily (*Lilium asiaticum* 'Black Charm') is an Asiatic hybrid reaching 2–3 feet tall. Its mid- to late-summer flowers are reflexed, trumpet-shaped, and 3.9–5.9 inches wide in dark red-purple that looks nearly black in bright light, held on stiff, strappy stems.

Black Ball Cornflower (*Centaurea cyanus* 'Black Ball') is an annual with thistle-like flowers 2–2.4 inches across, standing above mounds of fine, gray-green foliage from mid-spring into early summer.

Black Night Dahlia (*Dahlia* 'Arabian Night') is a tuberous perennial that forms bushy clumps around 4 feet tall, with pinnate foliage and fully double blooms 3.9 inches wide in deep burgundy that fade to near-black from midsummer until frost.

Blackout Viola (*Viola cornuta* 'Blackout') is a compact perennial reaching 6–10 inches high, forming a low mound of medium-green, glossy leaves beneath freely opening, velvety jet-black, five-petaled flowers with bright yellow centers from spring through autumn.

The Black Panther Peony (*Paeonia suffruticosa* 'Black Panther') is a semi-woody tree peony that reaches about 4 ft (3 ft 11 in) tall, with finely cut, fern-like foliage. Midseason, it produces semi-double to double, glossy maroon-black, fragrant blooms roughly 6 in across, each held aloft on sturdy stems.

The Arabian Night Dahlia (*Dahlia* 'Arabian Night') forms clumps about 3 ft 3 in tall, bearing 4 in-wide, double flowerheads of the deepest red-wine that fade to dusky maroon at the center. These blooms sit atop strong stems and dark green, lanceolate foliage from summer into autumn.

Hello Darkness Iris (*Iris germanica* 'Hello Darkness') is a tall bearded iris growing nearly 3 ft (2 ft 11 in) high with glaucous, sword-shaped leaves. In late spring it sends up flower spikes of ruffled, velvety purple-black standards and falls, each bloom measuring about 5 in across.

The Black Barlow Columbine (*Aquilegia vulgaris* var. *stellata* 'Black Barlow') is a clump-forming perennial standing 2 ft 4 in to 2 ft 6 in tall, with gray-green, lacy, divided leaves. In late spring to early summer, it bears fully double, upward-facing, spurless, dark plum-purple (almost black) blooms resembling starry pom-pons.

Fringe Flower 'Black Pearl' (*Loropetalum chinense* var. *rubrum* 'Black Pearl') is a semi-evergreen shrub about 3 ft 3 in to 4 ft 11 in high and equally wide. Its oval, leathery leaves range from deep purple-brown to nearly black, and in late winter to early spring, it produces clusters of fragrant, rose-pink, strap-shaped flowers that contrast vividly with the dark foliage.

Snapdragon 'Black Prince' (*Antirrhinum majus* 'Black Prince') is a bushy, short-lived perennial (often grown as an annual) reaching around 1 ft 6 in tall, with lanceolate, bronze-tinged leaves. From early summer into autumn, it carries dense spikes of tubular, two-lipped, deep crimson-black flowers ideal for borders and cut bouquets.

Love-in-a-Mist 'Black Beauty' (*Nigella damascena* 'Black Beauty') grows 1 ft 4 in to 2 ft tall, with finely divided, fennel-like blue-green foliage. In late spring, it bears single flowers 1 in to 1 ½ in across in rich purplish-black hues, surrounded by a lacy mist of bracts, later maturing to inflated, striped seed capsules filled with glossy black seeds.

Oriental Poppy 'Black Beauty' (*Papaver orientale* 'Black Beauty') sends up 2 ft to 2 ft 11 in stems topped with single, saucer-shaped blooms of deep, velvety red-black petals surrounding contrasting orange anthers.

Scabiosa 'Black Knight' (*Scabiosa atropurpurea* 'Black Knight') is a short-lived perennial growing 2 ft to 2 ft 11 in tall, with gray-green, finely divided foliage. Its wiry stems bear fully double, velvety pincushion blooms that open in a nearly black burgundy hue from summer into autumn.

Dahlia 'Black Jack' forms clumps 2 ft 11 in to 3 ft 11 in high, with dark green, pinnate leaves. From midsummer until frost, it displays striking semi-cactus flowers 6 in to 8 in across in a deep, velvety burgundy-black tone.

Zinnia 'Black Cherry' (*Zinnia elegans* 'Black Cherry') is an annual with bushy, branching stems 2 ft to 2 ft 11 in tall, crowned by 2 in to 3 in-wide, fully double blooms of rich cherry-black that sit atop sturdy flower stalks through summer.

Lily 'Night Rider' (*Lilium* 'Night Rider') is an Asiatic–Trumpet hybrid reaching 2 ft 11 in to 3 ft 11 in tall, featuring glossy, lanceolate leaves. It bears clusters of up-facing, trumpet-shaped petals in a lustrous, near-black purple, each bloom about 4 in to 6 in wide.

Yarrow 'Black Pearl' (*Achillea millefolium* 'Black Pearl') is a clump-forming perennial 1 ft 6 in to 2 ft tall, with finely dissected, dark bronze-black foliage. From midsummer into early autumn, it carries flat clusters of tiny, button-like, deep maroon-black flowers.

Hibiscus 'Black Dragon' (*Hibiscus acetosella* 'Black Dragon') is a tender shrub 3 ft 3 in to 5 ft 10 in tall, with glossy, deeply lobed, wine-black leaves. Through summer and fall, it blooms profusely with 3 to 4 in wide, velvety, deep burgundy flowers marked by an intense black eye.

Cranesbill Geranium 'Priestleyi' (*Geranium phaeum* 'Priestleyi') is a shade-loving perennial about 1 ft 4 in tall, with deeply cut, dark bronze foliage. In late spring to early summer, it holds loose sprays of nodding, bell-shaped, violet-black flowers.

Celosia 'Black Spider' (*Celosia cristata* 'Black Spider') sends up 1 ft to 1 ft 6 in upright stems topped with brain-like, crested flower heads of velvety black petals against a backdrop of green, lanceolate leaves.

China Aster 'Prince Noir' (*Callistephus chinensis* 'Prince Noir') grows 1 ft to 2 ft 11 in tall on branching stems clad in toothed, ovate foliage. From early summer into autumn, it bears 3 in to 5 in, fully double, velvet-black pompon blooms.

The Black Madonna Lily (*Lilium* × *hybridum* 'Black Madonna') pushes up 1 ft 8 in to 2 ft 11 in scapes clothed in glossy, strap-like leaves and opens wine-to-black, high-centered trumpet flowers 6 in to 8 in wide in summer.

Night Owl Gladiolus (*Gladiolus* hybrid 'Night Owl') forms 3 ft 11 in to 4 ft 11 in fans of sword-shaped leaves and nightly-opening, spicy-scented flowers of pale yellow, each 2 in to 3 in across, from late spring through midsummer.

Tulipa gesneriana 'Black Parrot'—commonly called the Black Parrot tulip—is a late-spring Parrot tulip prized for its flamboyant, deeply ruffled petals in velvety dark purple fading to near black. Plants reach 16–24 inches tall, blooming in full sun to reveal iridescent, flamed markings that mimic exotic parrot plumage—making them show-stoppers in borders, containers, or cut-flower arrangements.

Benary's Giant Black Zinnia (*Zinnia elegans* 'Benary's Giant Black') is a 2 ft 11 in to 3 ft 11 in annual bush with pinnate green leaves, crowned with 5 in to 6 in-wide, fully double, velvety, deep burgundy-black flowerheads on sturdy stems.

Black Diamond Lisianthus (*Eustoma grandiflorum* 'Black Diamond') produces 1 ft to 2 ft 11 in erect stems with gray-green, succulent lanceolate leaves. From early summer to fall, it bears 3 in to 5 in, rose-like, ruffled double blooms in near-black tones.

Black Panther Impatiens (*Impatiens walleriana* 'Black Panther') forms a 6 in to 1 ft mound of glossy, dark green, elliptic leaves. It freely opens 1 in to 1 ½ in-wide, velvety jet-black, five-petaled flowers spangled with bright yellow eyes in shade to part sun.

Black Adder Bee Balm (*Monarda didyma* 'Black Adder') grows as a 2 ft to 3 ft 3 in square-stemmed perennial, with opposite, serrated, aromatic leaves topped in midsummer by 1 in to 1 ½ in tubular, deep purple-black flowers in whorled clusters subtended by bracts.

The Black Beauty Sneezeweed (*Helenium autumnale* 'Black Beauty') sends up stems 2 ft 11 in to 4 ft 11 in tall with alternate, lanceolate leaves and late-summer to autumn heads of bright yellow, wedge-shaped rays surrounding domed golden-yellow centers.

Double Click Black Cosmos (*Cosmos bipinnatus* 'Double Click Black') is an annual that reaches about 1 ft 11 in to 2 ft 11 in in height, with feathery, pinnate foliage and roughly 3 in-wide, semi-double to double, ruffled button blooms in intense black from late spring until frost.

The Black Knight Tigridia (*Tigridia pavonia* 'Black Knight') emerges each summer with fans of sword-like leaves 1 ft 6 in to 1 ft 11 in tall and bears 5 in to 6 in-wide, up-facing, dark purple-black, spotted flowers that open for just one day mid-season.

Black Pearl Amaryllis (*Hippeastrum* 'Black Pearl') is a winter-forced bulb sending up 1 ft to 1 ft 8 in scapes above strappy evergreen leaves, each stem holding 6 in to 8 in-wide, velvety, near-black trumpet flowers—often two or more per bulb.

My Love Dahlia (*Dahlia* hybrid 'My Love') forms neat, tuberous clumps about 2 ft 6 in to 2 ft 11 in high and equally wide. From midsummer until the first frost, it produces lavish sprays of semi-double blooms 5 in to 6 in across in a deep rose-pink hue set against finely divided dark green foliage—perfect for mixed borders, containers, or long-lasting cut arrangements.

The Before the Storm Iris (*Iris germanica* 'Before the Storm') is a tall bearded iris growing to 2 ft 11 in with glaucous, sword-shaped leaves and late-spring spikes of ruffled, flaring falls and standards in a dramatic, near-black purple hue, scented sweetly.

The Raven ZZ Plant (*Zamioculcas zamiifolia* 'Raven') is a compact, evergreen houseplant sporting arching, pinnate leaves about 2 ft 5 in tall that emerge lime-green before maturing to a lustrous deep purple-black on thick, glossy leaflets above fleshy rhizomes.

Smoke Bush 'Royal Purple' (*Cotinus coggygria* 'Royal Purple') is a multi-stemmed shrub reaching 9 ft 10 in to 14 ft 9 in tall, with rounded, maroon-red leaves that deepen to purple and bear fluffy, pink-smoke plumes in late spring.

Black Bamboo (*Phyllostachys nigra*) is a running bamboo that grows 19 ft 8 in to 24 ft 7 in tall, its olive-green young canes turning jet-black within two to three years and topped by narrow, glossy green leaves.

Black Scallop Bugleweed (*Ajuga reptans* 'Black Scallop') forms a low groundcover just 3 in to 6 in tall, with rosettes of glossy, scalloped, near-black leaves and spring to early-summer whorls of violet-blue flowers.

Coral Bells 'Black Pearl' (*Heuchera* 'Black Pearl') is an evergreen perennial clumping up to 8 in to 10 in tall, with dense, ruffled, jet-black leaves edged in rosy purple and mid-summer sprays of white flowers in pink calyces.

Black Velvet Alocasia (*Alocasia reginula*) sends up petite, rhizomatous stems about 15 in tall, each topped with 6 in-wide, velvet-textured, heart-shaped leaves in deep green-black streaked with silvery-white veins.

Black Cardinal Philodendron (*Philodendron erubescens* 'Black Cardinal') is a self-heading tropical with burgundy stems 3 ft 3 in to 3 ft 11 in long, bearing large, glossy, arrow-shaped leaves that emerge deep red and mature to purple-black.

Onyx Odyssey Hellebore (*Helleborus* 'Onyx Odyssey') is an evergreen perennial 1 ft to 1 ft 3 in tall, with leathery foliage and fully double, cup-shaped blooms about 3 in across in slate-to-black purple.

Dark Opal Basil (*Ocimum basilicum* 'Dark Opal') is a tender annual herb 1 ft 6 in to 2 ft tall, with glossy, deep purple leaves, a sweet-anise fragrance, and terminal clusters of pink-lavender flowers.

Old Black Magic Iris (*Iris × germanica* 'Old Black Magic') is a tall bearded iris reaching 2 ft 11 in, with glaucous foliage and early-to-mid-season spikes of velvety, jet-black falls and standards accented by yellow beards and a sweet raisin scent.

Black Widow Crane's-bill (*Geranium phaeum*): a shade-loving perennial with back-turned, nearly black blooms that resemble mourning bonnets.

Crazytunia Black Mamba Petunia (*Petunia* 'Crazytunia Black Mamba'): a vigorous trailing petunia hybrid smothered in inky-maroon flowers all season long.

Clear Crystals Black Pansy (*Viola × wittrockiana* 'Clear Crystals Black'): jet-black petals rimmed in white, highlighted by bright yellow eyes—perfect for spring containers.

Black Charm Asiatic Lily (*Lilium asiatica* 'Black Charm'): star-shaped, reddish-black blooms on tall stems, ideal for dramatic cut-flower displays.

Black Pussy Willow (*Salix gracilistyla* 'Melanostachys'): striking purple-black catkins that emerge in late winter, adding early-season intrigue.

Black Pearl Coral Bells (*Heuchera* 'Black Pearl'): evergreen mounds of glossy, deep-purple foliage that glow even in low light.

Indigo Rose Tomato (*Solanum lycopersicum* 'Indigo Rose'): edible cherry tomatoes blushed deep purple-black, rich in antioxidants and garden drama.

Black Pearl Ornamental Pepper (*Capsicum annuum* 'Black Pearl'): upright habit with purple-black leaves and fruits that ripen to fiery red—eye-catching in mixed containers.

Black Cat Petunia (*Petunia* 'Black Cat'): an early-blooming, drought-tolerant petunia with sumptuous velvety petals that show no hint of fading.

Black Rose Aeonium (*Aeonium arboreum* 'Zwartkop'): succulent rosettes of burgundy-black leaves, striking in rock gardens or bright containers.

Dracula's Kiss Iris (*Iris* 'Dracula's Kiss'): A tall bearded iris reaching 36", featuring late-midseason blooms with ruffled, dark purple standards that darken to almost black falls around a bright tangerine beard. Honorable Mention 2011 and RHS Award of Merit 2013 recognize its dramatic color and form.

Black Mondo Grass (*Ophiopogon planiscapus* 'Nigrescens'): An evergreen, mat-forming groundcover producing dense, arching clumps of leathery, jet-black, linear leaves 8–12" long. In summer it bears small white, pink-tinged bell flowers and in fall glossy purple berries, thriving in sun to part shade on moist, well-drained soils and repelling deer and rabbits.

Black Lace Elderberry (*Sambucus nigra* 'Eva' BLACK LACE®): A deciduous multi-stemmed shrub 6–8' tall and wide, displaying deeply cut, purple-black pinnate leaves, fragrant lemon-scented pink umbels in early summer, and clusters of glossy blackish-red berries in late summer. It spreads by root suckers and self-seeds in moist, humus-rich soils.

Baptisia Dark Chocolate (*Baptisia* hybrid 'Dark Chocolate'): A false indigo forming a compact 3–3½' mound of blue-green foliage crowned in late spring by stout spikes of nearly black to charcoal-purple, pea-shaped flowers. Hardy in USDA zones 4–9 and resistant to deer and drought once established.

Dark Opal Basil (*Ocimum basilicum* 'Dark Opal'): A bushy annual 18–24" tall and wide, bearing glossy, nearly black-purple leaves with a mild licorice aroma. Produces spikes of small, tubular cerise flowers in summer and was a 1962 All-America Selections winner for culinary and ornamental appeal.

Black Pearl Ornamental Pepper (*Capsicum annuum* 'Black Pearl'): An 18–24" annual forming an upright, glossy mound of ovate leaves that emerge green and turn jet black under full sun. Bears purple blooms followed by ¾" round black fruits that mature to fiery red—edible but very hot—and was the 2006 All-America Selections Flower Winner.

Agave Black Widow (*Agave schidigera* 'Black Widow'): A slow-growing century plant forming a 12–16" rosette of green leaves edged with white fibers, each terminating in a sharp spine. Occasionally sends up a 3–5' pinkish-yellow flower stalk in autumn before the mother rosette dies. Hardy in USDA zones 8b–11; thrives in full sun with well-drained soil.

Heuchera Black Pearl (*Heuchera* 'Black Pearl'): A clump-forming evergreen coral bell featuring a dense mound of shiny, jet-black, scalloped leaves with rosy purple undersides. In midsummer, 18–20″ wands of delicate white flowers with pink calyxes rise above the foliage. Thrives in sun to shade on moist, well-drained soils; deer, salt, and drought resistant.

Summer Wine Black Ninebark (*Physocarpus opulifolius* 'SMNPMS'): A deciduous shrub 5–6′ tall and wide, bearing deep, nearly black new foliage contrasted by clusters of white flowers in spring. Tolerates a wide range of soils and exposures, requires minimal pruning, and excels as a striking specimen or mass planting in USDA zones 3–7.

Coleus 'Black Prince': a tender evergreen subshrub with nearly solid black, toothed soft leaves tinged with red, forming a dramatic mound up to 30 inches tall, and bearing small lavender-and-white flower spikes in summer.

Canna 'Tropicanna Black': boasts large, lance-shaped dark bronze to chocolate leaves and erect spikes of rich scarlet flowers that fade to orange, growing 4–6 feet tall and blooming from mid-summer to fall.

Sparkling Sangria™ Fringe Flower (*Loropetalum chinense* var. *rubrum* 'Sparkling Sangria™'): a large evergreen shrub up to 10 feet tall and wide, with vibrant deep burgundy foliage and profuse clusters of bright red, spidery flowers in spring that contrast beautifully with its dark leaves.

Ninebark Diabolo® (*Physocarpus opulifolius* 'Diabolo'): a deciduous shrub with deep purple, lobed, maple-like leaves, creamy-white spring flowers tinged pink that yield red seed capsules, and ornamental exfoliating bark, growing 4–8 feet tall and wide.

Black Lace® Elderberry (*Sambucus nigra* 'Black Lace®'): a large, upright deciduous shrub with finely dissected, purple-black lacy foliage, creamy-pink, lemon-scented flower umbels in early summer, and clusters of dark purple berries in fall, reaching 6–8 feet tall and wide.

Weigela 'Dark Horse': a dense, rounded deciduous shrub 2–3 feet tall and wide, with dark purple serrated leaves and profuse spring blooms of funnel-shaped pink flowers on last year's wood.

Weigela 'Tango': a compact, mounding shrub 2–2.5 feet tall with a slightly wider spread, bearing greenish-purple leaves and abundant rose-pink, tubular flowers with yellow throats in mid-spring.

Heuchera Northern Exposure™ 'Black': forms a medium-large mound of smoky chocolate-black, rounded, scalloped leaves that flash garnet-red underneath, sending up airy stems of white bell-shaped flowers from May through October.

Big Bluestem 'Blackhawks' (*Andropogon gerardii* 'Blackhawks'): an upright perennial grass with deep green leaves that turn dark purple to near-black, topped in late summer by purplish, turkey-foot-shaped flower clusters, growing 4–5 feet tall and 1–2 feet wide.

Mangave 'Black Magic': a compact succulent with 8–10-inch rosettes of flat, lance-shaped leaves so densely spotted they appear near-solid black, the tips arching over to a 20–24-inch spread in full sun.

Sedum Black in Black (*Sedum* 'Black in Black'): an upright, mounding succulent nearly 2 feet tall and wide, with almost black, rounded leaves supporting terminal clusters of creamy white blooms with dark red centers from August into September, thriving in full sun on dry to medium, well-drained soils.

Hillside Black Beauty (*Actaea simplex* 'Hillside Black Beauty'): a tall, late-season perennial reaching 4–6 feet with a 2.5-foot foliage mound of ferny coppery-purple leaves and fragrant 1–2-foot white bottlebrush flower spikes in early fall.

Smoke Tree 'Royal Purple' (*Cotinus coggygria* 'Royal Purple'): a multi-stemmed deciduous shrub 10–15 feet tall and wide, with rich maroon-red leaves that deepen to purplish-black in summer and bear large, feathery pink to purplish flower plumes that give a smoky effect.

Smokebush Winecraft Black® (*Cotinus coggygria* 'Winecraft Black®'): a rounded smokebush 8–10 feet tall with leaves emerging rich purple and maturing to near-black, adorned in early summer by large soft pink panicles that turn into hazy smoke and then red-orange fall color.

Black Diamond Crape Myrtle (*Lagerstroemia indica* 'Black Diamond'): a deciduous tree or large shrub 10–12 feet tall and 6–8 feet wide, with glossy black-purple foliage that endures year-round and abundant red, pink, or lavender flowers from late spring through fall.

Sweet Caroline Sweetheart Jet Black™ (*Ipomoea batatas* 'Sweet Caroline Sweetheart Jet Black™'): a vigorous annual vine with true jet-black, heart-shaped leaves on trailing stems up to 3 feet long, thriving in sun or shade as a container spiller or landscape groundcover.

Purple Fountain Grass (*Pennisetum setaceum* 'Rubrum'): a tender perennial grass 3–5 feet tall with arching burgundy-purple foliage and soft, fuzzy foxtail plumes of pinkish-purple flowers throughout summer.

Kodiak® Black Bush Honeysuckle (*Diervilla rivularis* 'Kodiak Black'): a native shrub 3–4 feet tall and wide with glossy dark burgundy-black lance-shaped leaves that glow red in autumn and clusters of yellow tubular flowers all summer, adaptable from full sun to shade.

DESANA® Bronze Sweet Potato Vine (*Ipomoea* hybrid 'DESANA® Bronze'): a trailing annual with a controlled habit of bronze foliage 6–10 inches tall and trailing 18–42 inches, featuring short internodes and excellent heat and humidity tolerance.

Cardinal Flower (*Lobelia cardinalis*): an herbaceous perennial 2–4 feet tall with lance-shaped green leaves and erect spikes of showy tubular two-lipped scarlet flowers from July to September that attract hummingbirds and butterflies.

Are you surprised there are so many black flowers? My dream is to own as many of these as possible. I'm sure it's your dream now, too!

Black Vegetables

Don't be afraid to think outside the box and plant vegetables and herbs with your ornamentals, shrubs, and flowers. This is a permaculture concept called "Don't Put All Your Eggs in One Basket." This principle, formally known as "Use and value diversity," advises against monocultures or relying on a single crop or plant. Cultivating and planting a wide range of species and varieties ensures against unexpected failures—whether from pests, disease, or weather extremes—ensuring that some portion of your garden always thrives. I interplant my herbs in my ornamental garden. But I keep the herbs out of my poison garden.

Here's a list of black heirloom vegetables that you can consider adding to a Garden for the Dead. Not only do they look cool, but heirloom plants are typically higher in nutrients and more flavorful than grocery store varieties.

Black Nebula Carrot (*Daucus carota* ssp. *sativus*)

Black Spanish Radish (*Raphanus sativus*)

Black Salsify (*Scorzonera hispanica*)

Shetland Black Potato (*Solanum tuberosum*)

Black Beauty Eggplant (*Solanum melongena*)

Gilo Eggplant (*Solanum aethiopicum*, Gilo group)

Black Beauty Tomato (*Solanum lycopersicum*)

Black Krim Tomato (*Solanum lycopersicum*)

Cherokee Purple Tomato (*Solanum lycopersicum*)

Paul Robeson Tomato (*Solanum lycopersicum*)

Black Hungarian Pepper (*Capsicum annuum*)

Black Beauty Zucchini (*Cucurbita pepo*)

Black Futsu Pumpkin (*Cucurbita moschata*)

Black Turtle Bean (*Phaseolus vulgaris*)

Cavolo Nero (Black Kale) (*Brassica oleracea* var. *palmifolia*)

Black Diamond Watermelon (*Citrullus lanatus* 'Black Diamond')

Blacktail Mountain Watermelon (*Citrullus lanatus* 'Blacktail Mountain')

Black Cherry Tomato (*Solanum lycopersicum* 'Black Cherry')

Midnight Bean (*Phaseolus vulgaris* 'Midnight')

Carolina Black Bean (*Phaseolus vulgaris* 'Carolina Black')

Kuromame Soybean (*Glycine max* 'Kuromame')

Black Mexican Winter Squash (*Cucurbita maxima* 'Black Mexican')

Black Diamond Kabocha (*Cucurbita maxima* 'Black Diamond')

Black Pearl Sweet Corn (*Zea mays* var. *saccharata* 'Black Pearl')

Hopi Blue Corn (*Zea mays* 'Hopi Blue')

Black Velvet Okra (*Abelmoschus esculentus* 'Black Velvet')

Black Seaman Collards (*Brassica oleracea* var. *viridis* 'Black Seaman')

Black Magic Kale (*Brassica oleracea* var. *palmifolia* 'Black Magic')

Black Groszolana Lettuce (*Lactuca sativa* 'Black Groszolana')

Black Seeded Simpson Lettuce (*Lactuca sativa* 'Black Seeded Simpson')

Bulgarian Black Pepper (*Capsicum annuum* 'Bulgarian Black')

Black and Dark Herbs

Black Basil – *Ocimum basilicum* 'Dark Opal'

Purple Basil – *Ocimum basilicum* 'Purple Ruffles'

Black Sage – *Salvia officinalis* 'Purpurascens'

Purple Oregano – *Origanum vulgare* 'Purpureum'

Chocolate Mint – *Mentha × piperita* 'Chocolate'

Perilla (Purple Shiso) – *Perilla frutescens* 'Purple'

Black Horehound – *Ballota nigra*

Black Cumin – *Nigella sativa*

Black Mustard – *Brassica nigra*

Purple Dead-nettle – *Lamium purpureum*

Blackcurrant Mint – *Mentha × piperita* 'Blackcurrant'

Amethyst Oregano – *Origanum vulgare* 'Amethyst Falls'

Black Mitcham Peppermint – *Mentha × piperita* 'Black Mitcham'

Black Knight Coneflower – *Echinacea purpurea* 'Black Knight'

Black Pearl Allium – *Allium sphaerocephalon*

Spooky Accent Plants

Moss, ferns, ornamental grasses, coleus, and hostas are welcome in any Garden of the Dead. I think of these as spooky accent plants. We need to break up all the flower blooms with splashes of green, white, and gray. Flowers mixed with moss, ferns, and hostas are particularly striking when plants with black and darker colored leaves are added. Add in some black mulch, and it's a gothic dream come true! If you live in a colder climate with a winter, these plants also look fantastic "dead" and create winter interest.

Spanish Moss (*Tillandsia usneoides*) is in the bromeliad family and hangs from tree branches. It has no true roots; instead, it absorbs water and nutrients through its leaves. It's a gorgeous silver-grey color—perfect as an accent between blooms and blossoms.

Other creepy mosses include *Hypnum imponens* (sheet moss), *Polytrichum commune* (haircap moss), *Sphagnum spp.* (peat moss), *Cladonia rangiferina* (reindeer lichen), *Thuidium delicatulum* (fern moss), *Leucobryum glaucum* (cushion moss), *Lycopodium clavatum* (running club moss), and *Amblystegium serpens* (star moss).

A Ghost Fern is a must-have in your Garden for the Dead. *Athyrium* × 'Ghost' (ghost fern) is a hybrid with upright fronds edged in pale silver and deep purple midribs. *Athyrium niponicum* (Japanese painted fern) has slender, lacy fronds in silvery gray with burgundy veins—one of Ghost Fern's parents. *Athyrium* × 'Frizelliae' (Frizell's painted fern) bears frilly fronds with a skeleton-like pattern and ghostly pale overlay. *Athyrium niponicum* var. *pictum* 'Silver Lady' (silver lady fern) displays broad, arching fronds with a metallic sheen and dark stems. *Osmunda regalis* (royal fern) unfurls tall, pinnate fronds like ghostly plumage. *Pteridium aquilinum* (bracken fern) spreads massive triangular fronds like spectral hands across your garden floor. *Phlebodium aureum* (blue star fern) offers waxy, blue-green fronds with an aquatic, spectral flow. *Asplenium nidus* (bird's nest fern) sends up shiny, undivided blades from a dark, funnel-shaped rosette—like a hidden nest. *Phlebodium mandianum* (bear's paw fern) shows rounded lobes along frond margins, lending a claw-like silhouette in dusky green.

These hostas bring an eerie, spectral vibe with ghostly variegation, deep shadows, and ominous names. Hosta 'Night Before Christmas' – silvery-white leaves with dark green veins; Hosta 'White Mouse Ears' – small, thick, bluish-white fuzzy leaves; Hosta 'Silver Bay' – dusty silver centers framed by deep green margins; Hosta 'First Frost' – blue-green bases with chalky-white edges; Hosta 'Silver Skates' – ghostly pale centers streaked with smoky veins; Hosta 'Abiqua Drinking Gourd' – puckered, deep blue-green leaves that curl like ancient manuscripts; Hosta 'Empress Wu' – enormous, dark emerald leaves that loom like tomb lids; Hosta 'Humpback Whale' – wavy, moon-pale green leaves resembling a creature rising from the depths; Hosta 'Ghost Brother' – milky white leaves speckled with charcoal-gray freckles; and Hosta 'Fire and Ice' – crisp white centers edged with steel blue margins.

Ornamental grasses lend a gothic garden an eerie presence as their slender blades sway and whisper. They conjure suspenseful soundscapes, and their dark foliage and dramatic seed plumes cast ghostly shadows. Low-maintenance perennials ensure haunting beauty all year. Recommended varieties include: *Panicum virgatum* 'Shenandoah' – blood-like, reddish-pink panicles above 4–5 ft of foliage in July–August; *Pennisetum alopecuroides* 'Burgundy Bunny' – creamy-white, feathery late-summer seedheads above dark red-tinged leaves; *Miscanthus sinensis* 'Purpurascens' – magenta-tinged plumes in late August, with foliage turning rosy purple in fall; *Panicum virgatum* 'Jamieson' – nearly black, wiry panicles in late summer resembling raven feathers; *Calamagrostis* × *acutiflora* 'Karl Foerster' – buff-tan early-summer plumes on tall, straight blades; *Deschampsia cespitosa* 'Goldtau' – nodding, silvery spring seed spikes that whisper like spirits; *Ophiopogon planiscapus* 'Nigrescens' – inky black leaves all season, creating an underworld-like carpet; *Imperata cylindrica* 'Red Baron' – dark green blades tipped with bright crimson, like blood-spattered blades.

Coleus

From moonlit chartreuse to blood-red veins, these plants thrive in shade and part-sun, making them perfect phantoms for borders, containers, and hanging baskets. Coleus refers to a group of ornamental plants in the mint family (Lamiaceae) grown primarily for their striking, multicolored foliage. Technically known as *Plectranthus scutellarioides*, these herbaceous perennials are treated as annuals in most climates. While they can flower—producing small blue or white spikes— gardeners almost always pinch blooms off to keep energy focused on leaf color. Victorians popularized coleus in elaborate "carpet gardens," and modern breeding has exploded to over 600 varieties spanning every imaginable foliage shade and pattern. Victorians seriously are the originators of the gothic garden. Coleus foliage showcases patterns such as borders, splashes, streaks, veins, splotches, and freckled or webbed designs, with leaf shapes ranging from scalloped and ruffled to lobed, elongated, fingerlike, or crinkled. I have a full shade garden at my house of only coleus…in every possible color I can find. This is my absolute favorite plant to mingle with the black flowers. Coleus offers endless possibilities for spectral gardens for the dead.

A Spectrum of Shades and Varieties

- Chartreuse, Green, and Lime: zesty foliage that lights up shadowy spots.

- Wine and Burgundy: deep, sanguine leaves adding gothic drama.

- Crimson and Ruby: Fiery reds that flicker like candlelight.

- Blush, pink, and Peach Soft: pastels evoking the rising sun.

- Variegated Blends: striking patterns in green, pink, and cream—each leaf a unique apparition.

Popular Cultivars

- Coleus 'Wizard Mix' Purple centers edged in neon green for maximum contrast.

- Coleus 'Kong Series' Gigantic foliage in bold reds, oranges, and purples— ideal for statement pieces.

- Coleus 'Henna' Matte bronze leaves veined with crimson, conjuring antique elegance.

- Coleus 'Fishnet Stockings' Bright pink veins traced on deep green for a lace-like effect. It looks just like fishnet stocking!

- Coleus 'Blackie' Nearly black leaves that absorb light, perfect for moody compositions.

  Your intent is important when selecting plants. Who is this garden for? We will discuss other factors that also influence what plants to grow (growing zone, budget, garden design, etc.) below in the Gardening 101 and Designing a Garden chapters. Now I will present the various types of Gardens for the Dead.

Gardens for the Dead

Memorial Gardens

A memorial garden refers to a purpose-designed natural space dedicated to remembering loved ones, commemorating significant events, or honoring communal and collective losses. Unlike cemeteries or graveyards, which are often prescribed by stricter traditions and regulations, memorial gardens offer remarkable flexibility and personalization, being established in public parks, religious grounds, community spaces, residential properties, and even digital landscapes. The core purpose, however, remains constant: to provide a locus for reflection, remembrance, and peace.

The concept of a memorial garden has been around since at least ancient Greece and Rome, when it was customary to inter the deceased in lush gardens adorned with sculptures, benches, and offerings. Eastern traditions, such as those in China and Japan, also developed profound connections between gardens and remembrance. Chinese ancestor gardens are sites for veneration, offerings, and reunion, while Japanese Zen gardens, though minimalist, foster contemplation, purification, and the ongoing cycle of life and death. In medieval Europe, Christian cloister gardens provided tranquil sanctuaries for meditation, prayer, and the assertion of a spiritual afterlife.

Historically, these spaces mirrored prevailing philosophies about life, death, and the cosmos. As we know, in Victorian England, the language of flowers became a means to express grief. In America, memorial gardens have been transformed with group garden clubs and civic initiatives, accelerating in popularity since the 20th century, with movements to create public, church, or children's remembrance gardens. The 21st century has renewed the relevance of memorial gardens as communities and individuals seek personal, sustainable, and emotionally resonant alternatives to traditional memorials.

Memorial Gardens can be both communal and individual, public and private. At their core, these gardens are living memorials. They assert that remembrance is a process, not a static event; that healing and grief, like seasons, ebb and flow. A planted tree or perennial bed becomes both a literal and metaphorical gesture of renewal, suggesting that life continues and transforms even in loss. When designing a memorial garden, it's most important to consider and honor your loved one's individuality and uniqueness and incorporate things that remind you of them, their personality, and interests.

Memorial gardens fulfill a range of purposes, serving as spaces for rituals or ceremonies—from anniversaries and religious traditions to community events—and providing a context for storytelling through educational signage or historical markers. Immersion in nature within these gardens can lower blood pressure, reduce anxiety, and lift depression, while the physical acts of digging, planting, and pruning offer a metaphorical process for working through loss, allowing expressions of love and remembrance through ongoing care. By committing to the nurture of a plant or a garden plot, bereaved individuals reclaim a sense of control and agency lost in mourning, creating a purposeful routine that restores meaning. The garden's flowering, growth, and fragrance become reservoirs of positive association, evoking specific memories and shared moments that hold emotional solace. Moreover, these spaces foster a connection with the natural world; their cycles of growth and decay gently remind us of the naturalness of mortality and the ever-present possibilities for renewal.

Thoughtful design is the heart of a meaningful memorial garden. While there is no strict criterion, a well-designed memorial garden stresses privacy by blending enclosed, intimate spaces with natural screens (trees, tall plants, low walls, fences, hedges, and/or pergolas with climbing plants), seating nooks, or gentle elevation changes to shape moments of quiet reflection gathering. Curved, meandering pathways invite visitors to wander and ponder, guiding them toward a carefully placed focal point—whether a memorial stone, sculptural piece, or tranquil water feature—that anchors the journey and gives the garden a visual heart. Layered plantings chosen for staggered bloom times and varied textures ensure year-round interest, reinforcing the theme of life's continual renewal. Finally, personalized touches—favorite color palettes, cherished objects, or living elements tied to the person or event commemorated—imbue the space with individual symbolism, making each memorial garden a unique celebration of memory and legacy.

Creating a seating area within the memorial garden provides visitors with a comforting refuge where they can sit, rest, and reflect. Consider adding a memorial bench dedicated to a loved one with a meaningful quote or personal message. Soft cushions and overhead shade from a pergola entwined with roses transform it into a serene alcove for quiet reflection. Personalized stepping stones engraved with names, life dates, or cherished sayings can lead guests along paths or frame flower beds, marking each step in the journey of remembrance. As dusk falls, solar lights with embedded photo markers cast a gentle glow, while glass suncatchers infused with cremation ashes catch the morning sun, celebrating enduring bonds. Wind chimes hanging from branches add a musical element, and lanterns tucked into trees provide warm light at twilight. Adding potted herbs for scent and planting a young memorial tree further enriches this living tribute, ensuring each feature resonates with individual memory and legacy. Sculptural and memorial art objects—angels, abstract forms, animals, or religious symbols—anchor the garden with visual and emotional resonance. Artistic input from family, friends, or local artists can make the space more unique and meaningful. You can include your loved one's favorite flowers, or any of the flowers discussed in the Flowers for the Dead chapter.

Incorporating personal touches into a memorial garden brings intimacy and resonance to the space. Wind chimes offer gentle, melodic reminders, evoking memory, presence, or even the symbolic voice of a loved one. Favorite objects can serve as heartfelt tributes—birdhouses for a nature enthusiast, artwork to honor a creative soul, or garden tools sculpted into thoughtful installations. Photographs and memory boxes nestled in weather-resistant frames or concealed in garden nooks invite reflection and interaction, allowing visitors to connect through keepsakes. More communal touches might include a memory pathway composed of stepping stones contributed by loved ones, walls or fences filled with written tributes, and shared garden beds where each visitor tends a chosen plant, weaving remembrance into the living landscape.

Cultural and spiritual traditions can also influence memorial garden elements.

Christian memorial gardens may incorporate biblical references, angels, or crosses, and be situated near or within church property.

Jewish and Islamic traditions may emphasize minimalism, the avoidance of figurative imagery, or the inclusion of inscribed stones and trees.

Eastern memorial gardens often integrate ancestor tables, altars for incense, and symbolic plants (e.g., cherry blossoms in Japan, which evoke the fleeting nature of life; lotus flowers in Buddhism, symbolizing spiritual rebirth and purity).

Indigenous memorial gardens may prioritize harmony with native ecology and be shaped by stories, oral tradition, and rituals intended to unite the human and natural worlds.

A pagan or witchy memorial garden is a sacred, evocative space that honors life's cycles—birth, death, and rebirth—through spiritual symbolism, natural elements, and personal ritual. Many such gardens are designed around the four classical elements: Earth, Air, Fire, and Water. These elements are often aligned with cardinal directions—North might include stones and evergreens, East adorned with wind chimes and airy herbs like lavender, South glowing with bright blooms and fire-associated plants, and West flowing with water features and moisture-loving flora. At the center, a fifth element—Spirit—may be represented by an altar or symbolic focal point.

The garden becomes a sanctuary for reflection and ritual with additions like a shrine or altar decorated with crystals, deity figurines, or photos of loved ones passed, and spaces defined by circles of herbs or stones for seasonal rites. Offering bowls may be placed throughout for herbs, libations, or flowers dedicated to ancestors. The memorial garden can feature spiral paths or pentagram layouts, rune-carved stones, and crystal grids. Wildlife is welcomed in such spaces, with bee, butterfly, and bat-friendly plants and bird baths inviting nature's messengers and spirits. Lighting aligned with lunar cycles, and moon dials or seasonal planting schedules, root the space in celestial rhythms. Every element works in harmony to create a place not only of mourning and memory but of magic, healing, and transformation.

Cremation Gardens

A cremation garden is a thoughtfully designed outdoor space where the cremated remains of loved ones can be legally and respectfully interred. I am going to write about scattering gardens and cremation burial gardens as separate entities. Cremation gardens provide a permanent, tangible focal point for remembrance while embracing the natural landscape. Unlike ash scattering, these gardens combine practical infrastructure with emotional support, offering families a serene environment for memorialization. Cremation gardens typically offer a spectrum of disposition choices to suit different wishes and budgets. Many families opt for in-ground urn burial, where a single or companion urn is interred in a lawn-level crypt beneath a flat bronze or granite marker. Above-ground columbarium niches provide a secure, sheltered home for one or more urns, each fronted by a personalized, inscribed plaque. Cremation memorial benches with built-in inurnment chambers let visitors pause for reflection right where their loved one rests. Some sites also feature communal ossuary walls—architectural structures housing multiple urns within recessed compartments—and lawn crypts, which are vaulted earthen graves designed specifically for urn interment. Whatever the preference—traditional inurnment, scattering, memorial seating, or living monuments—a well-designed cremation garden can accommodate every form of remembrance under one serene canopy of nature. The fundamental purpose is to provide a permanent location where loved ones can gather and reflect, ensuring ashes are deposited in a protected, legally sanctioned area.

Cremation gardens serve multiple roles: a place of final disposition, an outdoor chapel for memorial services, and an enduring landscape feature. Their naturalistic design fosters healing by situating mourning within the cycle of nature. Families benefit from the garden's permanence—unlike scattering ashes in open spaces, which lack a visitable site, cremation gardens offer a dedicated spot for ongoing remembrance. Furthermore, these gardens accommodate personal expression through customizable markers, tree dedications, and ecological plantings.

Creating a cremation garden begins with choosing a tranquil and private setting well away from high-traffic areas. Buffer the space with dense shrubs or a belt of trees—dogwood, serviceberry, arborvitae, or evergreen conifers—to soften road or cemetery noise and create a sense of enclosure.

Then define a unifying theme—perhaps a native woodland sanctum, a reflective water garden, a butterfly garden. or a rose garden. That concept will guide every decision, from the path materials to the urn niches you install later. Plant selection in a cremation garden should lean heavily on regionally adapted species to minimize upkeep and maximize ecological benefits. Under a canopy of trees—oaks or maples underplanted with serviceberries—layer spring bulbs like crocus and daffodil to welcome early visitors. In summer, lavender, echinacea, and blue hydrangeas provide both visual interest and pollinator forage. Autumn asters and goldenrods extend the season, while evergreens like rosemary circle columbarium walls as fragrant guardians. Embrace symbolic planting too: scatter forget-me-nots for enduring remembrance, lilies for innocence, and crimson roses for abiding love. Whenever I meet with families after a funeral, I give them forget-me-not seeds to scatter in memory of the loved one.

Hardscape elements transform this living memorial into an interactive, reflective space. Granite benches with laser-etched inscriptions give visitors a place to pause—choose a bench design that conceals a niche for two companion urns. Custom-engraved stepping stones set at intervals can bear names, words of endearment, quotes, or dates, guiding guests through the garden in slow, mindful steps. Wind chimes cast from brass or bronze add a softly musical tribute; each tone can be personalized with an inscription. Functional art pieces, like a bronze sundial calibrated to local coordinates or a sculpture by a local artist, become focal points that merge beauty, memory, and purpose.

Sheltered structures—gazebos or pergolas—provide gathering spots for memorial services or momentary respite on rainy days. Consider living roofs of wisteria or clematis to soften the architecture and merge it into the landscape. Select bronze-fronted niches for a patina finish, or glass-door compartments that let in light and allow families to view mementos placed alongside ashes. These walls can be set against a backdrop of climbing vines and flowering shrubs to weave in natural beauty.

Water features bring an extra layer of serenity to a cremation garden. A simple recirculating fountain near the scattering lawn masks distant noise and symbolizes the flow of life. Small ponds framed by natural stone or bio-locks invite waterfowl and frogs, while a shallow reflecting pool carved from slate lets the sky—and memories—be mirrored on its surface. Place urn-niche benches nearby so visitors can sit quietly, letting the gentle sounds deepen their reflection.

Finally, weave in cremation-specific elements that celebrate both remembrance and ecological stewardship. Install an ash-infused glass art wall where minute quantities of ashes are sealed in vivid panels, or create a labyrinth paved with stones that incorporate cremated remains in the mortar. Offer families the option of planting wildflower-filled urn planters—biodegradable vessels that bloom for a season before returning to the earth. Digital kiosks nearby can share life stories and photos, linking the physical garden to cherished memories. Altogether, these ideas transform a simple green space into a living tapestry of honor, beauty, and renewal.

Recommended Flowers and Plants for Cremation Gardens

- *Myosotis sylvatica* – Forget-Me-Not *Symbolic Meaning:* Enduring love, true remembrance *Ecological Benefit:* Supports pollinators; reseeds modestly
- *Lavandula angustifolia* – Lavender *Symbolic Meaning:* Serenity, calm, devotion *Ecological Benefit:* Drought-tolerant; attracts bees and butterflies
- *Chrysanthemum morifolium* – Chrysanthemum *Symbolic Meaning:* Honor, grief, celebration of life *Ecological Benefit:* Late-season nectar source; non-invasive
- *Tagetes erecta* – Marigold *Symbolic Meaning:* Comfort, warmth, friendship *Ecological Benefit:* Attracts pollinators; pest deterrent
- *Lilium candidum* – Lily *Symbolic Meaning:* Innocence, rebirth, purity *Ecological Benefit:* Bulbs naturalize; tolerant of varied soils
- *Rosa spp.* – Rose *Symbolic Meaning:* Love (red), purity (white), friendship (yellow) *Ecological Benefit:* Nectar source; supports pollinators
- *Viola × wittrockiana* – Pansy *Symbolic Meaning:* Thoughtfulness, remembrance *Ecological Benefit:* Cool-weather blooms; attracts pollinators
- *Lobularia maritima* – Sweet Alyssum *Symbolic Meaning:* Sweet memory, humility *Ecological Benefit:* Groundcover; beneficial insect habitat
- *Dianthus barbatus* – Dianthus *Symbolic Meaning:* Affection, remembrance *Ecological Benefit:* Permanent blooms; pollinator-friendly
- *Limonium sinuatum* – Statice *Symbolic Meaning:* Lasting remembrance, success *Ecological Benefit:* Drought-tolerant; long bloom period
- *Helianthus annuus* – Sunflower *Symbolic Meaning:* Loyalty, adoration *Ecological Benefit:* Nectar and seeds for wildlife; annual reseeder
- *Rosmarinus officinalis* – Rosemary *Symbolic Meaning:* Fidelity, remembrance *Ecological Benefit:* Evergreen foliage; aromatic; attracts bees
- *Cosmos bipinnatus* – Cosmos *Symbolic Meaning:* Peace, harmony *Ecological Benefit:* Grows in poor soils; attracts butterflies

- *Delphinium elatum* – Delphinium *Symbolic Meaning:* Cleansing, protection *Ecological Benefit:* Tall spikes attract bees; deer-resistant
- *Helleborus orientalis* – Hellebore *Symbolic Meaning:* Eternal renewal, serenity *Ecological Benefit:* Winter blooms; early nectar for bees

Scatter Gardens (Cremains)

A scattering garden is a designated area in a cemetery or a personal space in your yard where cremated remains are meant to be scattered. There is usually a wall or scroll with the names and dates of the individuals whose remains have been scattered there. You can also memorialize the dead with names and dates on stone or granite markers. A scattering garden gives the family a permanent and accessible place to remember, reflect, and share with future generations.

Interest in scattering gardens has grown in tandem with the rise of cremation, offering an eco-friendly alternative to traditional burials by avoiding land-intensive plots, embalming chemicals, and non-biodegradable materials. Families value these gardens for their ability to provide a personalized, contemplative environment that honors the deceased while promoting community gathering and solace in a shared green space.

Scattering gardens serve both private and public needs. Privately, homeowners create intimate remembrance spots in backyards or private estates. Publicly, cemeteries and memorial parks allocate sections—often landscaped with native and ornamental plantings—to accommodate multiple families, ensuring accessibility and communal legacy. This dual application underscores the flexibility and significance of scattering gardens as both personal and collective memorial sites.

Scattering ashes requires compliance with local, state, and federal laws. On private property, permission from the landowner is mandatory; on public lands, such as parks or beaches, permits are often required, and specific distances from water or trails may apply. For scattering at sea, the U.S. Clean Water Act mandates scattering a minimum of three nautical miles offshore and notification to the EPA within 30 days.

Some cemeteries now offer scattering gardens as part of their services. These gardens are subject to cemetery rules regarding booking, scattering procedures, memorial markers, and ongoing maintenance. Families should inquire about scattering time frames, acceptable urn types, and any documentation—such as death certificates—required by the cemetery administration.

As a gardener, I believe we are all stewards of nature (or at least we should be). We garden for beauty. We garden to protect the environment. We garden and understand we are in balance with nature and should not get upset when animals come into our yard and take a bite of the delicious treats we are growing. I know scattering ashes is a trend in deathcare, but it's important to know that cremains are not necessarily good for the environment.

Cremated ashes are alkaline and contain high levels of salts, calcium, and phosphorus, which can alter soil pH and nutrient balance. Cremated remains are extremely alkaline (pH ~11.8) and carry sodium levels 200–2000× higher than most plants can tolerate, which inhibits nutrient uptake and soil life. If you want to create a scattering garden, please try to mitigate cremains environmental impact through thoughtful site design, soil amendments, and plant selection that tolerates higher pH levels.

In your scattering garden, start by blending cremains with a specialized soil amendment—ideally one formulated to neutralize high alkalinity and dilute sodium—alongside high-quality organic compost or well-rotted manure, elemental sulfur, gypsum, peat moss, and biochar, then inoculate with compost tea or mycorrhizae. Let this mixture rest for 90–120 days so pH and sodium levels stabilize before planting.

When it's time to plant, use deep-rooted, alkali-tolerant perennials (like cypress or yarrow) in raised beds or mounded areas packed with your amended mix, allowing roots to access fresher earth layers. Maintain a gentle, consistent irrigation schedule to leach excess sodium below the root zone, top-dress with organic mulch to conserve moisture and feed soil life, and periodically apply slow-release, acidifying fertilizers (such as ammonium sulfate or chelated iron) to correct micronutrient lock-ups common in high-pH soils.

When creating a private scattering garden on residential property, prioritize accessibility and a meaningful setting. Ideal spots include a quiet corner of a backyard, near a favorite tree, pond, or rock formation, ensuring proximity to the house for ease of visitation. Evaluate sun exposure and drainage; aim for locations receiving morning sun and afternoon shade to balance plant needs and visitor comfort.

Design your private garden with flowing pathways—using materials like gravel, flagstone, or resin-bound surfaces—to guide visitors through the space without disrupting plantings. A gentle slope or curved path creates a contemplative journey, enabling wheelchair access where needed. Integrate a bench or small seating area as both a focal point and resting place, ideally situated with views of a scattering spot or water feature.

Select a mix of perennial and annual blooms to ensure year-round color. Surround the scattering area with low-maintenance groundcovers, ornamental grasses, and seasonal perennials such as asters, coneflowers, or black-eyed susans for a vibrant yet manageable display. Intersperse evergreen shrubs or small trees—like holly or dogwood—for structural stability and winter interest.

Personalize with engraved stones, plaques, or sculptural wind chimes to mark the scattering spot. Choose natural, eco-friendly materials—recycled wood, stone, or weathered metal—to complement the environment and ensure longevity.

Public scattering gardens should integrate seamlessly into existing cemetery master plans. Identify underutilized land—steep slopes, wooded areas, or meadowland—that is unsuitable for traditional burial plots. Master plan integration ensures visibility, respect for adjacent interment areas, and a balanced mix of scattering zones and conventional burial options.

To follow are the recommended species—each symbolizing death or remembrance and able to tolerate alkaline, sodium-rich soils typical of cremains.

- Chrysanthemum (*Chrysanthemum spp.*)

  - Symbolism: mourning, grief, rebirth

  - Soil tolerance and benefits: thrives in pH 6.5–7.5; hardy perennial whose fibrous roots break up compacted soil

- Marigold (*Tagetes erecta*)

  - Symbolism: Day of the Dead, guiding spirits

  - Soil tolerance and benefits: tolerates pH 6–7.5; dense root system suppresses pathogens and aerates heavy ground

- Asphodel (*Asphodelus albus*)

  - Symbolism: Greek underworld, everlasting regret

  - Soil tolerance and benefits: prefers pH 7–8; drought-tolerant bulb that endures poor, rocky soils and anchors ashes-laden earth

- Iris (*Iris germanica*)

  - Symbolism: messenger between worlds, hope beyond death

  - Soil tolerance and benefits: adapts to pH 6.5–8; spreading rhizomes improve drainage and reduce erosion

- Oleander (*Nerium oleander)*

  - Symbolism: caution, deadly beauty, remembrance

  - Soil tolerance and benefits: tolerant of pH 6–8 and high salinity; evergreen shrub that stabilizes slopes and filters sodium from runoff

- Yarrow (*Achillea millefolium)*

  - Symbolism: remembering the fallen, healing

  - Soil tolerance and benefits: thrives in pH 6–8.5; deep roots loosen soil, boost microbial activity, and survive in nutrient-poor ground

- Anemone (*Anemone coronaria*)

  - Symbolism: anticipation, fading life, remembrance

  - Soil tolerance and benefits: grows in pH 6.5–7.8; tubers enhance soil structure and bring early-season color to scattering sites

- Cypress (*Cupressus sempervirens*)

  - Symbolism: Eternal life, mourning, remembrance

  - Soil Tolerance and Benefits: Thrives in alkaline soils; deep roots stabilize and aerate compacted earth.

- Yew *(Taxus baccata)*

  - Symbolism: Death, longevity, resurrection

  - Soil Tolerance and Benefits: Adapts to a wide pH range; dense root network reduces erosion around burial areas.

- Rosemary *(Salvia rosmarinus)*

  - Symbolism: Remembrance, memorial

  - Soil Tolerance and Benefits: Prefers well-drained, slightly alkaline soil; evergreen habit binds soil and deters weeds.

- White Lily (*Lilium candidum*)

  - Symbolism: Purity, peace, soul's restored innocence

  - Soil Tolerance and Benefits: Tolerates pH up to ~7.5 when soil is amended; bulbs add vertical interest to the bed.

- Red Poppy (*Papaver rhoeas*)

  - Symbolism: Sorrow, remembrance of the fallen

  - Soil Tolerance and Benefits: Hardy annual that tolerates varied pH; its taproot helps break up dense soil layers.

Native species ensure ecological balance and low maintenance. Using native plants in your scattering garden is essential to preserving our ecosystems. Besides being hardy, drought-resistant, and pest-resistant, native plants attract pollinators, better absorb storm water, and balance the soil, making them ideal for a scatter garden. Temperate environments are regions situated between the tropics and the polar circles, where you get four distinct seasons—warm summers, cool autumns, chilly winters, and crisp springs—with moderate annual rainfall and generally fertile soils that support a wide array of deciduous forests, grasslands, and mixed woodlands. Day-to-day temperatures rarely swing to the extremes you'd see in tropics or arctic zones.

In temperate regions, consider the following plants, which are presented in layers to best mimic nature. From stately canopy trees to delicate groundcovers, these species stabilize soils, cycle nutrients, and provide food and habitat for wildlife.

Canopy and Understory Trees:

- White Oak (*Quercus alba*) Deep taproots break up compacted soils and sequester carbon in wood and roots.
- Sugar Maple (*Acer saccharum*) Brilliant fall color; its leaf litter slowly acidifies soil and boosts microbial life.
- Eastern Redbud (*Cercis canadensis*) Early spring blossoms feed bees; tolerates a wide pH range and drought once established.
- Serviceberry (*Amelanchier arborea*) Multi-stemmed understory tree whose berries support birds and small mammals.

Shrubs:

- Spicebush (*Lindera benzoin*) Host plant for spicebush swallowtail caterpillars; fragrant foliage tolerates clay and light alkali.
- Elderberry (*Sambucus canadensis*) Fast-growing, moisture-loving shrub that attracts pollinators and stabilizes streambanks.
- Inkberry Holly (*Ilex glabra*) Evergreen cover for wildlife; berries persist into winter, feeding resident birds.
- Ninebark (*Physocarpus opulifolius*) Tough, drought-resistant native with exfoliating bark that adds winter interest and habitat.

Herbaceous Perennials:

- Purple Coneflower (*Echinacea purpurea*) Long-blooming nectar source for bees and butterflies; seedheads feed finches in fall.
- Black-Eyed Susan (*Rudbeckia hirta*) Tolerates poor, dry soils; its tall stems and bright blooms add structure to scatter areas.
- Beardtongue (*Penstemon digitalis*) White tubular flowers attract hummingbirds; thrives in well-drained, rocky soils.
- Wild Bergamot (*Monarda fistulosa*) Mint family fragrance deters pests; superb for pollinators and aromatic tea-making.
- Asters (*Symphyotrichum spp.)* Late-season blooms that extend foraging into autumn; spreads slowly to fill gaps.
- Goldenrod (*Solidago spp.)* Keystone late-summer pollen source; deep roots improve soil structure.
- Yarrow (*Achillea millefolium*) Ferny foliage and flat flower heads draw predators of common garden pests.
- Butterfly Weed (*Asclepias tuberosa*) Milkweed species essential for monarch caterpillars; tolerates drought and alkaline patches.

Grasses and Groundcovers:

- Little Bluestem (*Schizachyrium scoparium*) Clumping prairie grass; brilliant copper tones in fall and superb erosion control.
- Prairie Dropseed (*Sporobolus heterolepis*) Fine, arching foliage with fragrant seedheads; drought-tolerant and low-maintenance.
- Woodland Phlox (*Phlox divaricata*) Spreads to form a fragrant carpet in shade; early spring blooms feed bumble bees.
- Virginia Creeper (*Parthenocissus quinquefolia*) Fast-climbing vine that shades soil, reduces evaporation, and provides fall food for wildlife.

Pet Cemetery/Pet Memorial Garden

Pet cemetery gardens serve as sacred spaces where we can both honor and remember our beloved animal companions. These gardens offer a dedicated location to reflect on the unconditional love pets provide and the joy they brought into our lives. Creating such a space can facilitate the grieving process by providing a tangible connection to the bond shared with a pet. You can bury either your beloved pet's body or their cremated remains in the garden.

Pet memorial gardens allow for personalized tributes, ranging from headstones and markers to plant selections that reflect a pet's spirit. When my husband and I lost our dogs Jasmine and Sesh, he worked through his grief by making each pet's headstone by hand. He made molds, poured concrete, and etched their names into them. He also embedded their name tags/dog tags into the headstones. They are lying in one of the memorial gardens. The act of designing, planting, and maintaining the garden can be a healing ritual, channeling grief into meaningful, living art that evolves with the seasons. Ultimately, these gardens stand as lasting legacies, commemorating the profound impact pets have on our lives.

Private pet burial laws vary widely across jurisdictions. Pet burials on private property can be allowed if the owner secures appropriate depth and distance from water sources. Municipalities may further restrict burials near property lines or water bodies to protect public health and the environment. Other states mandate that animal remains be treated as solid waste, requiring distances of at least 50 feet from property lines and 300 feet from water bodies. Before proceeding, pet owners should verify local ordinances, as some counties or homeowners' associations prohibit backyard burials. Consulting city or county health departments ensures compliance with state and municipal regulations, preventing potential fines and environmental issues.

When designing a private pet cemetery garden, consider the location's privacy, proximity to the home, and accessibility. A serene corner under a favorite tree or near a patio can become a comforting spot for visits. Defining the burial area with edging—such as stone or wood—creates a distinct boundary, protecting the grave and containing garden elements.

Memorial markers can range from hand-painted stones to custom granite headstones. For instance, DIY headstones painted on field stones provide a cost-effective tribute that can be refreshed every few years. Incorporating wind chimes, benches, or pet-safe water features adds soothing elements that invite reflection.

If you are burying your pet's body, use a garden spade to excavate the hole, targeting at least three feet of soil cover above the container to deter scavengers and prevent odors. Wrap your pet in a burial shroud or a blanket. You can also purchase or make pet caskets.

Place a stone slab, engraved pet headstone, or personalized plaque at the site. Customized granite markers ensure longevity and elegance. Surround the marker with ground covers, annuals, or perennials that thrive in your hardiness zone. Use mulch or gravel to define pathways and plant beds. Include your pet's collar, favorite toy, or handcrafted mosaic tiles. These personal items personalize the garden and make visits more meaningful. Integrate small fountains, birdbaths, or even miniature ponds to attract wildlife and add a calming auditory backdrop. Such features invite birds and butterflies, creating a living tribute to your pet's spirit.

Public pet cemeteries offer licensed burial plots and handle all regulatory compliance. I work at a cemetery that has a pet section. While some states permit private burials, public cemeteries provide an alternative when private land is unavailable or restricted. Many states require that public cemeteries follow solid waste disposal rules and maintain plot records, including ownership and burial documentation.

Selecting plants that resonate with your pet's spirit and your personal memories builds a meaningful tribute. Symbolic Plants for Pet Memorial Gardens:

- *Myosotis sylvatica* – Forget-Me-Not (Everlasting love)

- *Lilium candidum* – White Lily (Peaceful afterlife)

- *Rosmarinus officinalis* – Rosemary (Remembrance and healing)

- *Helianthus annuus* – Sunflower (Light and joy)

- *Lavandula angustifolia* – Lavender (Calm and tranquility)

- *Syringa vulgaris* – Lilac (Seasonal beauty, nostalgia)

- *Hydrangea macrophylla* – Hydrangea (Grace and heartfelt emotion)

- *Acer palmatum* – Japanese Maple (Elegance and transformation)

- *Cornus florida* – Flowering Dogwood (Renewal and beauty)

- *Rosa* (red cultivars) – Rose (Eternal love)

- *Bellis perennis* – Daisy (Innocence and cheer)

- *Tagetes erecta* – Marigold (Guidance and remembrance)

- *Zantedeschia aethiopica* – Calla Lily (Rebirth and purity)

- *Gypsophila paniculata* – Baby's Breath (Eternal innocence)

- *Chrysanthemum morifolium* – Chrysanthemum: Loyalty, honor, devotion

- *Hydrangea macrophylla* – Blue Hydrangea: Gratitude, sincerity

- *Viola odorata* – Violet: Faithfulness, affection

Creating a pet cemetery garden is both a heartfelt tribute and a healing practice. By combining legal compliance, thoughtful design, and meaningful plant selections, you can craft a lasting sanctuary that honors your pet's legacy and offers comfort to everyone who visits.

Graveside Gardens/Cradle Gardens

A cradle grave consists of a gravestone, a footstone, and two low stone walls connecting them, creating a rectangle designed to hold plantings to memorialize the person buried below. They were popular in the Victorian era but originated in the mid-1800s. Families filled the trough-like bed with living plants, treating it as a lush blanket laid over the deceased's resting place. The design visually echoes a baby's cradle, underscoring that era's belief that every soul remained a child of God, regardless of age. Some legends held that spirits lingered among the blooms, and tending a cradle garden could appease restless souls, ensuring peace for both the living and the dead.

Victorian gardeners chose blooms valued for their beauty, fragrance, and symbolism. Popular selections included:

Daylilies (*Hemerocallis*)

Roses (various heirloom and tea rose cultivars)

Iris (bearded and flag types)

Peonies (*Paeonia lactiflora*)

Bulbs: crocus, daffodil, hyacinth

Ferns and mosses for evergreen texture

Annuals: petunias, marigolds, begonias

These plantings formed a seasonal tapestry—spring bulbs heralded new life, summer perennials offered full color, and hardy evergreens provided winter structure.

Over time, many cradle gardens fell into neglect. Today, volunteer "cradle gardeners" have revived dozens of sites, researching burial records and replanting historically accurate heirloom varieties. Modern "adopt-a-grave" initiatives enlist volunteers to research the interred, select period-appropriate plants, and maintain cradle beds through the growing season. This labor of love restores historical landscapes, reconnects communities with local heritage, and transforms once-forgotten cemeteries back into living parks. Whether you're inspired to volunteer at a nearby historic cemetery or simply intrigued by this elegant Victorian tradition, cradle gardens offer a beautiful intersection of memory, myth, and horticulture. If your loved one's gravesite is not at a historical cemetery and you would like to create and maintain a cradle gravesite garden, please check with the cemetery to make sure you are abiding by that cemetery's rules and regulations, as some do not allow in-ground plantings.

Grave Blanket

Grave blankets are a tradition brought to America by Scandinavian settlers. Grave blankets are a decorative covering traditionally used in the Midwest, particularly in Minnesota, North Dakota, and Wisconsin. They are usually placed on gravesites before the first snow to serve as a symbolic gesture to tuck in a loved one and keep them warm during the winter.

Traditionally made from evergreen boughs arranged on a flexible wire frame, these blankets serve a dual purpose: they insulate and protect the grave from harsh winter weather while symbolizing continued care and remembrance for the deceased.

Grave blankets carry deep symbolism. They represent warmth, respect, and an ongoing connection with loved ones, visually conveying the message that the deceased are not forgotten. Placing a grave blanket is an act of honor and love, much like wrapping a living family member in a cozy blanket during cold months.

By drawing on centuries-old traditions, adapting to regional practices, and incorporating meaningful floral symbolism, grave blankets become more than just winter decorations; they stand as living testaments to love, memory, and the continuing bonds with those who have passed on.

Grave blankets use natural materials for both symbolism and functionality. The three key components include:

Evergreen Boughs: Branches from balsam, fir, white pine, or spruce symbolize eternal life and continuity due to their year-round greenery.

Metal or Chicken Wire Frame: This provides structure, maintaining the blanket's shape and sturdiness against weather elements.

Decorative Accents: Items like pinecones, berries, glitter, ornaments, and ribbons add personal touches and color to the predominantly green foundation.

My twist on the grave blankets includes hardy, cold-resistant blooms:

Winter Heather (*Erica carnea*): Features vibrant bell-shaped flowers in purple, pink, or white, with a hardiness of -10 °C to -15 °C and a low-maintenance appeal.

Cyclamen (*Cyclamen coum, C. hederifolium*): Offers charming tuberous blooms in late winter, thriving in the shade and pairing beautifully with snowdrops.

Snowdrops (*Galanthus nivalis*): These flowers push through frost and symbolize hope with their nodding white blossoms, emerging as early as January.

Hellebores or "Christmas Rose" (*Helleborus niger*): Known for sturdy blooms and evergreen foliage, they can tolerate temperatures down to -20 °C, providing continuous winter interest.

Pansies (*Viola × wittrockiana*): They deliver cheerful multicolored blooms even in light freezes and can resist temperatures as low as -15 °C while symbolizing remembrance.

Winter Aconites (*Eranthis*): Golden-yellow blossoms that emerge early, offering a cheerful splash and symbolizing renewal.

Here's a detailed, step-by-step guide to creating your own grave blanket:

1. Gather Materials: Collect evergreen branches—preferably sturdy ends about 2–3 feet long—along with smaller filler branches of 12–18 inches for fullness. Obtain a chicken wire panel (approximately 1x2 feet for a "grave pillow" or 2x4 feet for a full grave blanket) and floral or craft wire for securing greenery.

2. Prepare the Wire Frame: Cut the chicken wire to the desired size. Fold or bend it to form 3-4 layers for stability, ensuring the final dimensions will cover the grave evenly. Wear gloves to avoid wire cuts.

3. Attach Bough Ends: Poke the end branches through the wire mesh, one on each side, creating the blanket's perimeter. Position them opposite one another to define the blanket's rectangular outline.

4. Layer and Weave Filler Branches: Starting at the perimeter, weave mid-sized branches into the wire, filling toward the center. Alternate different types of evergreens—such as balsam and spruce—to add texture and color variation. Twist or angle some layers to increase bulk and hide the wire frame.

5. Lock in the Center: Continue inserting branches in the middle, pushing them through neighboring foliage until they lock in place. Use smaller filler branches to cover any exposed wire and fill gaps.

6. Secure with Floral Wire: Wrap floral wire around bunches of foliage or accents to reinforce their position. Anchor decorative elements—like bows or pinecones—by wiring them to robust branches near the center or edges.

7. Use Floral Foam Blocks to secure cold-weather flower arrangements and decorative elements in place. (optional)

8. Add Finishing Touches: Place a ribbon-wrapped branch at the blanket's focal point and attach berries, ornaments, bells, or feathers as personal commemorations.

9. Install at the Gravesite: Carefully transport the blanket to the cemetery using a sturdy sheet or tarp underneath. Stake down the corners with U-shaped garden pegs

or heavy rocks to prevent shifting in the wind. Remember, it is installed before the first snowfall.

Mourning Garden (Garden for Grief)

A mourning garden is a place to sit and reflect, meditate, and grieve as well as heal. It's recommended that we make these as much into a sensory garden a possible; engaging multiple senses (touch, sight, smell) to help us heal. Include highly aromatic plants, visually stunning plants, and plants that are soothing to the touch. Can make any of the flowers in the garden into flower essences to help you heal your heart, soul, and emotions while grieving the loss of a loved one. You may want to consider including a bench for sitting.

Flower Essences

Flower essences are the vibrational messages of flowers that are transmitted to water through a process called solarization. This allows the water to memorize the vibrational resonance of the flower. Flower essences are liquid infusions made from the blooming parts of plants, capturing the subtle "vibrational" energy or emotional signature of each blossom. They are used in flower therapy as gentle mood enhancers.

Bach flower essences were first developed by Edward Bach in the 1930s. These remedies contain a very small amount of flower material mixed in a 50:50 solution of brandy and water. Because the remedies are extremely diluted, they do not have a noticeable scent or taste of the plant. It is believed that these remedies carry the "energetic" or "vibrational" nature of the flower, which can be transferred to the user.

Bach flower remedies are considered vibrational medicines and are based on the concept of water memory. Bach theorized that the dew found on flower petals retains the healing properties of the plant. These remedies are primarily intended for addressing emotional and spiritual conditions, including, but not limited to, depression, anxiety, insomnia, and stress.

Choose a flower that you are drawn to or have read about and know its qualities.

Sit quietly with the flower, meditate, draw, or write.

Fill a glass or crystal bowl with fresh, living water. Do not use distilled water or water that is chlorinated or otherwise contaminated.

Cover the surface of the water with flowers, removing them at the stem and being careful not to touch the flower itself with your fingers.

Leave the bowl to sit in the sun for at least three hours.

At the end of its time in the sun, your water will be imprinted with the energetics and dynamics of your flower. You have created a "mother essence."

Remove the flowers. Do not touch the water with your fingers. Use a stick or twig.

To preserve this essence, pour the water into an amber glass bottle until it is half full. Fill the bottle to the top with the brandy alcohol.

Per tradition, you place four drops under the tongue or in a small glass of water, four times per day.

In a Mourning Garden, I would include any of the plants whose flowers look like tears:

Bleeding Heart – *Dicentra spectabilis*

Lily of the Valley – *Convallaria majalis*

Solomon's Seal – *Polygonatum spp.*

Snowdrop – *Galanthus nivalis*

Bluebell – *Hyacinthoides non-scripta*

Fuchsia – *Fuchsia spp.*

Bellflower – *Campanula poscharskyana* and others

Begonia 'Silver Teardrop' – *Begonia corallina* var. "Silver"

Foamflower – *Tiarella cordifolia*

Cyclamen – *Cyclamen hederifolium*

Siberian Squill – *Scilla siberica*

Snowflake – *Leucojum vernum*

Epimedium – *Epimedium grandiflorum*

Morning Glory – *Ipomoea purpurea*

Canterbury Bells – *Campanula medium*

Bleeding Glory-Bower – *Clerodendrum thomsoniae*

Bluebell Hyacinth – *Hyacinthoides hispanica*

Mourning Garden Trees

Weeping Willow – *Salix babylonica* 'Tristis'

Weeping Cherry – *Prunus × pendula* 'Rosea'

Weeping Japanese Maple – *Acer palmatum* var. *dissectum* 'Crimson Queen'

Camperdown Elm – *Ulmus glabra* 'Camperdownii'

Weeping Copper Beech – *Fagus sylvatica* 'Pendula'

Weeping Birch – *Betula pendula* 'Youngii'

Weeping Norway Spruce – *Picea abies* 'Inversa'

Weeping Nootka Cypress – *Xanthocyparis nootkatensis* 'Pendula'

Weeping Mulberry – *Morus alba* 'Chaparral'

Weeping Crabapple – *Malus* 'Louisa'

I would include these healing and highly aromatic herbs and flowers:

Lavender (*Lavandula angustifolia*) – Known for its calming scent, lavender supports relaxation and restful sleep.

Geranium (*Geranium spp.*) – A soothing herb that gently eases tension and promotes emotional balance.

Iris (*Iris spp.*) – With its graceful blooms, iris offers calming properties and has traditionally been used to ease anxiety.

Wood Betony (*Betonica officinalis*) and Skullcap (*Scutellaria lateriflora*) – Both members of the mint family, these herbs offer comfort and grounding during the tender early days of grief.

Rose (*Rosa spp.)* – A timeless symbol of love, rose helps heal the heart and soften emotional wounds.

Lemon Balm (*Melissa officinalis*) – Uplifting and heart-soothing, lemon balm gently restores emotional harmony.

Holy Basil (*Ocimum tenuiflorum*) – Revered in Ayurvedic tradition, holy basil supports the spirit and helps ease sadness and depression.

Oats (*Avena sativa*) – A gentle nervine, oats soothe frazzled nerves and bring calm to the body and mind.

Linden *(Tilia spp.*) – With its sweet-scented blossoms, linden eases tension and nurtures emotional well-being.

Borage (*Borago officinalis*) – Known as the herb of courage, borage lifts the spirit and brings lightness to heavy hearts.

Motherwort (*Leonurus cardiaca*) – A strong ally for the heart, motherwort calms anxiety and stress while offering emotional support.

Mimosa (*Albizia julibrissin*) – Often called the "tree of happiness," mimosa brings joy and emotional upliftment.

Hawthorn (*Crataegus spp.*) – A guardian of the heart, hawthorn helps mend emotional wounds and strengthen inner resilience.

Violet (*Viola spp.*) – Symbolizing remembrance, violet honors memory and offers gentle comfort.

Cherry Blossoms (*Prunus spp.*) – These fleeting blooms remind us of life's impermanence and the beauty *of each moment.*

I would include sensory plants with cool tactile sensations. Here's a selection of garden plants prized for the way they feel—offering unusual textures that invite touch and exploration. Healthy touch can be helpful for healing.

Lamb's Ear (*Stachys byzantina*): dense, woolly leaves that mimic rabbit fur—soft, downy, and unmistakably cool under your fingertips.

Silver Sage (*Salvia argentea*): broad silvery leaves with a light fuzz; substantial yet yielding, they hold a subtle chill even on warm days.

Hosta (*Hosta spp.*): large, waxy leaves that glide smoothly beneath your hand—perfect for shady spots where their cool surface contrasts with warmer surroundings.

Gardenia (*Gardenia jasminoides*): thick, glossy evergreen foliage and creamy petals feel firm and satiny, offering a cooling touch with every brush.

Eucalyptus (*Eucalyptus spp.*): round, silver-blue leaves coated in a natural wax bloom; their slick, almost slippery surface carries a refreshing coolness.

Scented Geranium (*Pelargonium spp.*): textured leaves with a velvety underside and smooth top release fragrance when stroked; the coolness intensifies the aromatic experience.

Aloe Vera (*Aloe barbadensis*): succulent leaves are thick and fleshy, retaining coolness and revealing soothing gel when pressed—an inherently tactile delight.

Mixed Succulents (*various spp.*): plump, water-filled leaves and rosettes range from glassy-smooth (Echeveria) to subtly ridged (Sedum), each holding ambient coolness.

Birch (*Betula spp.*): smooth, papery bark peels in thin layers—cool to the touch and offering a tactile contrast to leafy plants.

Ornamental Grasses (e.g., Blue Fescue): fine, arching blades feel crisp and gently cool, especially when gathered into a hand for a fleeting, rustling sensation.

Color therapy (chromotherapy) is the idea that colors create an electrical impulse in our brains. This stimulates the hormonal and biochemical processes in our bodies. These processes either stimulate or calm us. You can include flowers in the following colors to evoke healing emotions.

Blue: Darker shades of blue are also thought to have sedative properties and may be tried for people who experience insomnia or other sleeping disorders.

Green: Green is the color of nature, and according to chromatherapists, it can help relieve stress and relax a person.

Yellow: Yellow can be used to improve your mood and make you happier and more optimistic.

Orange: Orange, much like yellow, can be used to elicit happy emotions from people. The bright, warm color is also thought to be able to stimulate appetite and mental activity.

Charles Hall, Ph.D., is a professor and the Ellison Chair in International Floriculture in the Department of Horticultural Sciences at the College of Agriculture and Life Sciences in Bryan-College Station. He has conducted extensive research on how plants and gardening can enhance both physical and mental health. In an article published in the Journal of Environmental Horticulture, Hall outlines the numerous psychological benefits of plants and the activity of gardening across various categories. These benefits include:

• Anxiety and stress reduction
• Attention deficit recovery
• Decreased depression
• Enhanced memory retention
• Improved happiness and life satisfaction
• Mitigation of PTSD

• Increased creativity, productivity and attention
• Reduced effects of dementia
• Enhanced self-esteem

Dr. Hall stated that being in naturalized settings and engaging in activities like gardening has a positive impact on people's feelings of vitality and energy. He also noted that the activities of gardening and plant care help distract the mind and put it into a quieter and more relaxed state. So the act and practice of gardening can be healing to the bereaved.

A Garden for a Ghost

A Garden for a Ghost, or a Spectral Garden evokes an otherworldly, ghostly atmosphere through plant choices, color palettes, and layout. It's a space where ethereal whites, silvers, and pale greens dominate. The following are rare plants that earn their "ghost" moniker from their ethereal white forms, translucence, or uncanny shapes. Each of these plants relies on specific fungal or pollinator partnerships, making them exceptionally vulnerable. Seeing one in bloom is like glimpsing an apparition—rare, fleeting, and unforgettable. Here are the most hauntingly beautiful flowers that resemble ghostly, spectral figures:

Ghost Orchid *(Dendrophylax lindenii)* A leafless epiphyte native to Florida's swamps, its pure-white blossom seems to float mid-air, with two dangling "wings" that vanish at rest—as elusive as a specter.

Indian Pipe / Ghost Plant (*Monotropa uniflora*) Neither fern nor flower, this saprophytic herb emerges from forest duff in drooping, waxy white clusters. Lacking chlorophyll, its ghostly stems fade to black as they age.

Phantom Orchid (*Cephalanthera austiniae*) Found in cool Pacific Coast forests, this all-white orchid never photosynthesizes. Its upright, lantern-like spikes glow among dark understory ferns.

European Ghost Orchid (*Epipogium aphyllum*) A rarer cousin of the American ghost orchid, it surges from leaf litter only in optimal years, displaying a ghost-white, spidery flower and disappearing for decades.

Ghost Flower (*Mohavea confertiflora*) Native to the Mojave Desert, these creamy yellow blooms with darker veins lie close to sandy ground, mimicking the pale stones—almost camouflaged specters.

Queen of the Night Cactus *(Selenicereus grandiflorus)* Though not named "ghost," its single, snow-white blooms open after dusk for just one night—pale apparitions glowing against the desert dark.

Jamaican Ghost Orchid *(Dendrophylax fawcettii)* An even more elusive relative thriving on limestone trunks, its pure-white, irregular flowers drift on the humidity like silent phantoms.

Mix in silvery hostas and layer with creeping silver ferns or moss to reinforce the ghostly theme. Consider white-flowered perennials such as astilbes, lilies, and white anemones mixed with silver or gray-leafed plants like Artemisia, Dusty Miller, and Lamb's Ear. Pale foliage varieties, including chartreuse and cream variegated hostas, add an eerie atmosphere to your ghostly garden.

Additional design suggestions include white gravel or pale stones to reflect light, ground-level lanterns to cast ghostly shadows, and mist machines or strategically placed water features for hazy and foggy effects. To elevate the spectral ambiance of your ghostly garden, shadowy lighting is essential—lanterns swaying gently in the breeze, flickering LEDs hidden among the foliage, and dramatic uplighting beneath twisted trees all work together to cast elongated shadows and ethereal glows. Complement these moody effects with accessories that animate your garden with playful hauntings, such as ghost garden stakes. I also found ghost solar garden lights at the dollar store. A total score!

Necromancy Garden (Communicating with the Dead/Ancestors)

Necromancy is the art of communicating with or summoning the spirits of the dead for the purpose of divination, to gain knowledge or insights into the future. Necromancy is a form of magic that involves communicating with the dead, often seeking knowledge, or gaining insight from those who have passed on. It is typically associated with the practice of summoning spirits or souls to provide guidance or to uncover hidden truths. Historically, necromancy has been viewed with suspicion and often linked to dark practices. Necromancy is often misunderstood as raising the dead, reanimating corpses, or bringing people back to life. It can be found in various cultural and religious traditions, where it sometimes involves rituals or the use of specific tools to connect with the deceased. The concept has been present in literature and folklore, often depicting necromancers as individuals wielding significant power or as figures to be feared. The Greek word "mancy" (μαντεία) is derived from the root "manteia," which means "divination" or "prophecy." It comes from the verb "manteuō" (μαντεύομαι), which means "to prophesy" or "to foresee." "Mancy" is often used as a suffix in English to refer to various forms of divination or methods of predicting the future.

In the realm of divination, various "mancys" (derived from the Greek word for "divination") represent distinct methods or practices for obtaining insights or predictions about the future. Here are some notable types of mancy:

Cartomancy: The practice of divination using cards, typically tarot cards or playing cards. Each card has specific meanings that can reveal insights about the past, present, or future.

Geomancy: A form of divination that involves interpreting markings on the ground or patterns made by tossing a set of objects, such as stones or sand. It often involves creating geomantic figures based on random lines or patterns.

Hydromancy: Divination using water, often involving the observation of ripples, waves, or reflections in water to gain insight or predict future events.

Pyromancy: Divination using fire, such as interpreting the patterns of flames or the behavior of burning materials.

Rhabdomancy: Divination by using a rod or stick, often for finding water or minerals. This practice is also known as dowsing.

Somnomancy: Divination through dreams, interpreting the symbols or events within dreams to predict future occurrences or gain personal insight.

Besides incorporating any of the plants that have previously been talked about in this book, one can also include mood-altering plants that can facilitate necromancy.

The following plants can enhance psychic abilities and spirit communication and are ideal for a Necromancy Garden.

Mugwort (*Artemisia vulgaris*): Induces vivid, prophetic dreams and gentle anxiolysis. Traditionally smoked or brewed in tea to bridge waking consciousness with the ancestral realm.

Wild Lettuce *(Lactuca virosa)*: Delivers mild sedation and a soft euphoria. Historically used to quiet the mind for inner journeying and contact with subtle spirits.

Kanna (*Sceletium tortuosum*): Acts as a potent mood elevator and empathy enhancer. Chewed or infused to open the heart and commune with plant and guiding spirits.

Sage (*Salvia officinalis*): Sharpens mental clarity and lifts gloom. Burned as incense to purify space, ward off negative entities, and prepare for visionary work.

Morning Glory (*Ipomoea purpurea*): Seeds yield low-dose psychedelic effects—gentle visual shifts and a sense of cosmic unity. Used in divinatory ceremonies to glimpse other worlds.

Catnip (*Nepeta cataria*): Eases anxiety and inspires lighthearted joy. Placed on altars to invite benevolent household spirits and foster playfulness in ritual.

Yarrow (*Achillea millefolium*): Stabilizes emotions and grants a mild uplift. Employed in dream sachets to heighten intuition and receive guidance from nature deities.

Hyssop (*Hyssopus officinalis*): Calms the nerves and clears the throat—both literally and metaphorically. Burned or sipped to open the third eye and deepen spiritual insight.

Bay *(Laurus nobilis)*: Boosts confidence and mental focus. Bay-leaf divination (crack-reading) channels oracular messages from the divine.

Chamomile (*Matricaria chamomilla*): Provides gentle sedation and stress relief. Consumed before sleep to ease entry into dream-based spirit journeys.

Eyebright (*Euphrasia officinalis*): Clarifies physical and psychic vision. Used in eye washes or gazing rituals to sharpen sight in the spirit world.

Goldenrod (*Solidago canadensis*): Warms the heart and uplifts low spirits. Offered in ceremonies to call forth benevolent nature spirits and express gratitude.

Hazel (*Corylus avellana*): Grounds scattered energy and aids divination by dowsing. Hazel wands are said to detect hidden ley lines and elemental presences.

Hibiscus (*Hibiscus rosa-sinensis*): Opens the heart chakra and inspires affectionate euphoria. Petals used in love-focused rites and to commune with spirits of compassion.

Meadowsweet (*Filipendula ulmaria*): Soothes the emotions and gently enhances dream recall. Honored in water-spirit rituals to gain clarity on life's flowing currents.

Pennyroyal (*Mentha pulegium*): Sharpens focus and repels stagnant energies. A potent space-clearing herb—handle with care and respect.

Vervain (*Verbena officinalis*): Triggers trance and prophetic states. Sacred in ancient rites for invoking ancestral and elemental spirits.

Wormwood (*Artemisia absinthium*): Bitter tonic that stimulates lucid dreaming and divination. Used in purification ceremonies to open gateways to subtle realms.

Using plants to promote spirit communication is key as is including tools and techniques to communicate with spirit, particularly through scrying. Design elements in a necromancy garden may include gazing balls and mirrors (scrying) and bird baths (water scrying).

Scrying is a form of divination where you gaze into a reflective or translucent surface to receive intuitive messages, symbols, or visions. It's one of the most accessible magical practices and has been used across cultures for thousands of years to uncover hidden insights Scrying is also known as hydromancy, oculomancy, second sight, or peeping. The purpose of scrying can vary from personal guidance to prophecy, revelation, or inspiration. In the context of the Necromancy Garden, the aim is to communicate with loved ones in spirit.

Traditionally, scrying is done using a reflective surface, such as a mirror, water, or crystal globe. The term "scrying" originates from the Old English word "descry," which means "to make out dimly" or "to reveal." Thus, scrying is about uncovering the unseen through our intuitive second sight, also known as clairvoyance. This ability allows us to perceive things that cannot typically be detected through our five senses. Scrying encourages us to connect with our unconscious minds—the realm of the soul.

During the scrying process, we focus on an object until we lose focus and space out. By maintaining a fixed gaze, our eyes become blurrily unfocused. When we allow our physical eyes to relax, we enable our inner psychic eyes to open up and receive visions or information.

Psychic information isn't confined to second sight or "clairvoyance" alone—it can arrive through any of your senses: hearing, smelling, knowing, feeling, and yes, seeing. Remember that the "images" you perceive are created in your mind's eye, not captured by your physical eyes.

Scrying is a skill you develop over time. If you're just starting out, don't be daunted—there's no absolute right or wrong interpretation. What resonates with one person may not work for another, so give yourself permission to experiment. Even if you feel naturally gifted, you'll still encounter a learning curve before you experience real growth and a deeper understanding of the practice.

Scrying 101

To get started, choose a medium that resonates with you and your intentions. Typically, mirrors, crystals, or water are used. I have suggested scrying Necromancy Garden design elements below. The key is to pick something that holds your attention yet remains simple enough not to distract you. Experimenting with different tools will reveal which surface most effectively draws your mind inward.

Preparing your space is essential for a successful session. Find a quiet, comfortable spot free from interruptions, and adjust lighting to create soft, even illumination— candlelight, moonlight, or dim lamps work well. A brief cleansing ritual, such as smudging with sage or spritzing the area with a ritual spray, can help clear stagnant energy. Ground yourself through a few minutes of mindful breathing or meditation, allowing your body and mind to settle before you begin.

When you're ready, set a clear intention or question to guide your session. Gaze softly at your chosen medium, looking just beyond its surface rather than focusing too hard on any one point. Keep your posture relaxed and your mind open; if stray thoughts arise, acknowledge them and let them pass like leaves on a stream. Using low light reduces glare and invites subtle shapes or colors to emerge naturally. Be patient—initial impressions may be vague clouds or flickers of color, but with time, they often sharpen into distinct symbols.

As images, shapes, or sensations appear, record every detail immediately in a journal or voice memo. Note colors, movements, emotional undertones, and any associations or memories that surface. Avoid labeling impressions as good or bad. Instead, cultivate a neutral curiosity that allows your subconscious to speak freely. Over time, you'll build a personal lexicon of symbols and meanings that deepens your understanding of each session.

Finally, remember that scrying is a skill honed through consistent practice and a curious mindset. Be patient with yourself if nothing obvious appears at first— many practitioners report that breakthroughs come only after weeks or months of regular work. Feel free to switch tools, adjust lighting, or vary the time of day until you find what works best. Release any expectations about specific outcomes, and simply allow the images to unfold. With patience, openness, and dedication, you'll find that scrying becomes an increasingly clear channel to your inner wisdom.

Incorporating scrying elements into a garden can transform the space into a mystical realm that invites reflection, magic, and enchantment. At the heart of scrying lies the concept of gazing—using reflective or translucent materials to glimpse insight beyond the everyday. This can be achieved in the garden through mirrors, crystals, water, fire, and even light projections, offering a layered experience full of symbolic meaning and sensory allure.

Reflective surfaces play a foundational role in both traditional scrying and illusionary garden design. Outdoor-grade mirrors installed on fences or hidden among foliage can evoke the sense of alternate worlds, while mirror stepping stones and porthole-style features create optical surprises that entice the curious mind. Mosaic mirror arrangements cast fragmented reflections that speak to the multi-faceted nature of personal insight, and placing mirrors where they reflect key elements like the sky or moon can give even small spaces a magical expansiveness.

Crystals offer a dynamic blend of beauty and mysticism, serving as both visual focal points and energetic accents. Quartz or obsidian spheres on pedestals mirror the classic gazing globe, inviting contemplation and delight. Garden paths lined with chakra stones or crystal clusters lead visitors on symbolic journeys, while crystal grids in flower beds amplify intention-setting rituals. Hanging crystal prisms and wind chimes scatter rainbow light across the garden, echoing the shimmer of visions seen in crystal ball scrying. When embedded in steps or borders, gemstones provide a tactile connection between the physical and spiritual realms.

Water features embody the liquid mirror of ancient scrying traditions. Shallow reflecting pools, bowls atop columns, and dark-lined basins create hypnotic surfaces for stillness and divination. Enhanced with crystals or subtle lighting, these features become portals for personal exploration and ritual. Ultrasonic foggers and mist tunnels introduce drifting clouds that veil and reveal the garden in a theatrical fashion, while incense altars and fire bowls offer sensory richness and dynamic visual layers.

Spherical forms are universally symbolic of wholeness and mystery, making orb sculptures and gazing balls ideal additions. Whether floating in water or nestled in flower beds, these shapes can channel the energy of planets, spirits, and deep introspection. Polished stone spheres ground a space with tactile presence, while solar-powered globes cast moonlike glows that activate nighttime magic. Integrating fire—through cauldrons, crystal fire pits, or reflective flame glass— adds warmth and transformation, evoking ancient rituals and communal storytelling.

Light plays a crucial role in scrying-inspired gardens, with prisms and diffraction turning sunlight into kinetic displays. Hanging faceted crystals and prismatic wind spinners scatter vibrant color, creating visual joy and symbolic illumination. Moon gardens, filled with white and silver foliage, night-blooming flowers, and celestial-themed pathways, transform under lunar light into ethereal landscapes that whisper ancient secrets. Using LED "moonlighting" from high tree placements or installing moon-phase sculptures deepens the connection to cycles and celestial rhythm.

Interactive and multimedia scrying features blend tradition with technology. Water mirrors equipped with sensors or digital projections transform ponds into responsive art installations, capable of playing sound, light, or movement. Augmented reality overlays and choreographed fountain shows bring theatrical enchantment, allowing visitors to experience a garden as both sanctuary and portal. Leaf-shadow projections and pattern-casting laser lights turn ordinary surfaces into storytelling canvases.

Ancestral Garden

This is a garden with plants native to your ancestral land. We all have four ancestral lines: your mother's mother and father, and your father's mother and father. Start by defining whose story you want to honor—parents, grandparents, a wider lineage, or cultural homeland. Think about memories and traditions you'd like to preserve. Jot down a few keywords (heritage crops, family recipe ingredients, favorite colors, meaningful symbols) to guide your design.

Your garden's shape and circulation can echo ancestral worldviews and rituals. For example,

- A Sacred Circle or Medicine Wheel to symbolize life's cycles.
- An Herb Spiral for easy access to kitchen and healing plants.
- A Memory Path of stepping stones, each engraved with a loved one's initials or dates.

A Labyrinth or winding walk for reflection and storytelling.

Include artifacts, art, and elements that speak to your lineage and ancestral roots:

- A Memory Wall: mount framed photographs, family crests, or hand-painted tiles.
- An Ancestral Altar on a raised stone pedestal for offerings and candles.
- Carved Benches or tree-stump seating for elders to linger and share tales.
- Marker Stones inscribed with proverbs, blessings, or poems in your ancestor's tongue.

Please research your lineage and plants indigenous to your native lands. The following are just a few examples:

Scandinavian: Angelica for digestive tonics and folklore protections, yarrow for wound healing and divination, juniper for purification and flavor, rowan for protection against misfortune, heather to attract good luck, elderberry for immune support and seasonal remedies, mugwort for dream work, and arctic thyme for culinary and medicinal uses.

Celtic: Hawthorn as a sacred tree of love and healing, nettle for vitality and spring cleansing, mugwort for visionary rituals, meadowsweet for heart comfort and holy gatherings, hazel for wisdom and divining wands, oak saplings as emblems of strength, and bog myrtle for ceremonial smoke.

Baltic: Flax for linen weaving traditions, bilberry for eye health and wild jams, linden (basswood) for calming teas and community gatherings, Queen Anne's lace for lacework inspiration, rhubarb for hearty pies, St. John's wort as a sun-harvesting healer, and elderflower to mark midsummer celebrations.

Eastern European: Dill for pickling and protective charms, caraway for bread and digestive ease, beets for strength tonics, garlic for warding off illness and ill intent, chamomile for restful teas, elderflower for floral cordials, blackcurrant for vitamin-rich syrups, and tansy in folk remedies.

Mediterranean (Italian/Greek/Spanish): Olive trees as ancient peace symbols, rosemary for remembrance and culinary zest, basil for sacred kitchens, oregano for hearty stews, thyme for purifying rituals, lavender for calm and sleep, bay laurel for scholarly honors, fennel for digestive lore, and grapevines for communal harvest festivals.

Native American: Corn, beans, and squash intertwined as the Three Sisters of sustenance, tobacco for prayer offerings, sweetgrass for smudging and goodwill, echinacea for immune fortification, purple coneflower for long-standing herbal use, sage for purification, yarrow for healing, and Jerusalem artichoke as a famine food.

Egyptian: Date palms lining sacred groves, papyrus for ancient script and water purification, blue lotus for contemplative infusions, hyssop for temple incense, frankincense and myrrh from resin-bearing shrubs, and castor bean for lamp oil.

African: Baobab for powerful vitamin C fruit, marula for festive oils and skin care, sorghum and millet as resilient grains, Aloe vera for universal skin remedies, rooibos for antioxidant teas, hibiscus for tart drinks, devil's claw for joint support, and shea trees for communal butter.

Australian: Eucalyptus for aromatic oils and koala habitats, lemon myrtle for zesty teas, kakadu plum for super-rich vitamin C, wattle (acacia) for gum and cultural dye, quandong for tart jams, bush tomato for flavoring, and finger lime for caviar-like bursts.

Pacific Islands: Taro as the heart of culinary heritage, breadfruit for starchy sustenance, coconut palms for food and fiber, kava for communal ceremonies, ti plant for protective plantings, pandanus for weaving mats and flavor, noni for wellness tonics, and awapuhi (wild ginger) for traditional beauty rituals.

East Asian: Ginger for warming teas and culinary fire, ginkgo for longevity symbolism, chrysanthemum for floral teas and autumn festivals, bamboo for structural elements and grace, camellia sinensis (tea) for centuries-old rituals, peony for prosperity, and mugwort (ai ye) in moxibustion.

South Asian: Turmeric for golden immunity, neem for purifying skin care, holy basil (tulsi) for sacred daily offerings, cardamom for spiced blends, moringa for nutrient-dense leaves, curry leaf for classical cooking, ashwagandha for adaptogenic balance, and sacred fig (peepal) for meditative shade.

Latin American: Amaranth for ancestral grain breads, quinoa for high-protein bowls, cacao for ceremonial chocolate, chili peppers for heat and ritual offerings, vanilla for aromatic tribute, guava for vitamin-rich jams, and papaya for digestive enzymes.

Since many who venerate ancestors are deeply spiritual and ritualistic, here are some seasonal ceremonial ideas to practice in your Ancestral Garden.

Spring Planting Ceremony: Invite family to add seeds or seedlings.

Summer Story Dinners: Serve ancestral recipes while seated in your garden picnic style.

Autumn Seed Saving: Collect and label seeds for next year's planting stock.

Winter Candlelight Vigil: Light candles at the altar, share memories and hopes.

Herbal Garden for the Dead

An herbal garden for the dead is a living sanctuary where plants symbolically mirror life's final passage, serving as both a memorial and a conduit between worlds. In this context, "herbs of the dead" are botanicals selected for rituals of grieving, ancestor veneration, and spirit communication. Their life cycles—from seed to bloom and back to earth—echo human mortality and renewal, turning the garden itself into a commemorative altar of remembrance and respect. These herbs can be dried and made into a bundle for burning, used in incense, ritual, offerings to ancestors and death deities, and in spellwork. I have ideas on what to do with the herbs you grew in a later chapter on death witchcraft.

Across time and cultures, sacred gardens for the dead have flourished beside tombs, within monasteries, and at festival sites. Medieval European infirmaries grew sage, rue, and betony to ward off plague and protect the deceased from malevolent spirits. And during the Celtic Samhain, rosemary and bay leaf were burned or woven into wreaths to awaken ancestral presences and thin the veil between the living and the dead. In modern practice, these gardens support rites of purification, protection, and remembrance.

Here are suggested herbs for your Death Herbal Garden. I've included the herb's scientific (botanical) name, followed by its traditional magickal, witchy, and folklore uses tied specifically to spirit communication, death, dying, and the afterlife.

Basil. Botanical name: *Ocimum basilicum* • Spirit communication – Burn fresh or dried basil at night to thin the veil and invite ancestral guidance. • Death rites – Scattered on funeral pyres to honor the departed and aid their journey. • Folklore – In Italian lore, basil on a shroud attracts the soul's safe passage to the next world.

Bay (Bay Laurel). Botanical name: *Laurus nobilis* • Spirit communication – Smoke bay leaves during séances to open psychic channels. • Death and dying – Placed under pillows to induce visions of those who have passed. • Folklore – Ancient

Romans crowned heroes and buried bay leaves with their dead to protect their journeys in Hades.

Beet. Botanical name: *Beta vulgaris* • Necromantic inks – Boiled beetroot for red "blood" ink used in death-magic manuscripts. • Ancestral offerings – Roots interred at graves to "feed" ancestral spirits in folklore. • Underworld rites – Beetroots stuffed into skulls to symbolize rebirth of the spirit. (please note, beets are not an herb, but they are so cool that I include it in my herb garden).

Chamomile. Botanical name: *Matricaria recutita (or Chamaemelum nobile)* • Spirit communication – Chamomile steam inhalation to summon peaceful visitations. • Death and afterlife – Placed on tombstones to grant the dead tranquility in the next world. • Folklore – Egyptians used chamomile in mummification, linking it to safe passage of the soul.

Chives. Botanical name: *Allium schoenoprasum* • Protective ward – Chives hoops over doorways to keep malignant spirits from entering. • Death rites – Chives in burial sachets to guard the newly deceased. • Folklore – Medieval villagers believed chives washed away touches of the undead.

Cilantro. Botanical name: *Coriandrum sativum* • Spirit cleansing – Fresh cilantro sprigs burned to purify homes of hauntings. • Death and mourning – Cilantro bouquets laid on graves for ease of grief and guiding lost souls. • Folklore – Linked to Artemis, it was carried by those who ferried the spirits between worlds.

Dill. Botanical name: *Anethum graveolens* • Psychopomp herb – Dill bunches hung in doorways to guide spirits safely through thresholds. • Death vigil – Dill tea served at funerals to calm the living and honor the dead. • Folklore – Associated with Norse Valkyries, it was believed to mark paths of the fallen.

Dittany of Crete. Botanical name: *Origanum dictamnus* • Reviving balm – Dittany ointment applied to ghost-touched flesh to heal and exorcise restless spirits. • Death-magic ink – Dried and powdered in inks used in ancestral divination scripts. • Folklore – Named for Mount Dicte's caves, said to house underworld gateways guarded by spirits.

Fennel. Botanical name: *Foeniculum vulgare* • Psychic scrying – Burn fennel husks to enhance visions of the departed. • Tomb planting – Stakes of fennel around graves to protect the dead from malevolent forces. • Folklore – Romans believed fennel stalks marked safe crossing points to the underworld.

Heather. Botanical name: *Calluna vulgaris* • Faerie realm – Heather beds served as soft landing spots for souls visiting the living. • Death vigil – Sprigs laid on coffins to lend peaceful dreams to the dying. • Folklore – Celts planted white heather on burial mounds to guide souls home.

Holly. Botanical name: *Ilex aquifolium* • Psychic shield – Holly wreaths above windows to block psychic attachments from wandering spirits. • Funerary charm – Holly berries pinned to shrouds to illuminate the path to the afterlife. • Folklore – Romans used holly to crown the dead's graves, ensuring safe passage to Elysium.

Juniper. Botanical name: *Juniperus communis* (or other Juniperus species) • Ghost-banishing – Burn juniper cones to send unwelcome spirits away. • Ancestral call – Juniper smoke used to invoke grandparents' guidance at death anniversaries. • Folklore – Native shamans used juniper in rites to cleanse souls before their final journey.

Lavender. Botanical name: *Lavandula angustifolia* • Spirit-dreaming – Lavender sachets under pillows invite benevolent visions from beyond. • Fair-ground – Lavender crowns worn at Samhain to honor returning souls. • Folklore – Egyptians and Romans burned lavender at tombs to maintain soul's tranquility.

Lemon Balm. Botanical name: *Melissa officinalis* • Calming souls – Lemon balm tea offered to the living to soothe grief and ease communication with the dead. • Death healing – Poultices of lemon balm applied to grounds where tragedy occurred, aiding spirit rest. • Folklore – Believed to be tears of the moon goddess, linking it to the underworld's gentler aspect.

Mint. Botanical name: *Mentha spp. (e.g., M. spicata, M. piperita)* • Soul protection – Mint leaves scattered to repel phantom intrusions in homes. • Mourning blend – Mint, frankincense, and myrrh burned at funerals to guide spirits onward. • Folklore – Greeks tied mint to Hades' realm; it was strewn at death rites to honor the fallen.

Mugwort. Botanical name: *Artemisia vulgaris* • Astral travels – Mugwort tea and smoke used to escort the spirit body on out-of-body voyages. • Death revelations

– Dream pillows stuffed with mugwort to receive messages from the departed. • Folklore – Viking shamans carried mugwort to protect against malevolent spirits and underworld beasts.

Mullein. Botanical name: *Verbascum thapsus* • Spirits' lantern – Dried flower candles lit at gravesides to guide souls in darkness. • Path cleansing – Mullein smoke cleared poltergeist energy from the corridors of old homes. • Folklore – Ancient Hebrews used mullein torches to light night services for the dead. Please note, some authors write that this is a graveyard dirt substitute. It absolutely is not. Nothing is a substitute for graveyard dirt.

Oregano. Botanical name: *Origanum vulgare* • Afterlife fretting – Oregano smudge to quell restless spirits perplexed by mortal coils. • Tomb wards – Oregano sprigs laid on graves as compact protection against soul-stealing. • Folklore – Medieval monks carried oregano in pockets to avert demonic temptations at burial sites.

Parsley. Botanical name: *Petroselinum crispum* • Soul charmer – Parsley garlands woven to coax gentle spirits to speak at funerary feasts. • Death herb – Parsley tea brewed to comfort mourners and ease fear of the afterlife. • Folklore – Romans ate parsley at tomb visits, believing it honored heroes and kept ablaze Hades' fires.

Patchouli. Botanical name: *Pogostemon cablin* • Underworld gates – Patchouli incense dropped at thresholds to open portals for ancestral return. • Death rites – Patchouli oil anointed on caskets to mask decay and invite reverent passage. • Folklore – Southeast Asian tribes walked patchouli trails to scare off hungry spirits.

Rosemary. Botanical name: *Rosmarinus officinalis (or Salvia rosmarinus)* • Remembrance herb – Sprigs placed in hair or on graves to keep the memory of loved ones alive. • Soul guide – Rosemary smoke burns at dusk to guide wayward souls back to realms of rest. • Folklore – Greeks wove rosemary wreaths for the dead, believing the aroma kept nightmares from them.

Sage. Botanical name: *Salvia officinalis* • Soul cleansing – Sage smudging purges ancestral ties that no longer serve and readies the spirit. • Death protector – White sage bundles burned at funerals shield mourners from spiritual overwhelm. • Folklore – Native American elders used sage to honor the cycle of life, death, and rebirth.

St. John's Wort. Botanical name: *Hypericum perforatum* • Psychopomp aid – Placed on graves at Midsummer, it was believed to attract and soothe returning souls. • Dead's companion – Worn as garlands in death festivals to protect mourners from lich-like entities. • Folklore – Named for its bloom on St. John's Eve, it is steeped in healing and afterlife blessings.

Savory. Botanical name: *Satureja hortensis* (summer savory) • Death's ally – Savory tea served at wake services to calm fear of the unknown beyond the grave. • Soul fortifier – Garlanded around tombs to strengthen the spirit against underworld trials. • Folklore – Romans paired it with cucumbers at funerals, believing it eased the soul's final thirst.

Thyme. Botanical name: *Thymus vulgaris* • Heart's scent – Thyme sachets laid in caskets to perfume death's chamber and comfort the soul. • Step spells – Thyme leaves strewn at doors to prevent the restless dead from crossing thresholds. • Folklore – Druids plaited thyme crowns for the dead to ensure they passed gently into the Otherworld.

Valerian. Botanical name: *Valeriana officinalis* • Sleep passages – Valerian root pillows placed on graves to grant the dead peaceful eternal rest. • Veil softener – Valerian tea consumed by mediums to ease trance and unlock afterlife channels. • Folklore - it was strewn at nocturnal rites to soothe spirits in liminal spaces.

Vervain. Botanical name: *Verbena officinalis* • Departed's guide – Vervain draped around shrines to call benevolent spirits for counsel. • Last rites – Vervain crowned on heads of the dying to grant mercy and swift passage.

Wormwood. Botanical name: *Artemisia absinthium* • Shade of death – Wormwood sprigs thrown on pyres to honor Stygian paths of the soul. • Cursed bane – Repels malignant spirits and necromantic energies from graveyards and crypts. • Folklore – Greek necromancers burned wormwood to open gates to Hades

Cemetarium

A cemetarium is a cemetery-themed terrarium. These tiny indoor gardens are perfect for a windowsill facing west (land of the ancestors) or your altar. Craft a cemetarium with intent for grief and loss, for ancestor worship/veneration, for spirit communication, or as an offering to your chthonic/death deities, etc.

Creating a small-scale graveyard scene calls for plants that evoke moss-covered stones, weathered monuments, and somber beauty. You want to include ground covers, mini ferns, tiny evergreens, and dark accent colored plants. I have also planted the seeds of herbs that are correlated to death and dying, and these turned out fabulous (lavender, rosemary, thyme, mugwort, chamomile, lemon balm, tulsi, and meadowsweet).

Mood Moss (*Dicranum scoparium*) Forms tufted, cushion-like mounds that mimic aging tombstone bases. Thrives in high humidity and low, indirect light.

Baby's Tears (*Soleirolia soleirolii*) Delicate mats of tiny, round leaves that spill like centuries-old runner vine. Prefers moist substrate and filtered light.

Creeping Jenny 'Aurea' (*Lysimachia nummularia*) Golden-green coins that drape around miniature headstones, offering contrast while fitting a melancholic palette.

Selaginella kraussiana 'Gold Tips' Fern ally with fine, feathery foliage that looks like lichen on weathered masonry. Loves constant moisture.

Mini Maidenhair Fern (*Adiantum raddianum*) Lacy, fan-shaped fronds reminiscent of Victorian mourning art. Requires stable humidity and gentle light.

Peacock Fern (*Selaginella uncinata*) Iridescent blue-green fronds echoing twilight shadows in a crypt. Best in sealed or semi-sealed terrariums.

Button Fern (*Pellaea rotundifolia*) Round, leathery pinnae on wiry petioles that look like ancient coinage strewn across the ground.

Spikemoss (*Selaginella martensii*) Tight rosettes of dark green that hug the soil, perfect for "cracked" pavement effects.

Dwarf Japanese Cedar 'Globosa Nana' (*Cryptomeria japonica 'Globosa Nana'*) Slow-growing globe shape suggests a miniature churchyard cypress. Needs bright, indirect light and well-draining mix.

Mondo Grass 'Mini Green' (*Ophiopogon japonicus 'Nana'*) Tufts of grasslike leaves that frame tiny crypts and pathways. Tolerates lower light and cooler terrarium corners.

Boxwood 'Suffruticosa' (*Buxus sempervirens 'Suffruticosa'*) Naturally compact habit ideal for clipped hedges around mini mausoleums—prune to maintain scale.

Purple Wandering Jew (*sic*) Many people now call this plant Wandering Dude (*Tradescantia pallida 'Purpurea'*). Deep plum-purple foliage underlines gravestone borders. Trim back to keep it small.

Heuchera 'Palace Purple' Tiny ruffled leaves in burgundy-black that lend gothic flair around pathways.

Fittonia 'Black Magic' Dark, almost black leaves with silvery veins—like rain-slicked pavement in a moonlit graveyard.

Peperomia caperata 'Dark Form' Corrugated, heart-shaped leaves in charcoal green that cluster around miniature cuffs or lanterns.

How to Make an Open Terrarium

Choosing your container and plants is half the fun of making a terrarium. You can use almost any transparent (glass or plastic) container with a wide mouth to create a terrarium. Suitable containers include aquariums, goldfish bowls, Wardian cases, cold frames, bell jars, tureens, apothecary jars, cloches, mason jars, glass cookie jars, and even large brandy snifters. A wide opening allows you to fit your hand into the container to add drainage material, soil, plants, and decorative elements (shells, figurines, or ornaments).

Because terrariums don't have drainage, you will need to make a layer of pebbles at the bottom. Drainage layers help ensure excess water doesn't stay in the soil and cause root rot.

The next layer is ½ inch activated charcoal, which filters the air and water and keeps the terrarium clean.

You can either use cacti potting soil or soil with sand already mixed in it, or you can mix sand and sterile potting mix together.

Lastly, you plant your terrarium. Choose terrarium plants with various foliage forms and heights that are small enough to fit in your container, preferably without touching the sides of the terrarium. If you have chosen cacti for your open terrarium, you can either use tweezers, gloves, or an old newspaper around the cactus, so you won't hurt yourself planting it in the terrarium.

It is up to you how you want to decorate your terrarium. You can find some really amazing accessories in the craft stores around Halloween time. Mini headstones, spiders, pumpkins, ghosts, mini Victorian lamplights, angels, cherubs, iron fences, crypt entrances, skeletons, skulls, mini candles, twigs, etc. Have fun!!

Use a spray bottle or small watering can to water the plants so they are just damp, but not soaking wet. Use the spray bottle to clean off any dirt clinging to the glass sides of your container, which you can then wipe clean with newspaper or a paper towel.

How to Take Care of Your Terrarium

Succulents or cacti should be watered very sparingly, just as you would with these types of plants in any container, and keep an eye on any accumulated water. Remember, terrariums have no drainage holes, so when they feature arid plants, try only adding a dropperful of water at a time. Air plants will need to be taken out of the open terrarium, soaked in water for 20 minutes each week, then allowed to thoroughly dry out before they're returned to the terrarium. Aim for 60–80% humidity; mist lightly to keep mosses and ferns happy.

Never fertilize the plants in a terrarium. Terrariums provide their own nutrients through the natural decay of the potting mix.

Air plants thrive best in indirect light, while cacti grow best in bright sunny spots. Succulents thrive in bright indirect light. Most terrariums will do best in a location that receives plenty of filtered light, but not in harsh direct sunlight, where the terrarium can get hot enough to bake the plants inside. Slightly shaded south-facing windows can be ideal. If you don't have enough natural filtered sunlight—such as if your house is surrounded by shade trees—artificial grow lights will help your plants thrive. LED or fluorescent artificial lighting generally doesn't produce much heat, so your plants can get as much light as they need to thrive.

Scale and Pruning: Regularly trim fast-growing accents (Tradescantia, Creeping Jenny) to preserve miniature proportions.

Chthonic Garden: Gardens for Death Deities (Gods and Goddesses of the Dead)

These types of gardens can be used for Oracle Work and communicating with a death deity. These gardens can be crafted as a dedication or offering to one of the death deities. Chthonic (pronounced (k)THō-nik) means "concerning, belonging to, or inhabiting the underworld," and is often used to describe deities, spirits, or forces that dwell beneath the earth. Synonyms include infernal, nether, subterranean, and underworld.

Since we are reaching towards the underworld, these gardens are best created by digging a trench or a pit into the ground and then placing the plants and accessories into the pit.

Unlike other altars, which are typically placed up high, chthonic altars are placed on the ground or into a pit. Feel free to integrate a chthonic altar into your chthonic garden. Feel free to include statues and other iconography of the deities in their gardens. Many are also associated with animals, so animal statues and art are also welcome in their gardens.

The best plants for a Chthonic garden are the poisonous plants (Banes), plants that are tubers, bulbs, and rhizomes (plants that have underground stems), and mythology-specific plants.

Bulbs are compact stems surrounded by fleshy, nutrient-rich leaves (scales), anchored by a basal plate and often encased in a papery tunic. Common examples:

Daffodils (*Narcissus spp.*)

Tulips (*Tulipa spp.*)

Hyacinths (*Hyacinthus orientalis*)

Alliums (*Allium spp.*)

Lilies (*Lilium spp.*)

Garlic (*Allium sativum*)

Tubers are swollen stem or root sections that store food; they feature buds or "eyes" from which new shoots and roots develop. Common examples:

Potato (*Solanum tuberosum*)

Dahlia (*Dahlia spp.*)

Tuberous Begonia (*Begonia spp.*)

Caladium (*Caladium spp.*)

Rhizomes are horizontal underground stems that send out roots below and shoots above, enabling plants to spread laterally. Common examples:

Canna Lily (*Canna spp.*)

Bearded Iris (*Iris spp.*)

Ginger (*Zingiber officinale*)

Lily-of-the-Valley (*Convallaria majalis*)

In regards to the Death Deities, research their mythology! Themes, seasons, flowers, herbs, and plants associated with them. All plants have Gods who love them and have affinities to them. Some of these affinities are recorded in folklore, and some are not, and must be discovered by your experience (journeying, meditation, divination, oracle work, intuition).

Here are some death and underworld deities from around the world and plants associated with them:

Santa Muerte, also venerated as Niña Verde in Mexican folk Catholicism, is honored with corn for abundance, juniper for purification, rosemary for remembrance, and sage for protection.

Hecate, the Greek goddess of witchcraft, crossroads, and the underworld, is traditionally invoked with lavender to soothe and sharpen vision, mullein to guide spirits, belladonna and henbane for necromantic workings, dittany of Crete for protection, and hellebore for divination.

Persephone, the Greek queen of the underworld and goddess of spring's renewal, is symbolized by snowdrops heralding her return, narcissus marking her abduction, and the black tulip and black hyacinth embodying the beauty and mystery of death.

The Morrigan, the war-and-death goddess of Irish Celtic mythology, is honored with blackthorn for boundaries, belladonna for necromancy, juniper for purification, nightshade for underworld rites, mugwort for divination, yew for guiding souls, and dragon's blood resin to amplify her power.

Oyá, the orisha of winds, storms, and the cemetery realm in Yoruba and Afro-Caribbean traditions, is propitiated with camphor to clear paths, anise for protection, cinnamon for energy, carnations for death rites, calamus for cleansing, hibiscus for transformation, and geranium for ancestral communication.

San Pascualito, the folk Catholic "King of the Graveyard" venerated in Guatemala and Chiapas, is offered rosemary and sage for healing, juniper to ward off evil, and copal or tobacco to seal pacts and invoke his intercession in matters of life and death.

Baron Samedi, the loa of the dead in Haitian Vodou, is celebrated with tobacco and sugar cane as sacred plants, plus rum and hot peppers, to open the crossroads between life and death and secure his favors.

Exu, the trickster-messenger orisha in Yoruba, Candomblé, and Umbanda, is venerated with palm oil to open roads, hot peppers for power, tobacco for invocation, and red hibiscus blooms to signal his presence and clear spiritual pathways.

Hades, the king of the dead in Greek mythology, is symbolized by pomegranates (binding souls), cypress trees (funeral rites), mint (memory), narcissus (vanity and death), jasmine (night and underworld dreams), hemlock (poison), rue (protection), black roses (death's beauty), and poppies (sleep and oblivion).

Pluto, the Roman counterpart of Hades, likewise reigns over the underworld in ancient Roman religion and shares associations with pomegranates, cypress, mint, narcissus, jasmine, hemlock, rue, black roses, and poppies as emblems of wealth, death, and rebirth.

Hel, the Norse goddess of the underworld in Old Norse myth, is linked with elder for protection at crossroads, sycamore as a tree of spirits, yew for souls' passage, wormwood for banishing evil, and belladonna for visions and necromantic rites.

Kali, the fierce Hindu goddess of time, death, and liberation in Shaktism, is traditionally worshipped with red hibiscus flowers—and sometimes datura—in tantric rituals, symbolizing her blood-red tongue, ferocious power, and the cycle of destruction and renewal.

Anubis is the jackal-headed god of ancient Egypt, revered as the divine embalmer, protector of tombs, and guide through the underworld. He presided over mummification rituals and ensured safe passage for souls, embodying both the mystery of death and the promise of regeneration. plants. Acacia resin and wood were prized for their antibacterial properties and symbolic protection against decay, while cypress was burned as incense to mourn the dead and evoke eternal life. Juniper boughs lent their purifying smoke to funerary pyres and canopic jars, and the aromatic resins frankincense and myrrh cleansed sacred spaces and preserved flesh during mummification. Willow branches, emblematic of mourning, were woven into wreaths offered at Anubis's shrines, and papyrus stems and scrolls—inscribed with spells and guidance—steered souls safely through the duat.

Ah Puch, the Maya god of death in Classic Maya mythology, is honored with cypress sprigs at funerary rites and copal resin incense to guide souls through the underworld.

Mictlantecuhtli, the Aztec lord of the dead, is associated with sacred mushrooms for necromantic visions, marigold petals in offerings, and cypress trees planted in cemetery groves.

The Shinigami, Japanese spirits of death in Shinto and Buddhist folklore, are warded off with mugwort smudge sticks, willow branches for mourning, and bellflower blooms at gravesites.

Apophis (Apep) of ancient Egyptian myth is appeased by offerings of blue lotus flowers symbolizing rebirth, mandrake roots for protective magic, and rue incense to repel his chaos.

Maman Brigitte, the Haitian and New Orleans Vodou loa of the dead, is invoked with rum infused with hot peppers, tobacco leaves, rosemary for healing, and sage for cemetery blessings.

Azrael, the Guardian Angel of Death in Islamic and Jewish tradition, is memorialized by poppy wreaths for sleep and remembrance, frankincense for purification, and willow boughs for mourning.

Barnumbirr (Barnumbir), the Yolngu Morning Star creator in Australian Aboriginal myth, traces her ancestral songlines among eucalyptus groves, paperbark, ghost gums, and golden wattle blooms.

Epona, the Roman-Celtic horse goddess worshipped across the empire, is celebrated in stables with barley and oats, hawthorn hedges for protection, elderflower garlands, and wild rose offerings.

Freyja (Freya), the Norse Vanir goddess of love, fertility, and wealth, is linked to fields of daisies, wild strawberries, bluebells, rowan berries, and St. John's Wort in midsummer rites. In Norse myth, Freyja is deeply tied to death: as a chooser of the slain, she welcomes half of all warriors killed in battle into her hall Fólkvangr and, as a mistress of seiðr magic, guides fates and spirits between life and the afterlife.

Jizo (Kshitigarbha), the Japanese Buddhist bodhisattva of children and travelers, is surrounded by lilies for solace, chrysanthemums for remembrance, and lotus blossoms for spiritual safe-keeping.

Nephthys, the Egyptian funerary goddess and sister of Isis, is invoked with sprays of sycamore leaves, papyrus reeds, lotus buds, and myrrh to guard the dead on their final journey.

Isis, the supreme Egyptian goddess of magic, motherhood, and sovereignty, is intimately tied to the sacred blue lotus of rebirth, papyrus stalks for script and song, tamarisk branches in ritual offerings, and acacia wood in healing anointings.

Psychopomp Garden

My final idea for a Garden for the Dead is a psychopomp garden. A psychopomp is a guide whose primary role is to escort souls to the afterlife. They also assist in navigating various life transitions, such as birth. The term "psychopomp" originates from the Greek words "pompos," meaning conductor or guide, and "psyche," which translates to breath, life, soul, or mind. Stories of psychopomps are found in mythological tales, religious texts, sacred narratives, and real-life accounts from cultures around the world. Typically, this guidance ensures a successful transition for the soul; however, there are times when additional assistance is required. This has historically been a role for shamans and others who possess the ability to journey into the spirit realms and provide help to those in need.

Psychopomps appear in many mythologies globally, and as a result, the afterlife they guide souls into varies among cultures. Anubis (Ancient Egypt) guides souls and oversees embalming and judgment; Hermes (Ancient Greece) serves as messenger god and escorts souls to the underworld; Charon (Ancient Greece) ferries souls across the Styx; the Norse Valkyries choose the slain and escort them to Valhalla; Xolotl (Aztec) guides souls through Mictlan; Vanth (Etruscan) is a winged daemon guiding souls; Morana (Slavic) presides over death and seasonal cycles; Azrael (Islam/Judaism) is the Angel of Death who collects and comforts souls; Saint Peter (Christianity) acts as Heaven's gatekeeper, admitting righteous souls; and Daena (Zoroastrianism) self-guides the soul across the Chinvat Bridge.

Besides divine beings, I think hospice nurses, death doulas, exit guides, and soul midwives are modern examples of psychopomps. They are there to help you have a beautiful death and cross you over. Many mythologies also mention winged beings: bees, butterflies, bats, and birds as not only spirit messengers, but also psychopomps. My homage to the psychopomp, whether deities, a modern hospice worker, or a winged being, is to create a pollinator garden.

All of nature exists in harmony. When one part of the ecosystem is harmed, the entire system can be disrupted. Pollinators, such as bees and butterflies, are essential for our survival. Bees play a crucial role in pollinating most of the crops that provide our food. Without pollination, these crops cannot grow, leading to a shortage of food for animals, humans, and all living organisms that rely on plants and crops for sustenance. This could result in famine and economic instability.

Pesticides, herbicides, neonicotinoids, and genetically modified organisms (GMOs) pose serious threats to the survival of Monarch butterflies, honeybees, and bumblebees. These chemicals kill Milkweed, the primary food source for caterpillars. Additionally, they disrupt the bees' navigation and tracking abilities, causing them to become lost and unable to find their way home. Chemicals also weaken bees' immune systems, increase their stress levels, and are believed to be a major contributing factor to Colony Collapse Disorder, a phenomenon in which bees suddenly and mysteriously disappear from their hives. In recent years, beekeepers in the United States, Canada, Europe, Asia, Central America, and South America have all reported declines of over 50% in their bee populations. In the United Kingdom, three species of bees have already become extinct, and 90% of the wild bee population in the U.S. has vanished. Monarch butterfly numbers are also at their lowest point ever.

If we don't change our gardening and agricultural practices, we risk not only the extinction of bees and butterflies but also jeopardizing our food supplies and, ultimately, our own survival. As more people become interested in green and clean living—such as consuming organic food and using natural cleaning and body products—there is a growing need to translate this movement into our own backyards. Here are some actions we can take to support the survival of bees and butterflies and restore balance to the earth:

1. Respect the bees! Leave their hives undisturbed. Learn to distinguish between hornets, wasps, and bees—bees are not the bad guys and are generally not aggressive like wasps.

2. Consider becoming a beekeeper!

3. Embrace weeds! Many of us were taught that weeds are "bad." In reality, their presence is nature's way of balancing soil quality. Most weeds can also have medicinal properties. Weeds are also really just plants growing where you do not want them to be growing.

4. Use natural and organic gardening methods, including natural fertilizers (like guano, kelp, and bloodmeal) and natural pest deterrents (such as neem oil and essential oils like lemongrass and citronella).

5. Pull weeds by hand. This is not only great exercise, but also a great way to connect with nature.

6. Ensure that you only use organic seedlings or seeds in your garden. Plants from greenhouses may be treated with pesticides and chemicals.

7. Plant organic herbs that attract bees and butterflies. These plants will not only support our pollinator friends, but you can also harvest them at the end of the growing season to create delicious healing teas, tinctures, and balms for yourself and your family.

Herbs that Attract Bees and Butterflies

Milkweed (*Asclepias curassavica, Asclepias incarnata, Asclepias syriacea*)

Catnip (*Nepeta cataria*)

Bee Balm (a.k.a. Wild Bergamot) (*Monarda didyma, Monarda fistulosa, Monarda citriodora, and Monarda pectinata*)

Lavender (*Lavandula officinalis, Lavandula angustifolia*)

Echinacea (*Echinacea purpurea*)

Sage (*Salvia officinalis*)

Wild marjoram (*Origanum vulgare*)

Creeping thyme (*Thymus pseudolanguinosus*)

Anise hyssop (*Agastache foeniculum*)

Plants and the Butterflies They Attract

Achillea millefolium (yarrow) — Painted Lady

Anethum graveolens (dill) — Black Swallowtail; Anise Swallowtail

Angelica spp. — Black Swallowtail; Anise Swallowtail

Artemesia absinthium (wormwood) — Painted Lady

Artemesia dracunculus 'sativa' (French tarragon) — Oregon Swallowtail

Borago officinalis (borage) — Painted Lady

Carum carvi (caraway) — Black Swallowtail; Anise Swallowtail

Dictamnus spp. (gas plant) — Giant Swallowtail

Foeniculum vulgare (fennel) — Black Swallowtail; Anise Swallowtail

Glycyrrhiza spp. (licorice) — Silver Spotted Skipper

Helichrysum angustifolium (curry plant) — Painted Lady

Humulus lupulus (hops) — Gray Hairstreak; Comma; Question Mark; Red Admiral

Levisticum officinale (lovage) — Black Swallowtail; Anise Swallowtail

Melissa officinalis (lemon balm) — White Peacock

Mentha spp. (mint) — White Peacock; Painted Lady

Petroselinum crispum (parsley) — Black Swallowtail; Anise Swallowtail

Pimpinella anisum (anise) — Black Swallowtail; Anise Swallowtail

Ruta graveolens (rue) — Black Swallowtail; Giant Swallowtail (wear gloves— oils can burn sensitive skin)

Salvia spp. (sage) — Gray Hairstreak; Painted Lady; West Coast Lady

Symphytum officinale (comfrey) — Painted Lady

Tanacetum vulgare (tansy) — Painted Lady

Tropaeolum majus (nasturtium) — Cabbage White

Viola odorata (sweet violet) — Fritillaries

Nectar Plants

Achillea millefolium (yarrow)

Agastache foeniculum (anise hyssop)

Allium schoenoprasum (chives)

Angelica spp. (angelica)

Chamaemelum nobile (chamomile)

Coriandrum sativum (cilantro)

Heliotropum arborescens (heliotrope)

Hyssopus officinalis (hyssop)

Inula helenium (elecampane)

Lavandula spp. (lavender)

Melissa officinalis (lemon balm)

Mentha pulegium (English pennyroyal)

Mentha spp. (mint)

Monarda didyma (beebalm)

Monarda punctata (spotted mint)

Myrrhis odorata (sweet cicely)

Nepeta spp. (catmint)

Ocimum basilicum (basil)

Origanum laevigatum (oregano)

Origanum majorana (marjoram)

Prunella vulgaris (selfheal)

Pycnanthemum spp. (mountain mint)

Rosmarinus officinalis (rosemary)

Salvia spp. (sage)

Santolina spp. (lavender cotton)

Saponaria officinalis (soapwort)

Satureja hortensis (summer savory)

Scutellaria laterifolia (skullcap)

Tagetes spp. (marigold)

Taraxacum officinale (dandelion)

Teucrium spp. (germander)

Thymus spp. (thyme)

Trachelium caeruleum (throatwort)

Tropaeolum majus (nasturtium)

Tussilago farfara (coltsfoot)

Valeriana officinalis (true valerian)

Turn your Garden into a Bat Haven

Plant night-scented flowers. Moths, bats, and other nighttime pollinators are more attracted to flowers that are either white or very light in color:

Datura stramonium (jimsonweed)

Ipomoea alba (moonflower)

Yucca filamentosa (Adam's needle)

Nymphaea lotus (night-blooming water lily)

Cleome hassleriana (spider flower)

Eurybia divaricata (white wood aster)

Hydrangea arborescens (smooth hydrangea)

Hylocereus undatus (dragonfruit/pitaya)

Anemonella thalictroides (rue anemone)

Aloysia virgata (sweet almond verbena)

Oenothera biennis (evening primrose)

Cestrum nocturnum (night-blooming jasmine)

Philadelphus coronarius (Mock Orange)

Additional tips:

- Build a pond or another water feature
- Let your garden go a little wild
- Put up a bat box
- Create linear features, i.e., hedgerows/treelines
- Reduce or remove artificial lighting
- Keep cats indoors at night

Fireflies

It's a hot 80-degree night in July. I just let my dogs out before bedtime and had an otherworldly experience with some fireflies in my backyard. I believe that they, too, are psychopomps and spirit messengers. Some firefly species are at risk of extinction due to artificial lighting, loss of habitat, pesticides, and climate change. In Native American and Asian traditions, fireflies are considered spiritual guides or messengers from ancestors. In Japanese culture, fireflies symbolize the souls of the departed. I decided to include some gardening tips and plants to encourage them to visit your Psychopomp Garden.

Fireflies thrive in moist, undisturbed environments with plenty of shelter and food sources for their larvae. Here are some great plant choices to encourage them:

Grasses and ground cover provide shelter and moisture retention for firefly larvae:

- Eastern Gamagrass (*Tripsacum dactyloides*)
- Switchgrass (*Panicum virgatum*)
- Inland Sea Oats (*Chasmanthium latifolium*)
- Big Bluestem (*Andropogon gerardii*)
- Blue Grama (*Bouteloua gracilis*)

Wildflowers and perennials attract pollinators and create a biodiverse ecosystem:

- Goldenrod (*Solidago spp.*)
- Wild Bergamot (*Monarda fistulosa*)
- Joe-Pye Weed (*Eutrochium purpureum*)
- Swamp Milkweed (*Asclepias incarnata*)

- Evening Primrose (*Oenothera biennis*) Blooms at dusk, perfect timing for fireflies!
- Purple Coneflower (*Echinacea purpurea*)
- Black-Eyed Susan (*Rudbeckia hirta*)
- Boneset (*Eupatorium perfoliatum*)

Shrubs and Trees offer shade and leaf litter for larvae development:

- Buttonbush (*Cephalanthus occidentalis*) – loves wet areas
- Coralberry (*Symphoricarpos orbiculatus*)
- Sycamore, Pecan, and Pine Trees – great for egg-laying and shelter

Extra Tips to Boost Firefly Habitat
- Avoid pesticides and chemical fertilizers
- Keep areas of your yard damp or add a rain garden
- Let leaf litter and mulch accumulate naturally
- Reduce artificial lighting at night to help fireflies signal each other

Gardens of the Dead

The poem at the beginning of the book is Flanders Fields. The poppies in Flanders Fields in Belgium were not planted by anyone. They grew naturally over the graves of fallen soldiers during World War I. These are truly "Gardens of the Dead," blossoms nourished by blood and tears and the corpses of the deceased. Poppy seeds (*Papaver rhoeas*) had been lying dormant in the soils of Flanders for decades. The First World War's artillery and trench digging churned up the ground, bringing buried seeds to the surface. Exploding shells released nitrogen and lime, while the decomposition of fallen soldiers and animals enriched the soil. Together, these processes turned otherwise poor soils into nutrient-rich beds ideally suited to poppies. Literally human compost and a Garden made from the dead. The following *Gardens of the Dead* ideas use human remains as nutrients, with both cremation and whole body options.

Tree Urns and Tree Pods

Tree urns are biodegradable vessels designed to transform cremated remains into nourishment for a living tree. Rather than sitting in a niche, scattering, keeping at home, or buried in a traditional plot, these urns become part of the life cycle. Once planted, they break down and feed a seed or seedling, allowing a tree to grow where the urn was interred.

The two-piece urn consists of a lower capsule that holds the ashes and an upper section filled with a soil mixture—such as peat, vermiculite, or similar materials—along with a seed or young sapling. Once buried about two inches below ground, the biodegradable shell gradually dissolves over weeks to months, releasing nutrients into the surrounding soil. As those nutrients feed the seed or sapling, it germinates or establishes roots and grows into a living, lasting tribute.

Constructed from 100% biodegradable materials—ranging from recycled paper and coconut coir to plant-based composites—tree urns come in formats such as simple pods, full planting kits, and decorative planters. Many brands even allow you to choose the species best suited to your climate, with evergreens like pine or seasonal hardwoods shipped as seedlings timed to your planting zone. By returning remains to the earth, a tree urn creates a living, growing memorial rather than a static container, supports reforestation, and offers a tangible, lasting connection every time you visit. In this way, it becomes a powerful symbol of renewal, transformation, and the cycle of life.

Tree pod burial is an emerging green burial option designed to return human remains to the earth in a way that promotes new life, particularly through the planting of a tree above the burial site. Instead of using a traditional casket, the whole body is placed in a biodegradable pod that gradually decomposes, releasing nutrients to support the growth of the tree planted above it.

A young tree or seedling is positioned above the buried pod. As the pod's material breaks down over time, it enriches the surrounding soil with nutrients. While this practice is legal in designated green burial sites, there are currently no providers offering this service, and no pods are available for purchase on the market, making the concept still theoretical.

When using a tree pod or tree urn, try to focus on trees that are linked to death and dying through symbolism, myth, and doctrine of signatures.

Yew (*Taxus baccata*): The yew's dark evergreen needles and blood-red arils conceal a deadly toxin in its bark and seeds. Planted around churchyards and cemeteries for centuries, it came to symbolize both death and transformation, its evergreen persistence hinting at immortality even as the wood claimed the fallen.

Cypress (*Cupressus sempervirens*): With its soaring, spire-like form pointing toward the sky and unchanging foliage, the cypress became a fixture in funeral groves. Across the Mediterranean and beyond, its presence in burial grounds speaks to eternal life, sorrow, and the connection between earth and heaven.

Weeping Willow (*Salix babylonica*): The graceful, pendulous branches of the weeping willow resemble tears falling toward the water below. In literature and art, its drooping silhouette embodies grief and lamentation, standing watch over riversides and graves alike.

Elder (*Sambucus nigra*): Clusters of black berries—resembling decay—hang heavily on elder branches in late summer, while the tree's explosive regrowth from cut stumps hints at resurrection. European folklore often forbade cutting an elder, fearing it would bring misfortune or attract the dead.

Blackthorn (*Prunus spinosa*): Blackthorn forms dense, thorny thickets that blossom with stark white flowers in late winter. In Celtic and medieval lore, it stood for suffering and martyrdom, its blooms marking the turn of the year and the paths between the living world and the underworld.

Maple (*Acer spp.*): Maple trees, with their blood-red autumn foliage and sap that hints at the color of life's lifeblood, have long been planted in graveyards across Europe and North America. Their vivid fall display—followed by stark winter skeletons—serves as a potent reminder of mortality and the cyclical fading of life.

Birch (*Betula spp.*): Though often celebrated for renewal, the birch's ghost-white bark and its traditional use in funeral wands and coffins tie it to the boundary between life and afterlife. In Slavic lore, birches stand at the threshold of the otherworld, their pale trunks guiding souls on the journey beyond.

Eastern Red Cedar (*Juniperus virginiana*): Commonly found in colonial-era cemeteries across North America, Eastern red cedars were thought to guard the departed. Their dense, fragrant wood symbolized both perpetual mourning and the hope of eternal life, making them staples in 18th- and 19th-century burial plantings.

Acacia (*Acacia spp.*): In Egyptian myth and Masonic tradition alike, the acacia represents immortality and spiritual passage. Its thorny branches—rooted in earth yet reaching skyward—embody the soul's fragile bridge between the material world and the realm beyond, earning it a revered place in funerary rites and memorial symbolism.

Green Burials

Modern funerary practices are resource-intensive and environmentally problematic. Traditional burial consumes more than 4.3 million gallons of embalming fluid per year in the U.S. alone, including carcinogenic formaldehyde that may leach into soil and groundwater. Cremation is also terrible for the environment. The process uses industrial natural gas to fire the crematory, producing over 534 pounds (240 kg) of CO_2 per body (the equivalent of a 470-mile car journey or more). It pollutes the air by releasing mercury and other heavy metals from dental fillings and minor toxins. The cumulative environmental burden of these practices—given the roughly 2.8 million annual U.S. deaths—has turned attention to more sustainable alternatives, returning to practices that were always used up until 200 years ago.

Green burial is a return to ancient human traditions that honor the natural cycles of decay and rebirth. For thousands of years, most people were buried in simple shrouds or wooden coffins, without vaults, chemicals, or elaborate containers. This approach allowed nature's decomposers to reclaim our bodies swiftly and gracefully. Evidence of such burials, some dating back to Neanderthals, demonstrates not just a practical method of disposing of bodies, but also a spiritual acceptance of our own mortality and our interconnectedness with nature.

However, in the nineteenth and twentieth centuries, Western burial practices began to shift toward modern conventions. The introduction of embalming during the American Civil War, the popularity of ornate hardwood and metal caskets, and the widespread use of concrete burial vaults all contributed to a separation of death from the environment. These changes, initially driven by health, preservation, and ceremonial concerns, have since led to significant environmental issues.

The contemporary green burial movement gained traction in the late twentieth century as environmental and spiritual awareness increased. Pioneering organizations, such as the Green Burial Council (founded in the U.S. in 2005), established standards to restore burials to their ecological roots. This means avoiding toxins, non-biodegradable materials, and disrupting landscapes, in favor of practices that conserve, restore, and celebrate ecosystems. Conservation cemeteries, where burials actively contribute to land preservation, have emerged as models for how one's final act can support environmental stewardship.

Currently, there are roughly 220 natural burial cemeteries in the United States. Only a few are designated Conservation Ground burial sites that specifically aim to restore natural habitat. A large number are Natural Burial cemeteries, and then there are hybrid cemeteries that offer both traditional burial and green options together in the same cemetery. There are roughly 17,500 traditional cemeteries in the United States. As you can see, Green Burials are only a small fraction of final dispositions. We have a long way to go!

Green burials help prevent toxins from entering the environment and replenish healthy, organism-rich soil through organic decomposition. We are becoming increasingly conscious of how conventional cemeteries are wasteful, toxic, and contribute to the destruction of land and resources (Hello? Victorian Era? We literally ran out of room to bury the dead.) In an age shadowed by climate change, resource depletion, and an increasing yearning for sustainable living, society is compelled not only to reconsider its habits in life, but also in death. Bodies are interred without chemical embalming in biodegradable shrouds or simple coffins, often in conservation cemeteries that restore native habitats. Green burials prioritize the care of the deceased while promoting the restoration of natural resources and habitats. They aim to reduce carbon emissions and protect mortuary workers from the toxins associated with embalming. In green cemeteries, practices such as embalming, the use of vaults, non-biodegradable products, herbicides, pesticides, and fertilizers are not permitted. Instead, these cemeteries support sustainable management practices and creative, natural methods for marking graves.

In a natural burial, only biodegradable products are used for interment. Families often choose simple shrouds or eco-friendly caskets that decompose, made of pine needles, etc. They can also opt to be buried without a casket, wrapped solely in a burial shroud. Natural burials do not require cement or plastic vaults, and as a result, the burial holes are shallower—about 3 to 4 feet deep—minimizing soil disruption. In a green burial, the grave is closed in a way that harmonizes with nature and preserves the surrounding ecosystem. The soil excavated during the burial is carefully set aside in layers and then returned in reverse order, maintaining its original structure to encourage regrowth. The grave is filled naturally and often covered with straw, native plants, or biodegradable materials. In woodland settings, the root mat may be temporarily removed and then gently placed back to allow the landscape to heal. Graves are marked with natural elements—like stones or plants—or even GPS coordinates, rather than traditional headstones, minimizing visual disruption. Family and friends often participate in closing the grave, creating a meaningful ritual by shoveling earth or adding personal biodegradable mementos. Temporary wooden supports may be used for safety during the burial, but these are removed before the grave is fully closed. The result is a respectful and seamless return to the earth, allowing nature to reclaim the space over time. You can then plant directly on a green burial grave—provided you consult the cemetery's guidelines, select approved native species, use only biodegradable materials, and respect the natural-decomposition ethos of green burial. Most green cemeteries maintain an approved list of plants that can be installed on the burial mound. Green burial sites favor low-maintenance landscapes. Choose drought-tolerant and self-seeding species that require little to no supplemental watering or pruning. This whole process allows the earth to transform the human body into rich, healthy soil, which nourishes the ground and supports plants and animals.

Human Compost

Human composting, also called natural organic reduction, or terramation, is a process that transforms a human body into nutrient-rich soil through accelerated decomposition. It's a greener alternative to burial and cremation, designed to return the body to the earth. The process is inspired by composting practices long used in agriculture and gardening, but scaled and refined to safely, respectfully, and efficiently return a body to the earth.

Human composting is a new deathcare option. Like green burial, it transforms the human body into rich, living soil but at a much faster rate of 30-45 days. The process begins by wrapping the body in a biodegradable cloth and cradling it into a vessel, usually made of steel. Under and over the body is a blanket and bed of organic matter like alfalfa, wood chips, straw, and wildflowers. For about 30-45 days, funeral staff tend to the body and vessel. During the process, the temperature inside the container reaches about 140°, creating the prime environment for microbes to transform the body into soil. When the flesh is decomposed, bones and teeth remain. They are ground up just like in cremation, and returned to the soil. The resulting soil is carbon-rich, supports plant growth, aids water retention, and can be used in habitat restoration, reforestation, and other conservation projects. Loved ones can take home some or all of the composted soil to spread as a memorial in gardens, to create a garden, or to spread around trees. Some people choose to donate the soil to local land restoration projects.

As of mid-2025, human composting is legally available in 13 states: Arizona, California, Colorado, Delaware, Georgia, Maine, Maryland, Minnesota, Nevada, New York, Oregon, Vermont, and Washington. Several other states have bills pending or pilot programs underway to authorize natural organic reduction, and momentum suggests more will follow in the coming years.

While better for the environment, human composting is controversial. Some comment that it takes humanity and sacredness away from the funeral process and reduces human remains to just another material. The resulting soil, made from human remains, especially when used in gardening and land conservation projects, may be emotionally, spiritually, or theologically distressing to some.

Mushroom Suits and Mushroom Caskets

Fungi are the Earth's master recyclers. Mycelium, the thread-like root structure of fungi, forms complex webs beneath forest floors and within soils worldwide. These networks break down not only dead plants but also animal matter—including human bodies—transforming them back into essential nutrients through a powerful arsenal of enzymatic processes.

The mushroom burial suit, or "Infinity Burial Suit," was envisioned by artist and environmental advocate Jae Rhim Lee during her graduate work at MIT. She was inspired by mycoremediation research, developed the suit as an intersection of art, science, and sustainability. In 2011, Lee introduced her prototype through the now-famous TED Talk "My Mushroom Burial Suit." Later, through her company Coeio and the Infinity Burial Project, she commercialized the suit—the first to embed selected strains of mushroom mycelium within an organic fiber garment designed to accelerate decomposition and detoxification.

The contemporary mushroom burial suit is crafted from organic cotton or natural fiber, infused with a proprietary blend of mushroom mycelium and beneficial microorganisms. Upon interment, when the suit is placed in contact with the burial environment, the mycelium awakens, colonizing both the garment and the human body. Fueled by warmth, moisture, and nutrients from human tissues, the mycelium spreads, releasing enzymes that break down fats, proteins, cartilage, and even hair and nails. Over the span of two to three years, the body returns to the earth as humus, with the mycelium and associated microbes neutralizing hazardous compounds as they go.

Mushroom suits are available for both humans and pets. Celebrity endorsements and high-profile cases—most notably the burial of actor Luke Perry in a mushroom suit—have brought wider awareness and legitimacy to this approach. As of mid-2025, mushroom burial suits are legal and available in the U.S., Canada, parts of Europe, and Australia, but their use is still largely dependent on access to green cemeteries or natural burial grounds that allow such practice.

Biodegradable mushroom coffins, sometimes called "living caskets" or "mycelium coffins," bring the same ecological principles to a more familiar funerary form. Rather than manufactured like traditional wooden caskets, these coffins are grown from mycelium mixed with organic agricultural waste (often hemp fibers or sawdust). Over about seven days, the fungal network colonizes the organic substrate in a coffin-shaped mold, forming a lightweight but sturdy structure. The completed vessel is then dried to pause fungal activity until burial. Upon burial, ground moisture reactivates the dormant mycelium, which resumes growth and decomposition. Mycelium quickly infiltrates both the coffin material and the body inside, breaking down organic matter, neutralizing some toxins, and enriching the surrounding soil. The entire coffin typically degrades within 30–45 days—far faster than wooden, metal, or composite caskets, which may persist for decades or centuries. The process is designed to speed up body decomposition two to three times faster than traditional burial, with the body generally returning to soil nutrients within two to three years.

Mushroom caskets and mushroom suits improve soil quality at burial sites. The decomposition process creates nutrient-rich humus, facilitating the growth of plants and supporting microorganisms and invertebrates essential to vibrant ecosystems. Mushroom mycelium binds and breaks down heavy metals, hydrocarbons, pesticides, and synthetic compounds accumulated in human tissues over a lifetime, converting potentially hazardous materials into safer compounds. Mushrooms actively detoxify burial sites.

Biodegradable Urns

Biodegradable urns offer a beautiful and eco-conscious way to honor a loved one's memory while gently returning their remains to nature. Intended for water or earth burial, these urns are crafted from natural materials that break down over time. The same environmental challenges apply with biodegradable urns as with scattering of cremains. Please refer back to the last chapter on soil amending ideas if you choose to return your loved one to the earth using a biodegradable urn. While green burial options are not yet available at the cemeteries where I work, I do offer biodegradable urns to families that wish to place their loved one in a memorial garden at their home or private property. I am so intrigued by them and the materials that they come in. You can bury a biodegradable urn in your garden for the dead.

Common materials include:

Bamboo: Fast-growing grass with excellent tensile strength • Light yet sturdy for handling and transport • Decomposes in soil within 6–12 months

Recycled Paper and Cardboard: Made from post-consumer fibers, unlaminated, printed with soy-based inks • Often molded into rigid shapes or layered for thickness • Breaks down in 2–4 months in moist soil or water

Natural Plant Fibers (Cotton, Hemp, Wool): Textiles woven or felted into urn wraps or shrouds • Breathable, biodegradable within 3–9 months • Hemp's rapid regrowth and cotton's softness each carry distinct symbolism

Untreated Wood (Pine, Oak, Maple): Solid, dignified containers that reflect the forest's life cycle • Pine may decompose in 1–2 years; oak and maple can take 3–5 years • Ideal for earth burials; not suitable for water ceremonies

Clay or Cast Paper: Formulated to dissolve on contact with water • Commonly used in water urns—floats briefly before slipping beneath the surface • Residue is minimal clay or fiber, fully dispersing within hours to days

Compacted Peat and Coconut Shells: Compressed into dense bricks or shells for structural form • Adds organic matter to soil, enhancing nutrient content • Biodegrades in 3–6 months, attracting microorganisms to aid decomposition

Plant-Based Polymers (Cornstarch, Gelatin Blends): Molded like plastic but compostable under the right conditions • Decomposition in industrial or home compost ranges from 2–12 months • Offers more precise shapes and colors without synthetic additives

Sand: Blended from authentic beach sand and a plant-based gelatin, they feature tiny holes for graceful water ingress, floating momentarily, then dispersing ashes in water over three days, and breaking down in earth burials within roughly three months

Hemp Urns: Woven using sustainable hemp fibers and mulberry bark through a time-honored technique, these box-shaped urns dissolve naturally when interred, reflecting resilience and purity through a fabric of living fibers.

Himalayan Salt: These urns are hand-forged from pure Himalayan rock salt. They float briefly before gently sinking and fully dissolve in water within about four hours, or biodegrade in soil over a few months.

Pine Needle Basket: Crafted by hand with longleaf pine needles coiled and stitched into rustic baskets, they offer a woodland aesthetic and biodegrade directly in the ground, infusing the site with the forest's spirit.

When planning an eco-conscious farewell, families often weigh three main options: a biodegradable urn, opting for a green burial, or scattering ashes in a meaningful place. Each option carries its own meaning, environmental impact, and practical considerations. Understanding these differences can help you choose a final resting place that aligns with your values.

Biodegradable urns eliminate plastic and metal waste and can be personalized with eco-friendly coatings or embedded seeds that sprout into new life. Green burials allow the body to decompose naturally, returning nutrients to the soil and allowing native vegetation to flourish, transforming burial grounds into conservation areas or wildflower meadows. Scattering ashes is the most direct way to return cremated remains to air, water, or earth. This option eliminates the need for a burial plot or long-term memorial structure and offers tremendous flexibility in location choice. However, it's important to research local regulations, consider the high alkalinity of untreated ashes that can impact soil pH, and accept that there may be no physical site to visit in the future, as well as no memorialization.

Ultimately, the most meaningful choice depends on your spiritual beliefs, culture, family's traditions, the desired memorial site—whether a garden, grove, or seashore—environmental priorities, budget, and the level of ceremony you envision. Whether you seal ashes in a biodegradable urn, embrace the simplicity of a green burial, or cast remains to the wind or waves, each option can offer a gentle tribute that honors the cycle of life and aligns with your values. Each option, whatever you choose, is a garden of the dead, using our decaying bodies to create new life.

Gardening 101:
Turn that Black Thumb Green!

I am including chapters on basic gardening and garden design. I have taught thousands of classes over the decades. My biggest pet peeve is when people acquire information but fail to apply it. I don't just want you to read about cool gothic plants and gardens for the dead ideas, I want you to actually plant and maintain an epic garden that will make your neighbors and friends jealous, as well as cultivate a garden that the spirits will see from the underworld!

In all my gardening classes, I teach that horticulture means the ART, SCIENCE, MAGICK, INTUITION, EXPERIMENTATION, *and* PRACTICE of keeping a garden. Sometimes things do not work out the way we planned. But regardless, we learn a lesson about what we can do differently next time. I highly recommend keeping a garden journal, almost like a green witch's book of shadows. It allows you to track progress over time as well as help you identify patterns and learn from past experiences.

Keeping a garden journal is an easy way to plan and organize your work: you can note planting dates, seed types, garden layouts, and crop rotations. It also helps you learn by logging weather, pests, and what worked or failed each season. Journaling sparks your creativity when you sketch bed designs, jot down color schemes, or try new plant pairings. It encourages mindfulness and celebrates milestones like first sprouts and harvests, and it holds you accountable by tracking soil amendments, goals, and yield changes over time. To start, pick either a notebook or an app, use simple daily or weekly templates, write notes after each gardening session, and personalize it with photos, pressed flowers, or color codes. Over the seasons, your journal will become the roadmap to a more productive, beautiful garden.

In all my gardening classes, even more advanced classes, I always review the fundamentals. If there is a problem in the garden, it is almost always related to one of my core principles.

I teach that there are 6 essential ingredients to successful gardening:

1. Sun: Plants harness energy from the sun through photosynthesis and convert that energy into their tissues.
2. Water: Plants require internal water pressure to strengthen the stems and leaves. Plants need water to create energy and facilitate chemical reactions such as photosynthesis.
3. Nutrients: Plants need nitrogen (N), phosphorus (P), and potassium (K). These nutrients can either be derived from the soil or manually added through fertilizer or compost.
4. Soil: Provides structure and holds water/nutrients.
5. Understanding a Plant's Personality: Plants have personalities and specific likes. Some plants like it hot, humid, and sunny, while others like it cool, dry, and shady. Can take experimentation and research.
6. Using high-quality, non-GMO seeds and plants, as well as native plants, heirloom, and organic whenever possible.

Sun

First of all, please understand if your plant is full sun, part sun, part shade, or full shade. It is of utmost importance to put plants where they will thrive and in what type of sun they prefer. It is easier to work with the environment you have and find a plant that belongs there than it is to change an environment to adapt to a plant. Successful gardening starts with matching your plants' light needs to the sun exposure in each part of your yard. Here's how to decode Full Sun, Partial Sun, and Shade—and how orientation (East, West, South, North) affects light intensity and duration.

Sunlight Categories:

- Full Sun

Definition: At least 6 hours of direct, unfiltered sunlight per day. Ideal for: Tomatoes, peppers, lavender, most vegetables, and sun-loving annuals.

- Partial Sun / Partial Shade

Definition: 3–6 hours of direct sun, often during cooler morning hours (partial sun) or afternoon hours (partial shade). Ideal for: Herbs (basil, chives), leafy greens (lettuce, spinach), begonias, impatiens.

- Full Shade

Definition: Less than 3 hours of direct sun, with bright, indirect light or dappled shade the rest of the day. Ideal for: Ferns, hostas, ivy, and groundcovers like ajuga.

Orientation and Light Levels

East-Facing: Medium Light / Morning Sun

- Receives gentle, cooling sun from sunrise until midday.
- Best for plants that thrive on bright morning light but struggle in intense afternoon heat.
- Examples: Salad greens, peas, snapdragons, and many spring bulbs.

West-Facing: High Light / Afternoon Sun

- Gets strong, warming sun from midday until sunset.
- Can stress moisture-sensitive plants; ideal for heat-tolerant varieties.
- Examples: Peppers, okra, marigolds, and herbs like rosemary.

South-Facing: Full Sun / Maximum Light

- Bathed in sun from mid-morning through late afternoon.
- Warms soil quickly in spring; prime real estate for fruiting vegetables and drought-tolerant ornamentals.
- Examples: Tomatoes, squash, eggplant, lavender, and agastache.

North-Facing: Lowest Light / Full Shade

- Receives little to no direct sun; cool and consistently shaded.
- Perfect for shade-loving perennials and moisture-retentive foliage plants.
- Examples: Hostas, ferns, heucheras, and astilbes.

Tips for Matching Plants to Sunlight:

- Observe Your Garden: Track sun patterns over a week—note when and how many hours each bed gets direct light.
- Soil and Water Adjustments: More sun means faster soil drying; increase watering or mulch heavily in south/west beds.
- Use Shade Cloth or Screens: Provide filtered shade during peak afternoon hours for sensitive crops in west-facing areas.
- Plan Rotations: Move shade-tolerant crops into north beds during summer, then switch with sun-lovers in cooler months.

Water

Water is the lifeblood of every garden. It fuels the chemical engines inside plant cells, cools foliage on hot days, and creates the physical forces that hold stems upright. Without consistent moisture and balanced humidity, even the hardiest plants can wither, fail to flower, or fall prey to diseases.

- Plants split water molecules to release electrons and protons, driving the energy-capture reactions that build sugars.
- As water evaporates from stomata, it carries away heat, keeping leaf tissues from overheating.
- Nearly every metabolic process—from breaking down nutrients to synthesizing growth hormones—occurs in aqueous solution.
- Water dissolves minerals in the soil and ferries them, along with sugars, through xylem and phloem to every part of the plant.
- Source of turgor pressure. Cells swell with water, pressing against their walls to give stems rigidity, open stomata, and drive cell expansion.
- Growth regulator and temperature buffer. Consistent moisture levels moderate temperature swings in soil and air, stabilizing root zone conditions and signaling stress or dormancy cues.

Managing Water and Humidity

- Water deeply and infrequently. Encourage roots to grow downward by soaking the root zone, then letting the soil dry slightly before the next irrigation.
- Time it right. Water in the early morning or late afternoon to minimize evaporation and fungal risks.
- Mulch heavily. A 2–4-inch layer of organic mulch cuts the surface evaporation, cools the soil, and slowly releases moisture back to the roots.
- Match plants to moisture levels. Group moisture-loving specimens (ferns, begonias) in damp zones and drought-tolerant ones (lavender, sedum) in well-drained beds.
- Monitor and adjust humidity. In enclosed spaces or greenhouses, use hygrometers to keep relative humidity between 40–70%, reducing stress and pest pressure.
- Harvest rainwater. Collect runoff in barrels to reduce tap-water costs and supply plants with softer, chlorine-free water.

How much you need to water plants will depend on a few things. Hotter and drier air will pull moisture from plants and soils more quickly, so more watering will be necessary as the temperatures go up. The type of soil you have in your garden will also affect how much water is available to plants. A good rule of thumb is that plants should receive enough water to cover the ground with an inch of water each week, and it's better for plants to get all the water one or two times per week rather than a little bit each day. An easy test to see if plants have enough water available is to put a finger in the soil and make sure it feels moist two to three inches below the surface. When watering, it's best to use a watering can or sprinkler (dumping a lot of water on the plants all at once can damage them). Of course, if your area gets a lot of rain, you won't need to perform this chore often!

Watering Guidelines:

- Keep soil consistently moist for plants that need it. Stick to a regular schedule without letting the soil dry out completely—yet be careful not to overwater.

- Overwatering is the most common cause of root rot, so always check moisture before you water (the "finger test")
  - The "finger test" is an easy, no-tools way to check soil moisture before you water.
  - Insert your index finger about 1–2 inches into the soil around your plant.
  - Feel the soil at your second knuckle.
  - If it feels dry and crumbly, it's time to water.
  - If it clings together and feels cool or slightly damp, hold off.
  - If it's soggy or water drips off, let the soil dry out before watering again.
  - Use this quick check in multiple spots (especially around larger containers or garden beds) to get an accurate picture of your soil's overall moisture.
  - By relying on touch rather than a strict schedule, you'll avoid both underwatering and that most common killer—overwatering.
- Use lukewarm water to avoid shocking roots, and apply it evenly around the entire root zone rather than just at one spot.
- Never let pots or beds sit in standing water; good drainage is essential.
- For indoor plants, allow the top inch of soil to dry between waterings to prevent soggy roots.
- Boost humidity by misting foliage—especially helpful for tropical species.
- Remember that your water source (hardness, chlorine, pH) can impact plant health; consider rainwater or filtered water when possible.

Ensuring Proper Drainage

Plant roots need oxygen as well as water. Waterlogged soil deprives roots of air and leads to poor growth or rot. A simple drainage test helps you diagnose trouble before it kills your plants:

- Dig a 10-inch-deep hole and fill it with water.
- Let it drain completely, then refill the hole the next day.
- Time how long the second fill takes to disappear.

If water remains more than 3–4 hours after refilling, your soil likely has poor drainage—and you'll need to amend it with organic matter or install raised beds to give roots the air they need.

To promote sustainable water use and improve garden efficiency, implement the following strategies:

Rainwater Harvesting: Install rain barrels to collect runoff from rooftops during storms. This harvested water can be reused for garden irrigation, reducing dependence on municipal water and conserving natural resources.

Efficient Water Delivery: Utilize drip irrigation lines to deliver water directly to plant roots, minimizing evaporation and runoff. Pair this with self-watering planters that regulate moisture levels, ensuring plants receive consistent hydration without overwatering.

Water during cooler parts of the day (early morning or late evening) to reduce evaporation.

Regularly check for leaks or clogs in irrigation lines.

Use mulch to retain soil moisture and further reduce water consumption.

Nutrients

All plants require 17 chemical elements for life—essentially vitamins for plants. Carbon, oxygen, and hydrogen are needed in the largest quantities and are obtained from air and water. The remaining 14 essential elements (nitrogen, phosphorus, potassium, calcium, magnesium, sulfur, boron, chlorine, cobalt, copper, iron, manganese, molybdenum, and zinc) are provided by the soil. The primary nutrients are nitrogen (N), phosphorus (P), and potassium (K), which constitute about 0.5% to 3% of a plant's weight.

Primary Macronutrients
- Nitrogen (N): Drives leaf and stem growth, chlorophyll production
- Phosphorus (P): Fuels root development, flowering, and fruit set
- Potassium (K): Regulates water balance, disease resistance, and enzyme activation

Secondary Macronutrients

- Calcium (Ca): Strengthens cell walls, aids root and shoot growth
- Magnesium (Mg): Central atom in chlorophyll, activates many enzymes
- Sulfur (S): Integral to amino acids and vitamins

Micronutrients (trace elements)
- Iron (Fe), Manganese (Mn), Zinc (Zn), Copper (Cu), Boron (B), Molybdenum (Mo), Chlorine (Cl), Nickel (Ni)
- Though needed in tiny amounts, their absence can cripple photosynthesis, hormone balance, and cell division.

How Plants Absorb Nutrients

Root Zone Processes
- Nutrients dissolve in soil water, forming ions or small molecules
- Root hairs extend into pore spaces, increasing contact with nutrient solutions

Factors Influencing Nutrient Uptake
- Soil pH
- Optimal range: 6.0–7.0 for most vegetables; 5.5–6.5 for acid-loving shrubs
- Outside ideal pH, key nutrients become locked up or reach toxic levels
- Moisture Levels
- Water carries dissolved nutrients; drought halts uptake, waterlogging starves roots of oxygen
- Soil Temperature
- Microbial activity (which mineralizes organic matter) peaks between 60–85°F (15–29°C)
- Soil Structure and Organic Matter
- Loamy, well-drained soils with 5–8% organic matter deliver steady nutrition and aeration
- Competition and Stress
- High weed pressure or root damage reduces a plant's ability to forage for nutrients
- Stressors such as insufficient light, extreme temperatures, and disease can significantly hinder a plant's nutrient absorption.

Best Practices for Reliable Nutrition

Test and Amend Your Soil
- Conduct a comprehensive soil test every 2–3 years
- Adjust pH with lime (to raise) or sulfur (to lower) and apply missing nutrients

Incorporate Organic Matter
- Compost, aged manure, leaf mold, or green-manure cover crops boost CEC and microbial life

Choose Balanced Fertilizers
- Slow-release granular amendments or tailor-made blends support steady growth
- Liquid feeds and foliar sprays can correct acute deficiencies quickly
- Some organic fertilizers you can use include blood meal, bone meal, manure, compost, lawn clippings, and wood ash

Practice Crop Rotation and Diversity
- Rotate families (e.g., brassicas → legumes → solanums) to rebalance soil nutrients
- Interplant deep- and shallow-rooted species to exploit different soil layers

Monitor and Respond
- Recognize deficiency symptoms: yellowing between leaf veins (Mg), stunted growth (N), purple tints (P)
- Adjust feeding schedules through the season—heavy feeders like corn need side-dressings of nitrogen

Soil

Soil is a living, dynamic system made up mostly of mineral particles and about five percent organic matter. Its texture—how it feels and functions—is defined by the relative proportions of sand, silt, and clay, with loam (equal parts of each) universally prized for its balance of drainage, nutrient-holding capacity, and ease of cultivation. These particles originate in parent rock and have been refined over millennia by weather, water, and biological activity—from burrowing animals to fungi—while climate and topography continue to shape soil characteristics. Matching your plants to the right texture and pH ensures they thrive in the conditions they prefer.

Sandy soil, with the largest particles, feels dry and gritty. Its generous pore spaces allow water and air to move freely, so it warms rapidly in spring and is easy to dig—but it drains so quickly that seedlings struggle to access moisture or nutrients before they wash away. A simple field test—moisten a handful, attempt to form a ball, then watch it crumble—confirms sandy texture.

In contrast, silty soil feels smooth and almost soapy when damp. Its finer particles hold moisture longer and lend moderate fertility, but they pack tightly, making the soil cool, prone to poor drainage, and easily compacted. Avoid working silty patches when they're wet to preserve airflow around roots.

Clay soil contains the tiniest particles, which cling together tightly and retain water and nutrients exceptionally well. It feels sticky when wet and forms ribbon-like shapes when squeezed, but it also stays cold into spring and can become rock-hard in summer or heavy to dig when dry. Clay soil is black gold! It often benefits from generous organic amendments to improve structure and aeration.

Finally, soil pH governs nutrient availability: acidic soils register below 7.0 on the pH scale, while alkaline soils rise above it. Many garden plants flourish in the 6.0–7.0 range, where most essential nutrients remain soluble and accessible. Testing and adjusting pH—through lime to raise it or sulfur to lower it—helps unlock your soil's full potential.

Soil acidity plays a significant role in various chemical and biological processes occurring in the soil, affecting the availability of essential nutrients.

- Acidic soils have a pH of less than 7.
- Alkaline soils have a pH of more than 7.

To adjust soil pH, you can:

- Increase pH by applying lime.
- Decrease pH by applying sulfur.

Soil Sampling

Soil fertility is the ability of soil to supply water-soluble nutrients essential for healthy plant growth. To manage fertility effectively, you first need to know which nutrients are lacking and then supply them in the right proportions while keeping soil pH within the optimal range.

The only reliable way to uncover those nutrient needs is through a soil test. Plan to sample your soil every 2–3 years or sooner if plants show yellowing, stunted growth, or other deficiency symptoms.

Testing options:

- Send samples to a university or extension lab for a full analysis.
- Use do-it-yourself test kits from garden centers for quick, on-site results.

When collecting soil samples, consider the following steps:

1. Sample each distinct garden area separately.
2. Gather a composite sample from 5 different locations within the same area.
3. Dig down 4 to 6 inches to collect the sample.
4. Mix the soil from these locations in a bucket.
5. Indicate which plants you are growing on the sample information page.
6. Send the sample to a Soil Analysis Lab.

Important: Never apply more nutrients than your test report recommends, as this can stress or burn plants and potentially kill them. Excess nutrients can also harm the environment.

Compost

There is literally nothing better to add to your garden of the dead than compost. Compost is a perfect symbol of death and decay creating new life. Compost is a nutrient-rich soil amendment created through the managed, aerobic decomposition of organic materials such as food scraps, yard trimmings, and plant residues by microorganisms, including bacteria and fungi.

All organic matter eventually decomposes, but composting accelerates this process by providing an ideal environment for these microorganisms. The final product, known as compost or humus, resembles fertile garden soil. This dark, crumbly substance has an earthy smell and works wonders for all types of soil, supplying vital nutrients to help plants grow and thrive.

Decomposing organisms include bacteria, fungi, and larger creatures such as worms, sow bugs, and nematodes. For these organisms to thrive, they need four key elements: nitrogen, carbon, moisture, and oxygen. To achieve the best results, mix materials high in nitrogen—such as clover, fresh grass clippings, and livestock manure—with those high in carbon, like waste paper, dried leaves, and twigs. If there is a shortage of nitrogen-rich materials, adding a handful of general lawn fertilizer can help improve the nitrogen-carbon ratio.

Moisture typically comes from rain, but you may need to water or cover the compost pile to keep it damp without saturating it. Structuring the pile to maintain small air spaces ensures there is enough oxygen. Turning the pile frequently will also promote faster decomposition.

Cold Composting vs. Hot Composting

Cold composting moves more slowly in cooler climates and can take a year or longer to break down fully, depending on the materials you add and local conditions. You can build the pile gradually over time and leave it largely undisturbed.

Hot composting demands more active management—turning, layering, and monitoring moisture—but rewards you with finished compost in just a few weeks when temperatures are favorable.

Benefits of Composting

- Enriches soil structure, improving moisture retention and reducing disease and pest pressure
- Decreases reliance on synthetic fertilizers
- Promotes beneficial bacteria and fungi that convert waste into humus, a nutrient-rich material
- Cuts methane emissions from landfills, lowering your carbon footprint
- Saves money on soil amendments and waste disposal
- Enhances the soil's ability to hold nutrients over time

Essential Ingredients for Composting

All successful composting requires three components:

- Browns: Carbon-rich materials such as dead leaves, straw, branches, and shredded paper
- Greens: Nitrogen-rich materials like grass clippings, vegetable and fruit scraps, coffee grounds, and fresh plant prunings
- Water: Moisture helps microbes break down organic matter; aim for the consistency of a wrung-out sponge

Backyard Cold Composting Steps:

1. Choose a dry, shaded spot near a water source for your pile or bin.
2. Add browns and greens as you generate them, chopping larger items into smaller pieces.
3. Moisten each layer of dry materials as you build your pile.
4. Optionally turn the pile occasionally, or simply let it decompose in place.
5. Bury kitchen scraps at least 10 inches deep under fresh brown material to deter pests.
6. Cover with a tarp to retain moisture if your climate is particularly dry.
7. Compost is ready when materials at the bottom are dark and crumbly—a process that typically takes two months to two years.

Backyard Hot Composting

Hot composting aligns with the growing season when microbial activity is at its peak, but a well-managed pile can stay active into cooler months. Follow these guidelines:

- Mix browns and greens in roughly equal volumes for a balanced carbon-to-nitrogen ratio.
- Build a pile at least 120 cm on each side (smaller piles may not retain enough heat).
- Thoroughly water each layer as you build the pile.
- Turn the pile twice in the first week, then once every one to two weeks, keeping moisture at a wrung-out sponge level.

- Temperatures of 130–140 °F destroy most weed seeds and pathogens, producing safe, stable compost in as little as three to six weeks.

Additional Tips and Considerations:
- To troubleshoot slow decomposition, check moisture (should be damp but not soggy) and adjust the green-to-brown ratio.
- If your pile smells, add more browns and turn it to introduce air.
- Use finished compost as a top dressing, soil amendment, or in potting mixes to boost fertility and structure.

Indoor Composting

If you lack space for an outdoor compost pile, you can compost materials indoors using a special bin available at local hardware or gardening supply stores, or you can create one yourself. Be sure to manage your compost pile actively and keep track of what you add. A well-maintained compost bin will not attract pests or rodents and will not produce unpleasant odors. Your compost should be ready in two to five weeks.

What to compost:

- Fruits and vegetables
- Eggshells
- Coffee grounds and filters
- Tea bags
- Nut shells
- Shredded newspaper
- Cardboard
- Paper
- Yard trimmings
- Grass clippings
- Houseplants
- Hay and straw
- Leaves
- Sawdust
- Wood chips
- Cotton and Wool Rags
- Dryer and vacuum cleaner lint

- Hair and fur
- Fireplace ashes

What <u>not</u> to compost:

- Black walnut tree leaves or twigs - Releases substances that might be harmful to plants
- Coal or charcoal ash - Might contain substances harmful to plants
- Dairy products (e.g., butter, milk, sour cream, yogurt) and eggs* - Create odor problems and attract pests such as rodents and flies
- Diseased or insect-ridden plants - Diseases or insects might survive and be transferred back to other plants
- Fats, grease, lard, or oils* - Create odor problems and attract pests such as rodents and flies
- Meat or fish bones and scraps* - Create odor problems and attract pests such as rodents and flies
- Pet wastes (e.g., dog or cat feces, soiled cat litter)* - Might contain parasites, bacteria, germs, pathogens, and viruses harmful to humans
- Yard trimmings treated with chemical pesticides - Might kill beneficial composting organisms

Using compost:

- Mix 2 inches of compost into the top 6 to 8 inches of garden soil when planting seeds
- Use a 3-inch layer of compost as mulch and groundcover
- Sift ½ inch onto to lawn to enhance soil and add nutrients
- Make compost tea as a fertilizer
- Add to potting mix

Plant Personality

This is a concept that I have come up with. Twenty years ago, I read the book *The Secret Life of Plants* by Peter Tompkins. It completely changed the way I look at plants. Plants are living, sentient beings. They are highly intelligent. For example, climbing vines use touch-sensitive responses (thigmotropism) to "decide" optimal attachment points, enhancing their structural support and growth efficiency. Roots of many species forage selectively, growing faster into nutrient-rich soil pockets and redirecting growth away from poorer zones, a goal-directed foraging strategy. When under herbivore attack, some plants emit volatile organic compounds. Sunflowers track the sun (a behavior called heliotropism) by growing east-to-west during the day and reorienting themselves at night thanks to an internal circadian clock. Plants are so incredible! Plants are smart and have personalities and specific likes. Some plants like it hot, humid, and sunny, while others like it cooler, dry, and shady. Understand your plants' personalities and give them what they want. It's the best way to become friends.

These are all the elements that make up a plant's personality. Ponder each factor before choosing or caring for a plant.

Climate Adaptation
- Your USDA Zone defines the average minimum winter temperature your plant can tolerate, helping you pick species suited to your region. Understanding your USDA hardiness zone ensures plant survival.

Light and Exposure
- Sun and lighting requirements indicate whether a plant prefers full sun, partial shade, or deep shade to thrive.
- How much light specifies daily hours of direct or filtered light needed for healthy growth.

Watering Needs and Care Tolerance
- Water requirements describe the volume and frequency of watering—from thirsty to drought-tolerant.
- Dry vs. moist clarifies if the soil should dry out between waterings or remain consistently damp.
- Prefers Neglect or to Be Babied? Rates a plant's resilience; some bounce back from missed waterings, others demand consistent pampering.

Soil Preferences
- Soil Drainage: Outlines how quickly water moves through the soil—fast-draining, moderate, or heavy/retentive.
- Soil Requirements (Rich vs. Poor): tells you if the plant thrives in nutrient-loaded loam or lean, sandy, low-fertility mixes.
- Preferred Soil pH Range: Notes the acidity or alkalinity (e.g., 5.5–6.5) that maximizes nutrient uptake.

Growth Habit and Lifecycle
- Annual/Perennial/Biennial: Defines whether a plant completes its life cycle in one year, lives multiple seasons, or spans two years.
- Height of Plant: Provides mature stature to help with garden layout and spacing.
- Plant Spacing: Recommends the distance between plants to prevent crowding and ensure airflow.
- Planting Depth: Advises how deep to set seeds or seedlings for optimal root establishment.

Physical Characteristics
- Color of the Plant: Covers foliage, flowers, and stems to guide aesthetic choices.
- Texture of the Plant: Describes leaf or stem feel—silky, fuzzy, glossy, coarse—which affects visual and tactile appeal.

Planting and Location
- Planting Location: Captures microclimate details: next to walls, under trees, on slopes, or in containers.
- Ground vs. Pot vs. Raised Bed: Explains if a plant performs best in open soil, containers, or elevated beds for drainage and soil control.

Propagation Basics
- Germination Period: States days or weeks from sowing until seedlings emerge.
- Indoor vs. Outdoor Sowing: Advises whether to direct-seed outdoors or start seeds indoors under controlled conditions.

High Quality Seeds and Plants

Don't be tempted by the discounted, half-dead-looking plant on sale at the gardening center! Gardens for the dead are symbolic and dualistic. We are honoring death/dying by sparking rebirth and creating new life through planting and gardening. We can't do that with a stressed and unhealthy plant that is about to die. Leave those yellowing and wilted plants alone and just wait for the botanical grim reaper to cross them over. Focus on using high-quality seeds and high-quality plants. When paired with all the other gardening basics above (water, sun, nutrients, etc.) you will have majestic gardens resilient to disease and pests and other garden troubles. Focus on heirlooms, organic, non-GMO, and native plants.

Heirloom Plants

Heirlooms are cultivars preserved by gardeners and growers over generations, often within tight-knit communities or family lines. They predate modern large-scale agriculture and carry rich genetic diversity.

- True heirlooms generally trace back before 1951, the year hybrid seeds first took off commercially. Some varieties survive from much earlier periods, even prehistoric times.

- Under the strictest definition, an heirloom is a plant passed from one family member to another for decades or centuries, each generation selecting the best seeds.

- Thanks to years of local cultivation, heirlooms are finely tuned to regional soils, climates, and seasonal quirks. Their genetics often confer natural resistance to pests, diseases, and weather extremes.

- Heirloom fruits and vegetables are prized for intense, nuanced flavors and a spectrum of shapes and colors you won't find in mass-market hybrids.

Organic Plants

Organic nursery stock is grown without synthetic pesticides, herbicides, or fertilizers, promoting healthier soil and long-term garden wellbeing.

- Certified Practices: Look for recognized certifications (USDA Organic, OMRI Listed) that guarantee no prohibited chemicals were used in seed production or propagation.

- Soil Health: Organic growers build living soils rich in organic matter and beneficial microbes, resulting in stronger, more nutrient-dense plants.

- Ecosystem Benefits: By avoiding toxins, organic plants foster diverse insect populations, earthworms, and soil fungi—all crucial players in a balanced garden food web.

Non-GMO Plants

Non-GMO (genetically modified organism) labels assure you the plant's genetic makeup hasn't been altered in a lab through recombinant DNA techniques.

- GMO vs. Hybrid: Hybrids result from traditional cross-pollination of two varieties, whereas GMOs involve targeted gene insertions. Non-GMO simply means it isn't the latter.

- Verify Through Seed Suppliers: Choose reputable seed companies or nurseries that explicitly label their offerings as non-GMO, giving you confidence in the plant's heritage.

- Consumer Choice: For gardeners who prefer entirely natural breeding processes, non-GMO selections preserve ancestral genetics and biodiversity.

Native Plants

Native species evolved alongside local wildlife, making them foundational to a garden that supports pollinators, birds, and beneficial insects.

- Ecological Integration: Native flowers, shrubs, and trees provide the right pollen, nectar, and habitat for regional pollinators and wildlife.

- Low Maintenance: Adapted to local rainfall and soils, natives typically require less supplemental water, fertilizer, and care once established.

- Soil and Water Conservation: Deep root systems stabilize soil, improve infiltration, and reduce erosion—benefits that ripple outward to your entire landscape.

By prioritizing heirloom, organic, non-GMO, and native plants, you cultivate a garden for the dead that's environmentally responsible!

Seeds

Seeds are living organisms whose vitality begins to wane the moment they're harvested. Without special storage measures, most seeds will remain viable for about a year; however, when kept under ideal conditions, many varieties can retain strong germination potential for up to five years. Look at expiration dates on seed packets.

Moisture accelerates seed aging, so maintaining a relative humidity of around 30 percent or lower is crucial. An airtight container helps lock out damp air and keeps conditions uniformly dry, preventing the seeds from picking up excess moisture.

Including desiccants such as silica gel, calcium chloride, or even powdered milk can further reduce ambient humidity. To avoid chemical interactions, place these moisture absorbers in breathable pouches or wrap them in paper, ensuring they never directly contact the seeds.

Temperature and light control are equally important. Storing seeds at cool temperatures between 35 °F and 50 °F—most household refrigerators fall within this range—and keeping containers in absolute darkness will preserve seed energy and prevent premature germination, giving your seeds the best chance at sprouting successfully when it's time to plant.

Choosing Plants

Evaluate overall habit and form. Perennials, annuals, and vegetable transplants should look sturdy and compact rather than spindly or lanky. Trees and shrubs ought to have a balanced shape, well-spaced branches, and no double leaders or crossing limbs that can later cause structural failure.

Inspect foliage closely. Leaves should be vibrant, uniformly colored, and free of spots, blotches, or insect damage. A few minor blemishes are normal, but avoid plants with extensive leaf drop, yellowing, or wilting—signs of poor care or pest pressure.

Slip the plant gently from its pot (or tip it to peer beneath a burlap wrap) to examine the root ball. You want firm, white roots that fill but don't encircle the soil core. Avoid root-bound plants with massed, circling roots or those with roots protruding heavily from drainage holes.

Feel the soil: it should be evenly moist but well-drained. Plants sitting in bone-dry medium have likely been neglected, while overly wet pots encourage root rot. A healthy root substrate feels cool and slightly damp to the touch, never soggy or dusty.

Scan for pests and disease. Look under leaves, around stem junctions, and at the soil line for insects, eggs, mildew, or scale. Skip any plant showing active infestations or symptoms like sticky residue, moldy patches, or distorted new growth.

Finally, buy from reputable suppliers. Quality nurseries and garden centers will rotate stock regularly, label plants correctly, and maintain dialogue with local extension services. Their staff can recommend disease-resistant cultivars, verify provenance (organic, non-GMO, native), and help you select varieties proven in your region.

Keep your Quality Plants Healthy

When you first put seedlings into the ground, water them consistently to help their roots develop. Young plants haven't built sturdy root systems yet, so keep the soil evenly moist without oversaturating it. Be cautious with fertilizers at this stage— high nitrogen blends can easily burn tender shoots.

Once your plants have settled in, shift to watering only when the top inch of soil feels dry. Enrich the soil by mixing in compost or other organic matter every few weeks. Apply a layer of mulch around the base to retain moisture and suppress weeds. Periodically thin crowded areas to improve air circulation, and routinely scout for pests and diseases to nip issues in the bud.

Each season brings its own set of tasks to keep your plants healthy:

- Winter: Spread a protective layer of mulch to insulate roots from freezing temperatures.

- Spring: Remove dead foliage and debris to reduce disease pressure and welcome new growth.

- Summer: Water deeply during dry spells and mulch to conserve moisture. Deadhead old blooms. Remove yellowing and brown leaves.

Throughout the year, monitor soil moisture and pH, topping up with organic fertilizers or compost as needed to maintain vibrant, healthy plants.

Some vegetables and flowers benefit from regular harvesting to encourage continued production and prevent plants from bolting. Stay on top of weather forecasts—provide shade during heatwaves and cover delicate plants when frost threatens.

Mulch heavily around plants to conserve moisture, regulate soil temperature, and reduce weeds. Install drip or soaker hoses to deliver water directly to roots with minimal evaporation. Capture rainwater with barrels or swales, then use it during dry spells to lower your water bill and improve plant resilience.

Encourage beneficial insects—ladybugs, lacewings, and parasitic wasps—by planting pollen- and nectar-rich flowers like alyssum and yarrow. Scout weekly for early signs of pests and diseases; remove affected leaves or deploy row covers before outbreaks spread. Use organic controls (neem oil, insecticidal soaps) only when necessary to preserve beneficial bug populations.

Happy gardening! Now get out there and make a garden that's the talk of the town!

Handle with Care:
Gardening with Poisonous Plants

You may be unaware that many common plants in your garden are poisonous, toxic, and harmful to pets, humans, and the environment. Or, you may intentionally create and curate a poisonous garden as many of the poisonous plants are unique, gorgeous, and prized garden specimens. These flowers may be beautiful, but they can be deadly. Poisonous plants are known as Baneful plants, "The Banes," or Veneficium. They can cause death or severe illness in the hands of one with malicious intentions, and also simply by accident. Some of these are so dangerous that they should only be handled with gloves, as the toxin can enter your system through your skin, while others are only dangerous if certain parts are ingested. They can be poisonous, toxic, make you "high" narcotic, or entheogens (shift consciousness).

On the other hand, healing plants are called Worts or Balms. Balms refer to something that has a comforting, soothing, or restorative effect. Many Balm plants are in the mint family. For example, Lemon Balm and Bee Balm. A word with the suffix -Wort is often very old. The Old English word was wyrt. It was often used in the names of herbs and plants that had medicinal uses, the first part of the word denoting the complaint against which it might be especially efficacious (example: lungwort helped with lung ailments). By the middle of the 17th century, wort was beginning to fade from everyday use. St. John's Wort and Mugwort are common Worts.

What makes a Bane poisonous? It's chemistry! Anthraquinones are organic compounds found in some plants. Anthraquinones are potent laxatives and can be irritating to both the upper and lower parts of the gastrointestinal tract. Cardioactive glycosides such as digitoxin and convallotoxin have a strong, direct action on the heart. This chemical constituent is found in *Digitalis purpurea* (Foxglove) and *Convallaria majalis* (Lily of the Valley). Alkaloids vary widely from one plant to another in their components and their actions, but are all compounds that contain nitrogen. Most either sedate or stimulate. Alkaloids end in the suffix –INE. Examples: Caffeine, Ephedrine, Morphine, Berberine, Reserpine, Nicotine. They tend to have potent effects, and in some cases, are toxic in large amounts. They are often unsuitable for home use. They include morphine from the opium poppy, nicotine in tobacco, atropine in deadly nightshade, caffeine and theobromine in coffee, black tea and cocoa. Select Alkaloid-Rich Plants include *Banisteriopsis spp.* (ayahuasca), *Tabernanthe iboga* (iboga), *Papaver somniferum* (opium), *Camellia sinensis* (tea), *Coffea arabica* (coffee), and *Nicotiana tabacum* (tobacco).

Symptoms of poisoning include delirium, elevated body temperature, increased heart rate, abnormal behavior, dilated pupils, painful sensitivity to light, visual disturbances including halos and abnormal color vision (seeing yellow), drooling, weakness, tremors, severe abdominal pain, diarrhea, nausea, and seizures as well as heart arrhythmia and abnormal heart rate, hallucinations (particularly the sensation of flight), restlessness, a flushed appearance, vomiting, nausea and diarrhea, tingling sensation and numbness in the mouth and throat and a burning sensation of the abdomen. The numbness and tingling spread through the body, accompanied by weakness of the limb, sweating, dizziness, headache, confusion and difficulty breathing, arrhythmia, a drop in blood pressure, and finally paralysis of the heart and respiratory system. Survival is possible with supportive care, particularly if charcoal is administered within the first hour.

Other plants are baneful when the skin is exposed to the plant in sunlight. Phytophotodermatitis (PPD) is a cutaneous phototoxic inflammatory eruption resulting from contact with light-sensitizing botanical substances and long-wave ultraviolet radiation. The eruption usually begins approximately 24 hours after exposure and peaks at 48-72 hours. The phototoxic result may be intensified by wet skin, sweating, and heat. In other words, your skin erupts with blisters and itchy, burning red areas because you were in contact with plant chemicals (in this case, parsnip and carrot sap) and exposed to sunlight. You don't realize you're in trouble until several days after exposure.

Plants that may cause phytophotodermatitis include (but are not limited to):

• Parsnips (*Pastinaca sativa*)
• Carrots (*Daucus carota subsp. sativus*)
• Celery (*Apium graveolens*)
• Parsley (*Petroselinum crispum*)
• Wild Parsnip (*Pastinaca sativa*)

• Queen Anne's Lace (Wild Carrot) (*Daucus carota*)
• Giant Hogweed (*Heracleum mantegazzianum*)

If you are exposed to a phototoxic plant, seek medical attention. Like a standard burn, you can apply cool compresses to relieve the pain and try to keep blisters intact as long as possible to protect the tender skin underneath. Over-the-counter itch cream, like those for poison ivy, may also help, along with anesthetic creams like Aspercreme and hydrocortisone. Benadryl can be helpful, as well as calamine lotion. You can also use fresh plantain and yarrow leaves, mashed and applied as a poultice. As more blisters show up, you can coat the blisters with manuka honey to promote healing and fight infection.

I discussed many of the poisonous plants in the chapter on *Flowers for the Dead*. But here they are again for your reference:

- Hellebore (*Helleborus spp.)*
- Hemlock is the common name given to several plants in the carrot family, including the aptly named Poison Hemlock *Conium maculatum,* the water hemlocks *Cicuta spp.,* and the water dropworts
- Belladonna *Atropa belladonna,* a.k.a. Deadly Nightshade or simply Nightshade
- Daturas (*Datura spp.)* a.k.a. Moonflowers, Jimsonweed
- Henbane (*Hyoscyamus niger,* also black henbane and stinking nightshade)
- *Aconitum,* a.k.a. aconite, monkshood, wolfsbane, leopard's bane, devil's helmet, or blue rocket
- Elderberry plants Mandrake
- Mistletoe
- Wormwood
- Yew
- Morning glory
- Ricin/Castor
- *Delphinium spp.* Delphinium is also called Larkspur
- Mayapple
- *Nicotiana,* a.k.a. Tobacco
- Lily of the Valley
- Bitter Nightshade

- Dogbane
- Fleabane
- Witchbane
- Easter lily/True Lilies are very poisonous!! Especially to cats!
- Jessamine, also called woodbine and evening trumpet
- Oleander
- Gloriosa
- Angel's Trumpet/Brugmansia spp.
- Pokeweed
- Narcissus (Daffodils)
- False Hellebore
- Autumn Crocus
- Lantana
- Mountain Laurel
- Chinese Lanterns
- Stinging Nettle
- Giant Hogweed
- Yellow Dock
- Rosary Pea
- Rhubarb Leaves
- Wisteria
- Dieffenbachia (a.k.a. dumb cane and elephant ear)
- Hydrangea
- Rhododendron
- Azalea
- Poppy

Precautions and Considerations

Please take these seriously. I am an experienced Poisoner, and I accidentally poisoned myself while gardening both this year and last year. Here are my tips and suggestions for staying safe.

• Know your Plants! Be able to correctly identify plants!

• Some Banes are highly toxic and should not be ingested or used without proper knowledge and caution.

• Protective measures, such as long sleeves, pants, socks, close toed boots, gloves (preferably nitrile or latex—to prevent sap or toxins from contacting your skin), goggles and masks, should be taken when handling these herbs.

• Some of these herbs may be regulated or illegal in certain jurisdictions, so know the laws in your area.

• Personal Sensitivity…varying sensitivities or reactions to these herbs, so it's important to use with caution and in small quantities.

• The toxins can be absorbed through the skin. Always wear gloves!

• Some plants, like Henbane have "fumes" and narcotic aroma. Wear a mask when handling them!

• Do not plant these where pets or children can access

• Locate baneful plants in isolated beds or raised containers, away from high-traffic areas and play spaces.

• Label each plant using a plant stake and clearly include the plant's common and scientific names, along with a "poisonous" warning.

• If possible, fence off or add thorny border plants around the perimeter to deter accidental entry by children, neighbors, wildlife, and pets

• Dedicate a set of tools exclusively for use with baneful plants; do not let these tools mingle with those for edible or ornamental beds.

• After each use, decontaminate tools and gloves by rinsing with water, then washing with soap and hot water to remove residual toxins.

• Never handle baneful plants when alone; always have someone nearby who can assist in case of heavy exposure or injury.

• Avoid touching your face, especially your eyes or mouth, until you've thoroughly washed your hands and forearms.

• Immediately wash any exposed skin with cool water and mild soap; if irritation develops, seek medical advice promptly

• Clean gloves and tools before removing them; wash gloves separately from regular laundry.

• Disinfect work surfaces and buckets with a dilute bleach solution (1 part bleach to 9 parts water) after each session.

• Poison Control Number: 1-800-222-1222

• Keep a first-aid kit stocked with antihistamines, charcoal, and calamine lotion

• If severe ingestion or contact occurs—such as difficulty breathing, swelling of the face/throat, or systemic symptoms—call emergency services immediately.

Designing a Garden

Besides understanding and implementing the six essential tips for successful gardening discussed in Gardening 101, creating a visually dynamic living piece of art involves planning and problem-solving. Ask yourself:

What will be the main purpose of the garden? Consider your needs, uses, and goals.

How much time will I have to spend in the garden?
How much money will be in the gardening budget?
What do you want to be your focal point in the garden?
What types of plants do you want to grow? Why?
What amount of space and light do you have available for gardening?
How much time are you looking to spend gardening?
Are you trying to integrate into your current landscape?
What do you need to do to prepare the area?

Here are the foundational principles that can help you craft a space that's both stunning and meaningful.

1. Define your garden's purpose and intent.
2. Choose a garden style.
3. Sketch ideas or collect inspiration.
4. Establish Strong Structure ("Good Bones") by using paths, hedges, walls, and trees to shape the space.
5. Choose flowers and plants.
6. Diagramming your garden can help you determine what you can plant and how many plants and seeds you need before planting. Draw/write your plan up, including a map.

Landscape design is a creative problem-solving process that combines horticultural science, artistic composition, and spatial organization to create attractive and functional outdoor spaces. The design process considers the land, environment, plants, and your intent to create a visually pleasing garden design. Keep in mind these 10 landscaping concepts: repetition, variety, balance, emphasis, scale, form/shape, texture, color, and visual weight as essential for creating spaces, connecting them, and making them attractive.

Emphasis

Emphasis, or focalization, draws attention to a particular spot in the garden—an anchor that grounds the viewer's experience and gives the eye a place to rest. To me, this is the most important concept, and I built my entire garden around the focal point.

• Choose a statement tree, big/bold plant, sculpture, garden art, altar, gazing ball, memorial bench, or water feature at your design's focal point.

• Use contrasting color or texture (bright flowers, glossy foliage) around the focal area to amplify its impact.

• Frame the focal point with arbors or hedges so the view is "framed" like a living picture.

• Control sightlines with pathways or low walls that guide visitors directly to your emphasis.

Repetition

Repetition is the heartbeat of a unified design. By echoing shapes, colors, or materials at regular intervals, you create a visual rhythm that feels intentional and cohesive.

• Repeat plant species or foliage colors in groups to lead the eye through the garden.

• Use the same paving material or edging profile in multiple areas for consistency.

• Echo structural forms—like a curved bench matching arched trellises—to reinforce theme.

• Implement repetition in sequence (every third plant, every turn of a pathway) to establish pattern.

Variety

Variety injects vitality and keeps a design from feeling static. Introducing contrasting elements—whether in form, texture, or color—adds surprise and sustained interest.

• Pair coarse-textured shrubs with fine-textured groundcovers for tactile contrast.

• Mix flowering cycles (spring bulbs, summer perennials, autumn shrubs) for year-round dynamics.

• Incorporate both soft (plants) and hard (stone, metal) materials to balance natural and constructed elements.

• Shift leaf shapes—round, spiky, fronded—to play with shadows and light.

Balance

Balance ensures no single part of the landscape overwhelms the rest. Whether you choose symmetry for formality or asymmetry for a more relaxed feel, balance keeps the composition stable.

• Symmetrical balance: mirror identical plantings or hardscape on either side of a central axis for classic order.

• Asymmetrical balance: offset a large specimen tree with a group of smaller shrubs or boulders for a more organic equilibrium.

• Visual weight (dark vs. light, large vs. small) must be distributed so one side doesn't feel "heavier" than the other.

• Regularly step back and view your design from multiple angles to gauge true balance.

Scale

Scale is all about proportion—how the size of one element relates to its surroundings and to the human body. Getting scale right ensures the landscape feels comfortable and well-integrated.

• Keep pathways wide enough for two people to walk side by side; avoid corridors that feel too tight.

• Match planter heights to seating heights so transitions feel natural (12–18" tall containers beside 18" benches).

• Scale large trees or walls to the overall site size; a small garden overpowered by giant oaks will feel unbalanced.

• Layer plantings in height (tall at the back, medium in the middle, low at the front) to maintain clear sightlines.

Line

Lines define the skeleton of a landscape. They:

- Outline pathways, garden beds, and borders
- Draw the eye along sightlines or toward focal points
- Create patterns (curved for softness, straight for formality)
- Influence movement, inviting strolls or establishing containment

By varying line direction and rhythm (continuous vs. broken), you set the mood and flow.

Form

Form is the three-dimensional shape or mass of each element in the garden. It involves:

• The silhouette of trees, shrubs, sculptures, and structures

• Contrasting vertical (columns, tall evergreens) with horizontal (groundcovers, low walls)

• Geometric forms (spheres, cubes) for order versus natural, irregular shapes for an informal feel

Mixing forms creates depth, balance, and visual interest throughout the seasons.

Texture

Texture refers to the surface quality of plants and materials, from fine to coarse. It helps:

• Soften or sharpen transitions (fine-textured grasses next to broad-leaf perennials)

• Control perceived scale and distance (coarse textures appear closer; fine textures recede)

• Build unity or contrast (repeating similar textures versus pairing opposites for drama)

Intentionally layering textures keeps the eye moving and the design lively.

Color

Color adds vibrancy and mood through hue, intensity, and value. Effective color schemes include

• Monochromatic: different tints of one hue for a serene, unified look

• Analogous: neighboring colors on the wheel (e.g., blue-green to yellow-green) for harmony

• Complementary: opposite hues (e.g., purple and yellow) for bold contrast

Warm tones advance, cool tones recede—use this to highlight key features or create depth.

Visual Weight

Visual weight determines which features dominate your composition, by considering:

- Mass: large or dense plantings carry more weight than sparse elements. In a ghostly garden, group in odd numbers (3, 5, 7) to mimic natural clusters of spectral figures.

- Contrast: dark foliage or bright/white flowers draw the eye more strongly than muted tones

- Placement: central or foreground elements feel heavier than those tucked away. For example, place low-growing black mondo grass in front of taller burgundy-leaf varieties.

Balancing heavy and light components (symmetrically or asymmetrically) achieves stability and focus.

Permaculture

I am a fan of permaculture. Permaculture is an approach to land management and garden design that models the patterns and relationships found in nature. At its core, permaculture blends "permanent agriculture" and "permanent culture," aiming for systems that sustain themselves indefinitely by working with natural processes rather than against them. My favorite permaculture design concept is layering. Go out into the woods or forest and observe all the different layers and levels of plants naturally found...not man-made. We want to mimic this!

Layering in permaculture mimics a natural forest by stacking plants at different heights and depths to optimize sunlight capture, nutrient cycling, and space use. This approach maximizes overall yield and biodiversity while reducing maintenance and external inputs. By designing with multiple layers, gardeners create self-sustaining ecosystems that work with nature's patterns.

The Eight Layers of a Forest

1. Canopy Layer: The tallest trees—such as walnut or large fruit trees—form the overstory, providing shade and wind protection for lower layers.

2. Sub-Canopy (Understory): Layer Smaller fruit or nut trees (apple, pear) thrive beneath the canopy, filling mid-height niches and extending the harvest period.

3. Shrub Layer: Berry bushes and flowering shrubs (blueberry, currant) occupy the shrub stratum, offering fruit and habitat for beneficial wildlife.

4. Herbaceous Layer: Non-woody perennials and annual vegetables (kale, asparagus, culinary herbs) add under-story diversity and seasonal yields.

5. Ground Cover Layer: Low-growing plants (strawberries, creeping thyme, clover) function as living mulch, suppressing weeds and protecting soil moisture.

6. Root (Rhizosphere) Layer: Root crops (garlic, carrots, Jerusalem artichoke) exploit underground space and improve soil structure through their root systems.

7. Climber (Vine) Layer: Vining plants (grapes, beans, cucumbers, clematis) use vertical supports from taller layers to grow upward, adding another production zone.

8. Mycelial (Fungal) Layer: Mushrooms and beneficial fungi form a subterranean network that enhances nutrient exchange, soil health, and yields of other layers.

Ever-Blooming Garden

We want color and seasonal interest all year long. I am obsessed with ever-blooming gardens! An ever-blooming garden blooms with color from early spring through late fall (and even winter). The secret lies in layering bloom times, choosing hardy perennials, and mixing in annuals and shrubs for nonstop color.

Perennials form the foundation of gardens, returning each year with minimal care. Annuals and bulbs fill temporal gaps and add freshness each year. Mix evergreens and trees for year-round structure with perennials for seasonal color. Include plants with spring blooms, summer color, fall foliage, and winter interest (like bark or berries). Add ornamental grasses, evergreens, and deciduous shrubs for year-round appeal.

Below is a seasonal bloom plan with recommended combinations:

March–April: daffodils, tulips, hellebores, snowdrops, hyacinths
May–June: daylilies, lilies, elephant ears, gladiolas, peonies, irises, roses
July–August: dahlias, coneflowers, salvias, sedum, and zinnias
August–September: marigolds, black-eyed susans
October–November: asters, goldenrods, sweet alyssum, and chrysanthemums
December–February: evergreen shrubs and winterberry holly

Ever-Blooming "Memento Mori" Garden

Combine every seasonal bloomer into one continuous tapestry of life, death, and remembrance.

Early Spring Blooms:

- Daffodil (*Narcissus spp.*) – The crash between life's renewal and mortality; once an omen of misfortune, now a symbol of rebirth after death.

- Cowslip (*Primula veris*) – Believed to open a gateway between life and death, guiding lost souls.

- Anemone (*Anemone coronaria*) – Known as the flower of remembrance, an emblem of honoring departed loved ones.

- Hellebore (*Helleborus orientalis*) – Its downward-facing blooms evoke sorrow and contemplation of mortality.

- Snowdrop (*Galanthus nivalis*) – A quiet promise of hope and consolation emerging from winter's death.

196

- Snake's-Head Fritillary (*Fritillaria meleagris*) – Thought to guard graves, protecting the dead from restless spirits.

- Iris reticulata (*Iris reticulata*) – A whisper of resurrection and the soul's awakening beyond the grave.

- Pussy Willow (*Salix caprea*) – Catkins symbolize renewal beneath decay, life persisting through dormancy.

Late Spring Flowers:

- Red Poppy (*Papaver rhoeas*) – A remembrance of fallen soldiers; consolation for grief inspired by war's deaths.

- Asphodel (*Asphodelus spp.*) – Linked to the Elysian Fields; the flower of souls wandering after death.

- Perennial Carnation (*Dianthus caryophyllus*) – White and pink blooms stand for remembrance and pure love that transcends death.

- Bleeding Heart (*Dicentra spectabilis*) – Heart-shaped petals evoke unrequited love and the fragility of life.

- Columbine (*Aquilegia spp.*) – Signifies death's folly and the courage to face the unknown.

- Allium (*Allium spp.*) – Its spherical blooms represent the cycle of life, death, and rebirth.

- Lily-of-the-Valley (*Convallaria majalis*) – A return to happiness after loss, purity of the departed soul.

Early and Mid-Summer Spectacles:

- Black Rose (*Rosa spp.*) – The ultimate emblem of mourning, tragedy, and final farewells.

- White Lily (*Lilium spp.*) – Restored innocence and the peaceful passage of the soul.

- Gladiolus (*Gladiolus spp.*) – Spikes of strength in grief and unwavering moral integrity in death.

- Orchid (*Orchidaceae)* – White varieties convey reverence; purple denotes deep respect for the departed.

- Lavender (*Lavandula angustifolia*) – Used to cleanse spirits and soothe mourners in times of loss.

- Sweet Pea (*Lathyrus odoratus*) – A gentle farewell, gratitude for life's fleeting connections.

- Foxglove (*Digitalis purpurea*) – Poisonous beauty reflecting the thin line between healing and harm, life and death.

- Snapdragon (*Antirrhinum majus*) – Once believed to ward off evil and guide souls to the afterlife.

- Black Petunia (*Petunia × atkinsiana 'Black Velvet'*) – Velvety petals channel gothic elegance and mortality.

Late Summer Through Fall:

- Marigold (*Tagetes spp.)* – Guides spirits of the dead back to the living in Día de los Muertos traditions.

- Goldenrod (*Solidago spp.*) – Wards off evil spirits; woven into funeral garlands for protection.

- Red Spider Lily (*Lycoris radiata)* – The "death flower," planted on graves to bid farewell and guide souls.

- Chrysanthemum (*Chrysanthemum spp.)* – Universally placed on graves in autumn as a symbol of sorrow and comfort.

- Enchanter's Nightshade (*Circaea lutetiana)* – Ethereal blooms steeped in folklore of doom and enchantment.

- Zinnia (*Zinnia elegans)* – Bright petals symbolize thoughts of absent friends and enduring memories.

- Dahlia (*Dahlia pinnata)* – Layered blooms stand for dignity, commitment, and inner strength through grief.

- Black-Eyed Susan *(Rudbeckia hirta*) – Hardy resilience and the promise of hope after hardship.

- Sedum 'Autumn Joy' (*Hylotelephium telephium 'Herbstfreude'*) – As blooms fade, they mirror life's final, glorious flourish.

- Cosmos (*Cosmos bipinnatus*) – Represents harmony, peaceful endings, and the serenity of passing.

Winter Interest Plants for a Memento Mori Garden:

- Holly (*Ilex aquifolium*) Glossy evergreens and red berries symbolizing the blood of life spilled and the promise of eternal remembrance.
- Yew (*Taxus baccata*) A classic cemetery tree whose toxic seeds and longevity evoke both mortality's finality and hope for resurrection.
- Cypress (*Cupressus sempervirens*) Tall, columnar foliage long planted in graveyards to represent mourning, the soul's upward journey, and undying memory.
- Christmas Rose (*Helleborus niger*) Blooming amid winter's decay, it carries a name meaning "death," yet its delicate white flowers whisper of solace beyond loss.
- Winterberry (*Ilex verticillata*) Bare branches draped in bright scarlet fruit— a stark reminder of life's fragility and the persistence of spirit through dark months.
- Snowdrop (*Galanthus nivalis*) Nodding blossoms at the frozen soil's surface, offering hope and consolation as symbols of the soul's passage from death to rebirth.
- Witch Hazel (*Hamamelis virginiana*) Ribbon-like winter blooms thought to ward off evil spirits and guide lost souls, mingling protection with the uncanny.
- Mahonia (*Mahonia aquifolium*) Spiny evergreen leaves with fragrant yellow clusters in dead season—an emblem of perseverance amid hardship and mourning.

Color Combinations

The final garden design tip I want to mention before we deep dive into macabre and spooky accessories is color combinations. Color combinations influence mood, define style, and provide visual cohesion, and transform plants into a unified living work of art. When chosen deliberately, hues can guide the eye, emphasize focal points, and even make small spaces feel larger or more intimate.

When you consult a color wheel, complementary hues—such as purple and yellow—sit opposite each other, creating vibrant, high-energy pairings; planting purple salvia next to yellow coreopsis, for example, yields a striking border. Analogous schemes—colors that sit side by side, like blue and purple—feel soothing and harmonious; blending lavender, Russian sage, and catmint can transform a border into a cool-toned retreat. For a more dynamic effect, explore 3 or 4 palettes by selecting three or four evenly spaced colors on the wheel (red, blue, and yellow, for instance), but keep one hue dominant and use the others sparingly to avoid visual overload. To ensure your palette flows without gaps, map out each plant's flowering season and choose combinations that overlap. You might pair early alliums with spring-blooming tulips when they share similar color notes, or sow annuals and bulbs in weekly intervals so reds and pinks carry from late spring into early summer. Incorporating ever-bloomers or repeat bloomers—such as hardy geraniums or coreopsis—helps bridge seasonal shifts and maintains your chosen color story throughout the year.

Color shines brightest when paired with contrasting forms. Combine bold, sculptural blooms like dahlias or peonies with delicate foliage—fern fronds or heuchera leaves—to play with both form and color. Airy perennials and ornamental grasses such as Russian sage or miscanthus soften hard edges and introduce graceful movement. By repeating specific foliage textures throughout your beds (for instance, weaving spiky hostas around bright daylilies), you establish rhythm and unity across diverse plant groupings.

Neutral tones allow your vibrant hues to stand out while offering visual rest. White-flowering plants like Shasta daisies or white astilbe act as beacons that elevate surrounding colors, whereas silvery or gray foliage from lavender or artemisia provides a cool foil to hot reds and oranges. Evergreens and variegated leaves contribute year-round structure, ensuring that even in dormant seasons, your garden reads as an intentional, cohesive design.

Design Elements and Accessories

Now for the best part! Accessories! Here are gothic, dark, and macabre garden design elements and accessories to deepen your garden's narrative of remembrance, mortality, and reflection. Each idea ties directly into themes of death, dying, and eternal memory.

Wind Phones and Spaces for Whispered Words

My absolute favorite accessory for a Garden for the Dead is a wind phone. A wind phone is a simple, unconnected rotary or push-button telephone installed in a quiet, natural setting—often inside a small booth or mounted on a tree—where visitors can "call" someone who has passed away and speak their thoughts and feelings aloud without fear of interruption. A wind phone would be perfect in a Necromancy Garden.

The original Telephone of the Wind (kaze no denwa) was created in December 2010 by Japanese garden designer Itaru Sasaki in Ōtsuchi, Iwate Prefecture, after he lost his cousin to cancer. Sasaki set up a white, glass-paneled booth on a hillside overlooking the sea, installed a disconnected black rotary phone, and left a notebook for visitors to record messages of remembrance. In 2011, following the devastating Tōhoku earthquake and tsunami, he opened it to the public as a place of solace for fellow survivors.

Since then, more than 30,000 people have visited Sasaki's wind phone, and hundreds of replicas have sprung up around the world—located in cemeteries, parks, church grounds, hiking trails, and private gardens. These installations are free to use and provide a non-ritualistic space where mourners can externalize grief, find moments of peace, and feel a continued connection to lost loved ones.

Although rigorous scientific studies on wind phones are still forthcoming, grief counselors note that the act of speaking aloud—even to an empty receiver—can mirror therapeutic techniques like Gestalt chair work and letter writing. This one-way conversation promotes emotional expression, helps release tension, and can uncover subconscious insights, offering many users a deeply moving, life-affirming experience on their journey through loss.

Check out the Wind Phone website to find wind phone locations and help in creating your own wind phone: www.mywindphone.com/windphonelocations

Dripping Veils: Spanish Moss

Hang swathes of Spanish moss (*Tillandsia usneoides*) from pergola beams, statue shoulders, and low tree limbs to cast ghostly, gray-green curtains.

- Attach small lengths by gently draping over thin wires or tying with biodegradable garden twine so the moss appears to float.

- Position near seating or pathways so the tendrils brush shoulders—a tactile reminder of decay and renewal.

- Replace spent tufts every year to maintain density without smothering host branches.

Time-Worn Pathway: Sheet and Fern Moss

Plant sheet moss (*Hypnum spp.*) or delicate fern moss (*Thuidium delicatulum*) between irregular flagstones for an ancient, sunken route.

- Remove debris and lightly score grout lines in your stones to give the moss a foothold.

- Water daily until established, then switch to twice-weekly misting.

- In shaded areas, add a thin compost layer beneath the moss to enrich the substrate and encourage spread.

Fairy-Tale Cemetery Vignettes: Reindeer Lichen and Cushion Moss

Use reindeer lichen (*Cladonia rangiferina*) and cushion moss (*Leucobryum glaucum*) in shallow stone bowls or glass terrariums to evoke miniature graveyards.

- Choose weathered containers—broken urns or cracked bricks—to heighten the antique effect.

- Layer in sand, charcoal, and peat to mimic forest-floor soils, then nestle in small gravestone markers or rusted metal tokens.

- Keep these vignettes under partial shade to prevent bleaching and maintain soft, muted hues.

Texture Contrasts: Layering Different Moss Types

Combine soft, velvety mosses with coarser, spiky varieties to create visual drama and tactile intrigue.

- Pair *Hypnum cupressiforme* (soft, pillowlike) with *Polytrichum commune* (erect, bristly).
- Cluster each type in small "islands," allowing edges to blur so one texture seems to bleed into the next.
- Alternate between bright chartreuse and deep emerald species for a shifting palette that feels both alive and spectral.
- Moss thrives in humid, stable conditions—replicate a woodland understory by:
- Installing a low-pressure misting system on a timer, delivering short bursts in early morning and evening.
- Grouping potted mosses and containers closely to create shared microclimates.
- Placing shallow trays of water or damp gravel beneath planters to boost ambient humidity through evaporation.
- Avoiding direct midday sun and winds that dry the foliage; use shade sails or natural canopy where possible.

Labyrinth Pathway

Create a winding stone or gravel labyrinth that visitors walk slowly, mirroring life's journey toward an inevitable center and back out.

Use dark slate or black basalt to underscore contemplative steps, with edging in bleached white pebbles as a reminder of life passing into death.

Moon Gate or Arched Entry

Install a circular "moon gate" at your garden entrance to symbolize the cycle of life, death, and rebirth.

Frame it with climbing black roses or white clematis to merge architectural symbolism with seasonal bloom.

Reflecting Pool or Shallow Basin

A black-tiled reflecting pool offers still water for quiet meditation, reflecting sky and passing clouds as metaphors for impermanence.

Surround with ghostly white water lilies or silver-leafed Artemisia to heighten the spectral effect.

Memorial Wall or Collage Niche

Build a weatherproof niche in a stone wall for framed photos, engraved plaques, or small mementos—each item a permanent testament to a departed soul.

Accent with trailing "mourning" vines like black ivy (*Hedera helix 'Purpurea'*) to suggest the intertwining of life and loss.

Sculptural Focal Point

Choose a statue—an angel in repose, a guardian figure, or an abstract form cracked in two—to embody grief, protection, or the soul's fracture at death.

Position it under a lone yew or cypress, linking evergreen longevity with human transience.

Seasonal Sound Features

Add a set of custom-tuned wind chimes in bronze or bamboo. Their random, ephemeral tones become audible "moments" that echo the fleeting nature of life.

Install a small, hand-cranked calliope or rusted bell for occasional ceremonial ringing, calling visitors to pause and remember.

Hidden Remembrance Niches

Carve small hollows into rock outcrops or beneath low stone benches as secret spots for placing handwritten notes, dried flowers, or personal tokens.

These micro-shrines invite intimate reflection, as though uncovering memories buried beneath earth.

Texture-Rich "Faux Ruin" Walls

Erect short, cracked limestone or reclaimed brick walls overgrown with ghostly white vinca or silvery woolly thyme to evoke an ancient cemetery or abbey ruin.

Use weathered mortar and occasional lichen patches to heighten the sense of age and decay.

Seasonal Fire Pit or Candle Hearth

A simple, fire-hardened stone circle can host controlled evening fires or pillar candles, symbolizing the soul's spark amid darkness.

Gather around it for memorial ceremonies or solitary contemplation under winter skies.

"Night Garden" Lighting

Integrate low-voltage amber uplights at the base of yews, statues, or moon gates to cast long shadows—reminders of mortality's looming presence.

Use concealed pathway lights to guide gentle footsteps, mimicking lanterns for wandering spirits.

Sensory "Farewell" Walk

Line a narrow path with aromatic plants tied to remembrance—tobacco (*Nicotiana alata*), whose scent fades at dawn, or rosemary, whose strong odor cleaves memory to mind.

Alternate patches of soft moss, bare gravel, and crushed charcoal to create tactile and olfactory contrasts.

Interactive Memory Stones

Scatter smooth river stones near seating areas with permanent engravings or leave them blank for visitors to inscribe their own messages in chalk.

These living memorials can be taken home or left behind, creating an evolving tapestry of remembrance.

Graveyard Dirt and Symbolic Soil

Graveyard soil carries the spiritual resonance, characteristics, and energies of those buried beneath it and has been used in folk magic for both benign and malignant intentions. In a Garden for the Dead, a small buried vial or subtle mound of graveyard dirt becomes a potent symbol of mortality and connection to the underworld. I also include a small vial of graveyard dirt in my cemetariums.

Gargoyles, Grotesques, and Gothic Statues

Stone gargoyles and grotesque figures once served as both ornament and protector of medieval cathedrals. In a gothic garden, statues of gargoyles, mythic beasts, or even cherubs can line pathways or perch atop stone plinths to cast ominous silhouettes as dusk falls. Pairing such figures with aged, mossy stones or repurposed architectural salvage (arches, columns) heightens the sense of an ancient, secret place.

Chthonic Deity and Underworld Statuary

Evocative statuary of underworld deities—Hecate, Persephone, Anubis— reinforces themes of death and rebirth. Garden shrines to Hecate, triple-faced sculptures, or small altars can be created using resin or 3D-printed figurines with patina finishes. Clustering these statues within a "temenos" of black gravel, skeletal vines, and candlelight creates a ritual space for nocturnal rituals or silent reflection.

Animal Bone Decor and Skeletal Forms

Animal bones—skulls, ribs, vertebrae—evoke the fragility of life. Cleaned and bleached bone fragments can be artfully arranged in shallow containers or embedded into stonework to form macabre planters. Fine examples include real or replica bird skulls displayed among ferns or perching on wrought-iron stakes for an unsettling, surreal effect. These installations should be subtly integrated so that they surprise rather than overwhelm.

Wrought-Iron Fixtures, Arbors, and Gates

Ornate wrought-iron gates, arbors, fencing, and trellises are quintessential gothic elements. Their curling filigree and pointed arches echo medieval architecture, guiding visitors through hidden garden rooms and creating theatrical entrances. Overgrown with dark-leaved vines (ivy, clematis), these fixtures take on a sense of haunted grandeur, promising secrets behind every turn.

Meandering, Sinister Pathways

Avoid straight lines. Instead, create winding pathways with unexpected twists and turns so visitors never see the full garden at once. Use cracked flagstones or aged bricks set in moss to suggest a forgotten ruin. Secret nooks and "pocket gardens" appear around each bend, perfect for secluded shrines or solitary benches cloaked in clematis and ferns.

Crumbling Walls, Aged Stonework, and Ruins

Weathered stones, broken columns, and half-ruined walls lend authenticity. Apply a "yogurt and moss" paint technique—mix plain yogurt with moss fragments and brush onto new stone to encourage real moss growth and patina within weeks. Alternatively, arrange bricks or stones salvaged from old buildings to form low walls around burial mounds or raised beds.

Burial Mounds and Earthworks

Raised earthen mounds, topped with simple stone markers or rough-hewn crosses, evoke ancient barrows and tombs. Plant them sparsely with dark seasonal bulbs— tulips, anemones—so blooms emerge like ghosts from the earth. Surround mounds with low lighting or circle them with a ring of smooth black pebbles for an eerie boundary.

Gothic Hardscaping and Reflecting Pools

Stone benches carved in gothic motifs provide seating and contemplation spots. Introducing a shallow, still reflecting pool—lined in dark plaster or black EPDM liner—captures moonlight, sky, and surrounding statues for a mirror-like illusion of depth and infinity. Place it amid deadleaf litter and skeletonized stems to amplify the spectral quality.

Lighting, Candles, and Soundscapes

Use wrought-iron lanterns with flickering LED "gaslight" bulbs or real candles in hurricane glass for soft, haunted illumination. Uplight statues and walls to cast ominous shadows, and string dark-hued fairy lights in tree branches for a starry, nocturnal canopy. Enhance ambiance and encourage transition between worlds with wind chimes made of metal keys, old skeleton keys hanging from tree limbs to tinkle in the breeze. For soundscapes, add subtle recordings of distant church bells, owl calls, or whispered voices carried on hidden speakers.

Climbing Vines and Dark Foliage

Vines transform ironwork into cloaked arches. Black-ivy (Hedera helix 'Black Lace'), *Clematis vitalba*, and moonflower (*Ipomoea alba*) swirl around trellises to create shady corridors. For annual thrills, plant sweet potato vine (*Ipomoea batatas 'Black Heart'*) in containers to spill charcoal-black leaves over pot rims.

Skeletonized and Dried Botanicals

Collect dried seed-heads—*Echinacea purpurea* heads, teasels (*Dipsacus fullonum*), and *Nigella* pods—to place in urns and atop walls. Their spiky silhouettes suggest skeletal forms and reinforce the theme of death, particularly when dusted with faux cobwebs for Halloween.

Layout and Structural Anchors

Paths and intersections guide visitors through your vision of the underworld.

- Create a Crossroads: A central intersection of gravel or flagstone paths symbolizes choices between light and dark, life and death. Mark each axis with a tall, wrought-iron signpost or weathered milestone inscribed with cryptic directions ("Silence," "Echoes," "Memory," "Oblivion").

- Wrought-Iron Fixtures (Gates, Trellises, etc.): Use rust-patinaed gates to define entry, climbing iron trellises twined with black roses or ivy to frame alcoves. Gently corrode metal with vinegar and salt for authentic aging.

Memorial and Ritual Objects

Mourning becomes an immersive act when graveside artifacts mingle with the living landscape.

- Gravestones: Scatter compact, moss-covered headstones along winding borders. Choose Gothic arches, Celtic crosses, or skull-topped markers in slate or limestone.

- Coffins and Caskets: Partially bury a reclaimed wooden coffin at the garden's edge as a sculptural seat or low planter. Line its interior with black velvet and drape trailing vines (e.g., black mondo grass) over the lip.

- Urns: Cluster classical stone or metal urns on plinths near seating areas. Fill them with late-blooming flowers or dried arrangements of pampas grass and dark hydrangea heads.

- Outdoor/Chthonic Altars: Dig a shallow pit or use a flat-topped stone slab as an altar on the ground. Surround it with half-buried candleholders, smoldering incense, and offerings—bones, feathers, blackened gemstones.

Sculptural and Mythical Accents

Bring Gothic literature and folklore into the garden's bestiary.

- Gargoyles: Perch small cast-stone gargoyles on walls or trellises, their contorted forms guarding the space against malevolent spirits. Let creeping moss soften their edges.

- Angels, Fairies, and Cherubs: Juxtapose a broken marble cherub dripping lichen with a delicate steel fairy perched on a branch. Use faded patinas to suggest these beings are relics half-forgotten.

- Mythical Creatures (Vampires, Centaurs, etc.): Commission or repurpose statues: a crouching vampire at dusk, a centaur leaning on a spear. Position in twilight corners to play with shadows as the sun sets.

- Skeletons: Place life-sized resin or stone skeletons reclining in undergrowth, clutching a wilted bouquet or a tarnished chalice. For a dynamic tableau, drape thin gauze webs to imply movement.

Living Decay and Natural Textures

Embrace rot as an ally—an aesthetic of transformation.

- Mushrooms and Rot: Encourage saprophytic mushrooms on old stumps or logs. Create a damp enclave by a small water feature or shaded grove; species like oyster mushrooms or turkey tails add color and shape.

- Spider Webs: Hang fine, faux webs spun between branches and trellises. In the morning light, dew will catch and glisten, evoking an abandoned, enchanted ruin.

- Lifeless Shrubs and Fallen Limbs: Instead of clearing every dead branch, weave them into low fences or lean them against walls for skeletal sculptures. Use bleached trunks as pedestals or bird perches.

Ruins and Stone Work

Crumbling Statues and Ruins

- Salvage broken architectural fragments (capitals, columns, wall sections) from architectural salvage yards or cast resin reproductions.

- Position fragments in lightly shaded groves so creeping ivy and moss can claim their surfaces over time.

- Arrange a partially toppled statue atop a low pedestal, letting its missing limbs and weathered face suggest stories forever lost.

Aged Stones

- Collect flagstones or plinths with natural cracks, or artificially distress new stone with acid washes and chisel marks.

- Use them as edging for beds, low seating ledges, or as foundations for urns and lanterns.

- Scatter pebbles between pavers for a brittle, crunched-leaf crunch underfoot.

Cairns

- A cairn is a human-made pile or stack of stones erected for purposes such as marking a trail, commemorating a site, or forming a burial mound. Cairns range from small, loose conical heaps to elaborate megalithic structures, and have been used since prehistory across Eurasia. The term comes from the Irish carn, reflecting its Celtic origins.

- Build small cairns at decision points along paths to evoke ancient boundary markers or memorials.

- Vary heights (from ankle-high to waist-high) and stone types (slate, granite, quartz) for an improvised, ritual feel.

- Top with a single, distinctive stone (black obsidian, fossilized wood) as a focal "offering."

Natural Decay and Overgrowth

Vines and Moss

- Plant hardy, shade-tolerant vines like *Parthenocissus quinquefolia* (Virginia creeper), *Hedera helix* 'Black Knight' (dark-leaved ivy), or *Rosa* 'Black Baccara' on walls and trellises.

- Keep soil moist and slightly acidic to encourage sheet moss, cushion moss, or rock cap moss on stones and statues.

- Hand-place loose patches of sphagnum moss into crevices for instant age and texture.

Skeletons of Long-Dead Plants

- Leave bare stems of perennials (e.g., Echinacea, Rudbeckia) for the season: their dried cones and ribs become sculptural.

- Wilted hydrangea heads, bleached seedpods, or skeletal fennel fronds whisper of former life—tuck them into urns or latticework.

- Combine with faux spider webs for extra drama in late fall and winter.

Whimsical Covered Walkway

- Erect an arched timber or wrought-iron pergola draped in climbing plants: wisteria for ghostly blossoms, black honeysuckle for fragrance that turns unsettling at dusk.

- Hang tattered fabric strips, lanterns, or chthonic charms from crossbeams.

- Line the ground with crushed gravel or bark, leading visitors into a tunnel of shifting light and shadow.

Light and Mystery

Lanterns, Dragon Statues, or Ghostly Objects

- Install battered metal lanterns (kitchen-jar style or Moroccan pierced-metal) on posts or hang them from tree limbs. Use flickering LED candles for safety.

- Place ceramic or cast-stone dragon figures near focal points, their fierce silhouettes guarding hidden corners.

- Scatter mirrored or smoky-glass orbs on pedestals—catch glints of light and glance back like specters.

Spiritual Communication Objects (perfect for your necromancy garden)

Spirit Trumpet

- Source an actual 19th-century spiritualist "spirit trumpet" or fashion one from a polished brass megaphone.

- Mount it horizontally on a low pedestal or embed it into a wall alcove aimed at a chosen "listening" spot.

- Encourage visitors to whisper into its narrow end and move to the flared opening to "hear" the departed.

Spirit Board

- Carve or paint a durable wood or stone spirit board (alphabet, numbers, "Yes/No," sun/moon symbols) onto a garden table or bench seat.

- Weather-proof with clear epoxy and antique-finish paints.

- Place near a secluded altar or circle of stones; provide a smooth disc or stylus on a chain so guests can gently "invoke" messages.

Garden Follies

- Ornamental structures (miniature towers, ruined temples, hermit's cottages) that serve no practical purpose but stir the imagination.

- Materials and Finish: Salvaged stone, reclaimed timber, cast-resin casts distressed with acid washes or patina sprays.

- Placement and Effect: Set one folly at the end of a winding path to create a narrative destination. Let climbing vines and moss soften cracks, hinting at a once-grand purpose now reclaimed by nature.

Ravens and Crows

- Sculptural Birds: Bronze or wrought-iron raven statues perched on posts or tree limbs. Apply a dark patina for an aged look.

- Live Silhouettes: Hang lightweight acrylic silhouettes that sway in the wind—an unsettling nod to real birds.

- Auditory Role: Scatter small seed dishes nearby; the occasional crow call adds an ominous, living soundtrack.

Iron Arches

- Design and Material: Heavy-gauge steel or wrought iron arches with Gothic tracery or pointed tops. Let rust form naturally or accelerate it with vinegar treatments.

- Vine Pairings: Train dark-leafed climbers like black-ivy or passionflower over the arch to create a tunnel of shifting shadows.

- Placement: Use as dramatic gateways between "real" and "spirit" sections, marking transitions in mood.

Eerie Illumination

- Focal Lighting: Low-voltage spotlights with amber or red gels to cast fleeting shadows on statues, ruins, and trees.

- Moonlight Simulation: Install cool-white LED floodlights high in the canopy to mimic pale moonbeams filtering through branches.

- Candle Effects: Cluster weatherproof LED candles in lanterns or cauldrons, letting their flicker dance across nearby stones at dusk.

Stained Glass

- Sourcing Panels: Reclaimed church windows or small stained-glass mosaics from artisan shops. Choose jewel tones—deep reds, purples, and greens.

- Mounting Options: Hang panels from iron trellises or embed shards in concrete garden walls.

- Light Interaction: Position where sunlight (or a spotlight) will shine through, painting colorful patterns on stone floors or foliage.

Unexpected Wind Chimes

- Material Choices: Use hollow metal pipes for hollow, echoing notes; or threaded wooden dowels and bone-like resin pieces for dry, hollow clinks.

- Placement and Variation: Hang near seating areas, under iron arches, or from tree branches at different heights for layered melodies.

- Mood: Let irregular chimes mimic ghostly whispers on a still day, adding an auditory layer of mystery.

Weathered Wood Bench

- Construction: Reclaimed oak or cedar beams with uneven edges. Distress further by sandblasting or hand-carving runes.

- Aging Techniques: Leave untreated outdoors; over months it will grey naturally. Tuck moss or lichen into seat cracks for added life in decay.

- Siting: Nestle in a quiet clearing beside a reflecting pool or at the foot of a ruined column—an invitation to linger in contemplation.

Tree Roots

- Natural Sculpture: Expose sections of root by gently removing soil under mature trees or planting species (like bald cypress) that reveal buttressed roots.

- Integration: Weave low-lying ruins or skeletal planters among roots, as if the earth is swallowing ancient relics.

- Effect: Creates a primeval, half-buried feel—nature reclaiming artifice in slow motion.

Cauldrons

- Types and Sourcing: Large cast-iron pots, vintage blacksmith vats, or concrete replicas painted to resemble iron.

- Uses:

1. Planters for trailing dark foliage (e.g., black mondo grass, purple heuchera).
2. Fire pits with ember-glow lighting at night.
3. Bowls for floating candles and smoky incense.

- Arrangement: Group uneven sizes on flagstone pads to suggest ritual gathering spots.

Dark Reflecting Pools

- Dig shallow basins lined with black EPDM pond liner for mirror-flat water.
- Edge with jagged stones or broken slabs to maintain the ruin aesthetic.

- Surroundings: Encircle with low, moss-covered walls or half-buried urns. Plant water-loving species with dark foliage at the margins.

- Ambiance: The glassy surface captures sky, shadow, and statue reflections—an invitation to peer into another realm.

Fallen Trees as Coffin-Shaped Garden Borders

Transforming fallen trees into coffin-shaped borders adds a poetic, somber frame to your Garden for the Dead. We had fallen trees after a storm at my house. We trimmed them up and made several coffin-shaped gardens. Spooktacular!

Glow in the Dark Stepping Stones

Strategically embed glow-in-the-dark river stones at pivotal junctures—entrance thresholds, ring intersections, and seating alcoves—so that once twilight falls, their soft, eerie glow charges by moonlight and guides phantom footsteps along the labyrinth's winding path. Transform ordinary stones into luminous pathway markers with two simple methods: painting existing rocks or mixing glow powder into fresh concrete.

Materials Needed:

- Smooth, flat rocks or river stones
- Glow-in-the-dark spray paint or brush-on paint
- White primer (optional but recommended)
- Glow powder formulated for concrete
- Concrete mix (if making new stones)
- Water and mixing container (wheelbarrow or bucket)
- Paint brushes or spray can
- Clear concrete or paver sealer
- Soap, water, and a scrub brush
- Gloves, mask, and protective covering for your work area

Method 1: Painting Existing Stones

1. Clean the stones

    - Rinse each rock with water, then scrub off dirt and debris using soapy water and a brush.
    - Wipe them down with isopropyl alcohol or acetone and let fully air-dry.

2. Apply a base coat (optional)

    - Brush on a thin layer of white primer to seal porous surfaces and enhance glow brightness.
    - Let the primer cure according to the label.

3. Paint with glow-in-the-dark paint

    - Shake your spray can or stir brush-on glow paint thoroughly.
    - Apply a thin first coat, holding spray about 6–8 inches away or using smooth brush strokes.
    - Wait 10–15 minutes between coats.
    - Repeat for 2–3 coats for maximum luminosity.

4. Seal the stones

    - Once paint is fully cured, spray or brush on a clear concrete sealer to protect against weather and wear.
    - Allow sealer to dry completely before handling.

Method 2: Mixing Glow Powder into Concrete

1. Prepare concrete mix

    - Empty your bag of ready-mix concrete into a wheelbarrow or bucket.

    - Add glow powder at a ratio of roughly 15% glow powder to 85% concrete by volume (e.g., 1.5 gal powder to 8.5 gal concrete).

2. Add water and combine

    - Pour in water gradually, mixing until a sludge-like consistency is reached.
    - Avoid overly wet mixes to prevent settling issues.

3. Mold and cure

    - Lightly coat molds with petroleum jelly for easy release.
    - Fill molds to a consistent depth, tapping to remove air bubbles.
    - Let stones dry undisturbed in a warm, dry area for at least 24 hours.

4. Demold and finish

    - Gently remove stones from molds once fully hardened.
    - Smooth any rough edges if desired, then seal

Stone Circles

My last idea as an accessory in your *Garden for the Dead* is a stone circle. I am currently slowly building one on the west part of my property as the west is the direction of the ancestors. At the largest stone I have forget-me-nots growing. Part remembrance, part ritualistic, and part my salute to the TV show *Outlander*!

Stone circles in many prehistoric cultures were intimately tied to burial and ancestor veneration. Archaeological excavations have revealed that in a number of Late Neolithic and Early Bronze Age rings, cremated and inhumed human remains lie within or immediately around the stone settings, indicating their use as communal cemeteries and memorial sites rather than purely astronomical observatories. For three weeks in April/May 2023, I visited stone circles in Ireland, England, and Scotland. CHANGED MY LIFE!

Beyond serving as burial grounds, the very permanence of stone was symbolically charged—standing monoliths embodied the eternal presence of the dead and marked liminal thresholds between life and the spirit world.

Integrating a Stone Circle into a Garden for the Dead

Creating a stone circle in a funerary or memorial garden brings ancient symbolism, architectural drama, and a contemplative focal point for visitors. Below are the steps and considerations.

1. Concept and Symbolism

- A circle has no beginning or end, symbolizing the cycle of life, death, and rebirth.

- In many megalithic traditions, stone circles mark liminal spaces and portals—thresholds between the living realm and the spirit world.

- The open center invites small rituals, silent meditation, or group remembrance ceremonies.

2. Site Selection and Orientation

- Choose firm, level ground or a gently sloping knoll. Avoid waterlogged soils that could shift heavy stones.

- Align the circle's center-axis to sunrise on the solstice or to a notable lunar event for added mystical resonance.

- Frame the circle with existing trees, ruins, or garden features so it feels "discovered" rather than artificially imposed.

3. Stones: Selection and Preparation

- Material Types: Slate or bluestone for a dark, somber palette. Sandstone or limestone for weathered, age-worn surfaces.

- Aim for 6–10 standing stones (monoliths) ranging from 2–5 feet tall. Irregular, hand-hewn edges enhance the ancient feel.

- Lightly distress new stones with acid wash or sand-blasting. Encourage moss and lichen growth by misting with a moss slurry.

- Space evenly, or cluster pairs for an asymmetrical, "ruined" arrangement.

- Leave one or two gaps to suggest a broken portal or entrance.

4. Plants and Accents

- Underplanting: Black mondo grass and *Ajuga reptans* 'Black Scallop' for midnight-dark groundcover. White Anemone or ghost orchid (*Epipogium aphyllum*) for spectral contrast.

- Accent Features: A shallow, dark reflecting pool at the circle's center. A single, wrought-iron bench just outside the ring for silent vigil.

- Sound Elements: Hang wind chimes at one opening in the circle so passing breezes "sing" into the sacred space.

5. Ritual and Usage

- Personal Remembrance: Encourage visitors to place small offerings—feathers, stones, or handwritten notes—at the base of each monolith.

- Group Ceremonies: Use the open center for candlelit vigils, guided memorial services, or small musical performances (soft harp, singing bowls).

- Silent Meditation: The circle can serve as a quiet zone: phones off, voices lowered, attention focused inward.

6. Seasonal Dynamics and Maintenance

- Spring/Summer: Let ferns and moss flourish between stones. Trim back vigorous vines to prevent overpowering the monoliths.

- Autumn/Winter: Allow fallen leaves to rest in the circle; their decomposition adds fertility and deepens the sense of natural cycle.

Death Witchcraft:
Gardens for Ghosts, Spellwork, and Magick

Now that we just discussed stone circles and you are contemplating where to put one on your property, you are all warmed up to read more about magick, spellwork, and death witchcraft!

Death witchcraft is a branch of modern witchcraft that centers on the transformative power of death, dying, and endings. It views death not as a finality but as a threshold that can be crossed in both literal and symbolic ways. Practitioners work with the energy of decay and renewal, forging relationships with departed spirits, underworld deities, and the unseen forces that guide souls. By embracing these liminal spaces, death witches learn to navigate change, grief, and personal rebirth with intention and respect.

At its heart, death witchcraft rests on the belief that endings seed new beginnings. Honoring the dead involves ritual offerings, ancestral altars, and ceremonies that ease spirits onward. Symbolic deaths—such as shedding old habits or phases of life—function as potent rites of passage, clearing stagnant energy and making way for transformation. By integrating literal and metaphorical death work, practitioners cultivate resilience and deeper self-understanding.

Common practices blend together spirit communication and ancestor veneration. A death witch might begin a session by calling on specific spirits for insight, using tools like tarot cards, pendulums, or a spirit board to receive messages. Working with deities and psychopomps is a cornerstone of this path. Many death witches invoke gods like Hades, Anubis, Persephone, or Hecate to guide souls and protect the living during ritual journeys. Psychopomp and death walking practices focus on escorting newly deceased spirits to the afterlife. Some may also work as death doulas. Seasonal observances—most notably Samhain—offer natural portals when the veil between worlds thins, though lunar and equinox alignments can also anchor these workings year-round.

Gardens for the Dead Ritual and Spellwork

Your garden is a magickal tool! The more you work in it, spend time in it, and cultivate it, the stronger it gets! Your garden can become a living altar—an ever-evolving tool that honors departed loved ones, beckons chthonic energies, and channels healing through the cycles of life and death. Below is step-by-step ritual for crafting a *Garden for the Dead* and weaving potent spellwork into every seed, leaf, flower, tree, and stem.

1. Set Your Intent

A Book of Mirrors is a witch's personal development journal—a private space where you record your inner reflections, magical experiences, and spiritual insights as they occur. Unlike a Book of Shadows, which serves as a reference for spells, correspondences, and ritual recipes, the Book of Mirrors is entirely unique to each practitioner and focuses on self-examination, intuition-building, and the evolution of your craft. Begin by answering these questions in a journal or Book of Mirrors to crystallize your purpose:

- What is the heart of this garden? What type of garden? (Mourning, ancestral communication, necromancy, memorialization, etc.)
- Who or what will this space serve? A specific ancestor, a loved one in spirit (ghost), the forgotten dead, a spirit guide, a death deity such as Hades, Anubis, or Hecate, etc.
- Where will you locate it? Consider the Western quadrant of your yard or indoor altar (for a cemetarium) for ancestral alignment.
- Which plants will you choose and why?
- What landscape ideas will you utilize?
- What additional accessories do you choose?
- What outcome do you desire? Open a dialogue, release grief, charge a sacred space, spirit communication, etc.

Write down a concise intention statement—one sentence that captures your highest aim—and revisit it throughout the process.

2. Gather Your Tools

Collect everything you'll need before you begin:

- Plants, seeds, or bulbs
- Quality soil and compost
- Gardening tools (trowel, gloves, watering can)
- Containers or raised beds if you're not planting directly in the ground
- Candles (black for endings, white for guidance)
- Offering bowls or vials for libations (wine, milk, oil)
- Sea Salt or Himalayan Salt
- Smoke-cleansing materials (dried sage, cedar, or mugwort bundles)
- Sound-cleansing tools (bells, chimes, singing bowls)
- Protective crystals (obsidian, smoky quartz)
- Journal, pen, and small shovel or trowel for burying petitions
- Tarot Deck or Oracle Deck

3. Establish Sacred Ground

Choose a quiet spot where you can work undisturbed. Mark the perimeter with:

- A ring of smooth river stones or edging pavers
- A salt circle

Arrange a small table or stump near your planting area as an altar for offerings and ritual tools.

4. Cleanse the Space

Before touching soil or lighting candles, purify the area to clear old energies:

- Light a smoke bundle and walk counterclockwise around the garden's perimeter, letting the smoke drift into corners. When you want to banish, break down, or clear unwanted energy, you move widdershins—that is, counterclockwise. This unravels stagnant or negative currents and sends them away. It symbolically "undoes" what's been done. In most Western esoteric and folk traditions, widdershins is the motion of banishment, purification, and release.

225

- Ring a bell or chime three times at each cardinal point.
- Play a singing bowl or chime for 30–60 seconds to dissolve stagnant energy.

Set your intention aloud: "I clear this ground for sacred work with the spirits and deities of death."

5. Cast Your Circle of Protection Clockwise

Creating energetic boundaries ensures respectful, focused work. One elemental method:

1. Face East (Air). Visualize gusts swirling around you. Say: "Element of Air, I call to you."

2. Turn South (Fire). Feel warmth and crackling flames. Say: "Element of Fire, I call to you."

3. Face West (Water). Imagine streams and waves flowing near your feet. Say: "Element of Water, I call to you."

4. Face North (Earth). Sense solid rock and fertile soil. Say: "Element of Earth, I call to you."

5. Look up to the sky, arms outstretched (Spirit). Feel a surge of energy come down from the heavens, stars, sun, and moon. Say: "Oh great spirit, I call to you."

6. Still facing North, root your awareness into the earth. Draw a pillar of white light up through your feet, filling the circle. Say: "By earth, air, fire, water, and spirit combined, I cast this circle of protection and purpose. Three by three this circle is now cast so mote it be."

Remain within your circle until you close the circle.

6. Invoke Chthonic Deities and Ancestors

With your circle established, open a dialogue with the powers of the Underworld and your familial spirits:

- Pour a small libation of wine or honey onto an altar plate.

- Speak your offerings aloud: "Hecate, guide of crossroads, join me here. Ancestor [Name], I honor your presence."

- If you have photographs or personal tokens, place them beside candles.

- Allow a moment of silence, breathing deeply as you feel their responses.

7. Perform Your Spellwork

Customize your ritual to match your intent:

- Write your grief, question, or petition on a scrap of paper. Concentrate on its energy as you fold it.

- Bury the paper beneath your chosen plant or in a small offering pit, consecrating it as you press the soil with your fingertips.

- Recite chants, blessings, or invocations that resonate with your purpose— for example: "Through root and soil, death and birth, I plant this seed to heal the earth."

- Another option is to create a Sepulcher-Seed Burial. Write your intention—release of grief, ancestral petition, protection—and tuck the paper into seed-filled eggshells or hollow gourds. Plant the shells in your garden. As the seeds germinate, they "sprout" your spell into the living world to manifest.

- Meditate or enter a trance, envisioning the roots of the plants drawing ancestral wisdom upward into the living world.

- If you wish to speed transformation, perform this work under a waning moon; for new beginnings, choose a waxing phase.

- Feel free to choose a tarot card or oracle card for a message.

8. Tend the Garden/Raise Energy

After your spellwork, raise energy to feed your spell. We raise the energy with the act of creating the garden, cultivating the garden, and working in the garden. This is when you can rake, plant seeds, water, weed, mulch, transplant, etc. Gardening is magick. Spellwork continues with every act of care:

- Each time you till, weed, or water, speak your intention softly to the soil.

- Sprinkle ashes of incense or charcoal around the base of plants to honor endings that fuel new life.

- Place small offerings—coffee grounds, salt, flower petals, compost, egg shells,—at the plant's root every dark/new moon.

9. Close the Circle Counterclockwise

When your ritual concludes, release the energies with gratitude:

1. Face the Sky: "Spirit, I thank you for your power. I release you."
2. Face North: "Earth, thank you for your strength. I release you."
3. Face West: "Water, thank you for your flow. I release you."
4. Face South: "Fire, thank you for your transformation. I release you."
5. Face East: "Air, thank you for your clarity. I release you."
6. Return North: "Spirit, I release this circle back to the earth. The circle is open but never broken."

Extinguish candles mindfully, imagining the flames carrying thanks to the otherworld.

10. Offerings and Aftercare

To deepen your bond and sustain the garden's magic:

- Leave offerings of tears (small glass vial), a drop of your blood (sterile pinprick on paper), or libations (pomegranate juice, wine, mead, honey, incense) at your altar on a regular basis.

- Journal shifts in dreams, synchronicities, or messages from spirits.

- Recharge the circle at each major sabbat (the most important are when the veils are thinnest at Samhain and Beltane) or quarterly. You can also recharge every 28 days on the new moon/dark moon, as that is associated with death and dying, as it symbolizes the dark void before rebirth. As the moon vanishes from the sky, it invites us to release what no longer serves: old habits, painful memories, and stagnant energies. This liminal phase also resonates with the underworld's quiet power.

- As plants wither, harvest and dry herbs for spell bags or incense, transforming endings into new charms. Ideas for using the plants you grow and harvest are below.

By integrating these steps, your *Garden for the Dead* becomes more than a plot of earth—it transforms into a living, breathing portal where the realms of the living and the dead converge in mutual respect and healing.

Dedicating the Garden of the Dead

Once your garden is created, it is time to dedicate it to your ghost (loved one in spirit), deity, or ancestor. I suggest following a 3-part ritual of cleansing, consecrating, and dedicating.

1. Cleansing the Ground

Preparing the soil physically and spiritually ensures old, stagnant energies are swept away before inviting the dead.

- Timing • Perform between Samhain (Oct 31–Nov 1) or the next Dark Moon, when veils thin in folklore.
- Physical Clearing • Remove weeds, fallen leaves, broken twigs; rake in spirals outward to symbolically draw impurities up. • Turn soil gently with a fork or spade—just enough to "wake" it without disturbing burial layers.
- Spiritual Purification • Cast a circle of sea salt or burnt ash around the perimeter to repel unwanted spirits and energies. • Smudge the entire garden with smoke of mugwort, rosemary, or common folk's sage—walk counterclockwise, letting the smoke drift into every nook. • If near running water, sprinkle well water or rainwater gathered at midnight or moon water, invoking the cleansing flow of ancestral streams.

2. Consecrating the Garden

Consecration dedicates the space to ancestors and protective spirits, marking it as hallowed ground.

- Casting the Sacred Boundary
    - Using an athame, wand, or hawthorn staff, trace a circle or spiral from east to south to west to north, returning to east.
    - At each quarter, face that direction, sprinkle consecrated water or herbal oil, and speak an invocation: "By Sky and Sea, Earth and Flame, I hail the watchful dead. This ground I make sacred, hallowed by their name."
- Calling the Guardians • In each direction, call the Four Winds or Celtic Four Treasures (Sky, Sea, Land, Underworld) alongside household spirits or clan ancestors. • Visualize a ring of ancestral light rising from the soil, binding the space in a web of remembrance.
- Sealing the Consecration • Plant four memorial stones—one at each compass point—anointed with elderflower oil or salt, inscribed with a family rune or name or sigil. • Offer a libation (milk, mead, wine, or black tea) poured over a central stone or bench, sealing the vow of protection and remembrance.

3. Dedicating to the Dead

Dedication transforms the garden into an active memorial and meeting place for souls and spirits.

- Take time to define exactly why you wish to dedicate this garden to this spirit. Are you seeking guidance, expressing gratitude, or forging an ongoing bond? State a concise statement of intent out loud.
- Seasonal Offerings (Gifts): Lay out bread, cakes, shellfish, or roasted venison—foods of both hearth and tomb in folk tales—on a low stone altar. • Scatter marigold petals or yarrow—plants traditionally said to guide souls—along flagstone paths or around plantings. Ancestral spirits may welcome home-cooked bread or family mementos.
- Planting Memorial Herbs: Sow calendula (pot marigold) around the stones; plant rosemary, yew sprigs, or autumn crocus in drifts to draw

ancestral presence. • Place living memorials—ash, elder, or rowan saplings—at compass points, their roots linking you to Celtic Otherworld lore.

- Final Invocation: Light a single black or dark purple candle at dusk. Stand in silence until the flame casts ancestral shadows. • Speak your dedication: "Spirits of kin and kind, dwell here among these living roots. Teach us, guard us, walk these paths until veils renew." • Let the candle burn for a half hour, then extinguish it with earth (don't snuff)—returning it to the ground it consecrates.

Beyond the Ritual:

- Maintain the garden through Imbolc (Feb 1) and Beltane (May 1) with fresh offerings or new plantings.
- Invite family and friends each Samhain to leave tokens—ribbons, feathers, written prayers—to strengthen communal bonds.
- Keep a spirit log: record dreams or signs you perceive in the garden, deepening your dialogue with the dead.

Magickal Uses for Harvested Herbs and Flowers in Death Witchcraft

The following are ideas on how to use the herbs and flowers you grow in your Garden for death-centered spellcraft and spirit work. Each method invites the energies of ancestors, chthonic deities, or the restless dead while offering layers of symbolic and practical power.

1. Offerings for the Dead, Ancestors, and Chthonic Deities

- Select herbs and flowers traditionally linked to the Underworld— marigold, yarrow, mugwort, rosemary, rue, etc. and leave in offering bowls or on your altar.

- Scatter petals or leaves in a spiral atop graves or around a home altar to guide spirits back to the world of the living.

- Burn small bundles as loose incense or in a charcoal brazier; let the smoke carry your intentions downward.

- After the ritual, gather any unburned remnants and bury them at a crossroads, inviting continued communion.

2. Burning as Incense

- Create custom incense blends for funerary rites: base of frankincense or myrrh for purification, plus powdered yew or juniper for protection. Include any of the other plants you are growing in your garden of the dead.

- Mix finely ground herbs with a resin binder like charcoal dust.

- Offer smoke to deities of the dead by wafting it clockwise around headstones or ancestral portraits.

- Store in airtight jars to preserve potency and charge each batch under a waning moon.

3. Brewing Death Teas

- Combine any of the following: mugwort, damiana, chamomile, yarrow, hops, blue lotus, rosemary, clary sage, and a pinch of dried rose petals for dream-work and spirit communication.

- Steep herbs in boiling water for 10–15 minutes; sip at dusk or just before divination to open psychic channels.

- Use leftover tea as an offering—pour into a shallow bowl on your death altar, calling forth ancestors through taste and scent. You can also use leftover tea to water the plants in your Necromancy Garden.

4. Mixing into Gravesites or Graveyard Dirt

- Harvest topsoil from consecrated burial grounds and mix in your own blend of dirt with crushed memorial herbs (rosemary, thyme, etc).

- Leave a small pile of this "gravesoil" by your ritual circle; use it in necromantic spells or anoint candles.

5. Bouquets on Gravesites and Funeral Floral Arrangements

- Weave a bouquet of any of the flowers discussed in this book.

- Tie with black ribbon or twine; place on a headstone at twilight to honor the fallen.

- For funeral rites, integrate white lilies (rest), yarrow (protection), and night-blooming jasmine (spirit flight).

- Encourage mourners to pluck a bloom as a keepsake—each petal sealed in a letter or tucked into a pocket.

6. Protective Charms Against Unwelcome Spirits

- Stitch small pouches from black or deep purple cloth; fill with dried petals from the black colored flowers.

- Carry the charm in your coat pocket when wandering through old cemeteries or atop burial mounds.

- Anoint the outside of the pouch with a drop of salt-infused oil to reinforce its warding power.

- Replace the herbs every Samhain, offering the spent material to your ancestral altar.

7. Infusing Oils

- Macerate dried flower petals in a neutral oil (olive, sweet almond) for 4–6 weeks under a waning moon.

- Strain and use this "Mourner's Oil" to anoint ritual tools, candles, or the body of a death-doula client during bedside vigils.

- Label each bottle with moon phase and intended use—for example: "Anointing of the Departed"

8. Crafting Beads for Malas, Rosaries, or Memento Mori Jewelry

- Pulverize a selection of dried herbs and flower petals and mix into natural clay.

- Roll into small beads, poke a hole in them using a needle, bake or air-dry until firm, then string on black cord alongside jasper or onyx "death stones."

- Each mala lap becomes a mantra for release: with every bead count, honor a different ancestor or spirit guide.

- Wear close to the heart as a living talisman that bridges life and death.

9). Graveyard Oil

Ingredients:

- ½ cup carrier oil (olive, sweet almond, or jojoba)
- 1 tbsp dried mugwort (Artemisia vulgaris)
- 1 tbsp dried wormwood (Artemisia absinthium)
- 1 tbsp dried graveyard thyme (Thymus serpyllum)
- 1 tsp dried patchouli leaves (Pogostemon cablin)
- 5 drops vetiver essential oil (Vetiveria zizanoides)
- 5 drops cypress essential oil (Cupressus sempervirens)

Step 1: Cleanse and Prepare

1. Sanitize a small glass jar and lid with hot water or by passing a flame under the rim.

2. Set your intention: hold the jar in both hands and visualize drawing ancestral or underworld energies into your offering.

Step 2: Infuse and Charge

1. Combine the carrier oil and dried herbs in the jar.

2. Seal tightly and shake gently while speaking a dedication such as: "By shadowed earth and silent stone, I bind this oil to worlds unknown."

3. Can charge under the dark moon.

4. Optional cemetery charge: bury the sealed jar at the foot of a permitted, undisturbed grave (or in a consecrated plot) from dusk until dawn. You can also bury it in your *Garden for the Dead* as all soil and dirt has energy.

Step 3: Strain and Finalize

1. After 24–48 hours of charging (burial or simple moonlight exposure), retrieve and unseal the jar.

2. Strain the oil through fine muslin or a coffee filter into a clean container, pressing the herb matter to release every drop.

3. Discard plant remnants respectfully (bury them or burn them in ritual).

4. Add vetiver and cypress essential oils, then seal and gently invert several times to mix.

Usage and Storage:

- Anoint candles, ritual tools, or pulse points (wrists, throat) before graveyard workings, ancestor altars, or shadow magic.

- Store in a cool, dark place. Replace every 6–12 months to maintain potency.

Safety and Ethics:

- Do not ingest. For external use only.
- Patch test for skin sensitivity.

- Only bury the jar where allowed—never disturb human remains or break any local regulations.
- Always approach cemetery magic with respect, clear intention, and gratitude.

10. Cooking into Food Offerings

- Bake seed-cakes using ground poppy seed, calendula petals, and honey to leave at an ancestor's place at the table (the Dumb Supper tradition).

- Infuse funeral breads with rosemary sprigs for remembrance and thyme for purification.

- Serve at memorial gatherings—each slice is a blessing for souls passing back into flesh.

- Reserve a portion for birds or animals near burial mounds, trusting nature to carry your offering onward.

11. Sewing into Poppets or Spirit Dolls

- Embed dried herbs and flowers into the stuffing of a small cloth doll, symbolizing a specific deceased soul.

- Stitch with black thread and embroider its face with a symbol meaningful to that person—runebinding or ancestral sigils.

- During Samhain, drape the poppet over a candlelit altar; as it weathers, so too may it carry messages between worlds.

- Bury the doll near an old tree when finished, returning its essence to Earth's cycle.

12. Ritual Baths for Divination and Death Rites

- Scatter dried lavender, rose petals, mugwort, and wormwood into a warm bath to thin the veil before hedge-crossing or spirit-doula work.

- Add a handful of sea salt and a few drops of graveyard-infused oil for an extra boundary-breaking effect.

- Soak at midnight; meditate on your ancestors' faces as you imagine their presence swirling in the water.

- Use the same water to wash ritual tools, consecrating them for further necromantic practice.

13. Drying into Amulets

- Press and dry single blooms or flowers between book pages; once brittle, encase in resin pendants.

- Fill tiny bottles with seeds, dried herbs, and flower petals and then seal with wax.

- Wear these as amulets during Séances or while tending to burial grounds to keep unwanted energies at bay.

- Recharge under the new moon—hold to the earth and whisper your protective intent three times.

14). Crafting Herbal Death Candles

- Melt beeswax or a black-tinted vegan wax and stir in finely crushed herbs and petals.

- Pour into pillar or taper molds, then press additional whole petals onto the warm surface.

- Carve the name or initials of the deceased (or a sigil) into the cooled candle's side.

- Anoint the finished candle with your graveyard-infused oil, charging it under a new or waning moon.

- Burn the candle during vigils, funerary rites, or Samhain observances—let the herb-laden smoke carry messages to the dead.

15). Mourning Jar

A Mourning Jar is a jar-spell crafted to help you navigate grief, honor a lost loved one, and invite healing energies into your heart. By combining personal tokens, herbs, and ritual actions, you create a living talisman that holds space for sorrow and transformation. Place it in your memorial garden or mourning garden or on your altar.

Purpose and When to Use It:

- To hold and transmute raw grief into acceptance
- To honor an ancestor or recently departed soul
- To provide a focal tool for nightly or weekly grief-working meditations
- To gradually release sorrow by emptying and cleansing the jar over time

Ingredients:

- A small glass jar with a tight-sealing lid
- A pinch of sea salt or black salt (cleansing)
- A few chips of onyx or obsidian (grounding)
- Personal memento—photo, note, scrap of clothing, handwritten name on paper
- A dark candle (black or deep purple) for sealing
- Blackthorn bark: Protection on spirit journeys
- Rosemary: Remembrance and purification
- Mugwort: Dreamwork and spirit contact
- Lavender: Calming and emotional soothing
- Yew needles: Transition and rebirth
- Bone or shell: Physical link to the dead
- Onyx or obsidian: Grounding and shielding
- Frankincense: Soul-lifting incense smoke

- Your tears
- Hair of the deceased (optional)
- Cremains (optional)
- Teeth (optional)
- Graveyard dirt or Graveyard Oil (optional)

1. Cleanse the jar. Wash out any old contents under running water. Smudge inside and out with sage, palo santo, or mugwort.

2. Set your intention. Hold the empty jar and speak aloud: "I dedicate this vessel to hold my grief and guide me toward peace." Write the name of the departed or a grief-affirming phrase ("I allow my tears to flow toward healing") on a slip of paper.

3. Layer your ingredients.

   1. Begin with a thin layer of sea salt at the jar's base.

   2. Add the grounding stones.

   3. Tuck in the personal mementos and folded name-slip.

   4. Layer herbs: rosemary for memory, lavender for calm, mugwort for visions, yew for transformation.

   5. Place the blackthorn bark or bone/token on top.

4. Seal and anoint. Drip warm beeswax or candle wax around the lid's rim, locking in your intentions. Anoint the lid with a drop of frankincense resin, whispering, "May this smoke lift my sorrow to the ancestors above."

5. Charge the jar. Light your dark candle. Circle it around the jar three times, then set it beside the jar to burn safely. Meditate on the flame, visualizing grief transforming into a gentle, warming light within the jar.

Activation and Aftercare:

- Keep your jar on your altar or beside your bed. You can also put it in your garden.

- Each night, hold it, breathe deeply, and speak a short mantra ("I am held by love beyond death").

- As grief eases, remove a single herb sprig or stone weekly—thank it, then bury it in earth or scatter it in running water.

- When the jar is empty, rinse it, re-smudge, and refill for continued work, or retire it under the new moon by burying it at a crossroads.

16). Funeral Rites and Memorialization with Your Herbs and Flowers

Across civilizations, fresh herbs and flowers have long been woven into funerary rites. They purify the space, guide the departed, and bring comfort to the living. Harnessing the energy of plants you've grown and nurtured invites a deeply personal, meaningful tribute for those who've passed.

Sachet Handouts: Fill small muslin bags or cheese cloth bundles with dried herbs and flowers. Give them to mourners to carry through the funeral or memorial ceremony as personal talismans of cleansing and remembrance.

Petal Release Ceremony: Invite guests to scatter petals at the gravesite or into flowing water. The drifting petals form a gentle pathway for the spirit and signify collective love, sending the deceased on their journey.

Pressed Flower Bookmarks: Press and dry petals and sprigs between weighted books, then laminate between clear sheets for bespoke bookmarks that friends and family can use daily. You may wish to include your loved one's obituary on it.

Pressed Flower Art and Framed Collages: Arrange flattened petals and small sprigs into meaningful shapes—initials, hearts, or abstract patterns—then frame as wall art that tells your loved one's story.

Herbal/Floral Grave Blessing: Steep petals in hot water, let cool, then gently sprinkle on gravesites or urns as a blessing.

Floral Smoke Cleansing: Blend dried herbs and petals in a heat-safe bowl. Can also use a mini cauldron with charcoal. As the smoke rises, visual its dual power to purify and to guide the departed into the next realm.

17). Using Your Herbs and Flowers for Samhain Rituals

Samhain marks the Witch's new year when the veil between worlds is thinnest and ancestor energies are closest. Herbs and flowers amplify release, divination, and honoring the dead during this transitional sabbat.

Spirit-Powered Incense Blend: Mix equal parts mugwort, bay leaf, and rosemary. Burn in a fireproof bowl before divination to thin the veil and call ancestors.

Ancestor Altar Decoration: Arrange fresh lavender, marigold garlands, and rosemary sprigs around ancestral photos. Scatter chrysanthemum heads to form a protective circle.

Circle of Release: Scatter dried marigold or chrysanthemum petals around a candle in counterclockwise motion. Speak what you wish to release as the petals fall into the flame.

18). Using Your Herbs and Flowers in Communicating with the Dead

Using aromatic botanicals can open channels to benevolent spirits and ancestors, inviting clear messages and honoring presence.

Top Botanicals for Spirit Contact:

- Mugwort helps induce vivid, prophetic dreams and spirit visions when placed under the pillow or in a sachet.

- Yarrow drives away malignant entities while strengthening psychic awareness; carry a small pouch during séances.

- Angelica offers purification and protection; hang bundles at doors or windows to safeguard spirit work.

- Rue heightens emotional receptivity; add sprigs to ritual smoke bundles to invite gentle spirit voices.

- Bay Laurel opens ancestral gates; tuck leaves into offerings or lay under altar cloths when calling the dead.

- Cedar calms and uplifts; burn as smoke to honor spirits and clear space before contact.

- Tobacco serves as a classic ancestral offering; sprinkle dried leaves around an offering dish or burn sparingly outdoors.

- Frankincense and Myrrh resin purify and sanctify, guiding benevolent spirits into your sacred space.

Dream Sachet: Fill a small cloth bag with mugwort, yarrow, and lavender. Place beneath your pillow to receive nocturnal messages.

Spirit Smoke Bundle: Bind fresh rue, cedar, and angelica into a tight bundle. Light until it smolders and waft smoke around your workspace to invite spirits.

Offering Dish: Arrange bay leaves, rosemary sprigs, and a pinch of tobacco on a dedicated plate. Add a drop of frankincense resin for resonance.

Ritual Tea: Brew a gentle infusion of mugwort and chamomile. Sip quietly before a séance to calm nerves and open intuitive channels.

19). Funeral Candle Dressing

Dress black or dark-red candles with death-potent petals.

Anointing (or "dressing") a candle infuses it with your intention, magnifying the energy of your spell or ritual. Below is a clear, step-by-step guide to prepare your candle with oil, herbs, and focused will.

1. Cleanse the Candle: Remove any residual energies by passing the candle through incense smoke or wiping it with a bit of salt water.

2. Prepare Your Oil: Blend a few drops of essential oil into your carrier oil—never apply undiluted essential oils directly to the wax. You can also anoint your candle with Graveyard Oil.

3. Anointing Directions: There are two widely used methods; choose the one that fits your tradition or intuition:

- Drawing Energy In: Rub oil from the base up toward the wick (or from both ends toward the center). • Visualize your desire flowing into your life with each stroke.

- Banishing or Sending Energy Out: Rub oil from the wick down toward the base (or from the center out to both ends). Envision negativity or obstacles being pushed away as you work.

4. Carve Your Intent (Optional) Use a toothpick or small knife to inscribe names, symbols, or single words into the candle's surface. This physically "locks in" your petition before oiling begins.

5. After the candle is dressed in oil, roll it in a selection of dried herbs associated with death and dying.

6. Charge and Light the Candle: Hold the candle between your palms, speak or silently chant your intention, then place it on a heat-safe holder and light it.

20). Death Dust for Thresholds

Create a powdered blend to ward off unwanted entities or seal doorways.

- Ingredients: Ground herbs and flowers, black salt.

- Application: Sprinkle a thin line across door sills or around grave markers to protect and contain.

21). Necromantic Grief Cord Binding

Necromantic cord binding is a powerful ritual for sealing endings—whether grief, death, or the loss of something or someone. Each component carries symbolic weight, and every knot you tie anchors intent into the earth.

Materials:

- A Black Cord represents the void, protection, death, and dying. Choose a sturdy natural fiber (cotton or hemp) about 3–5 ft long.

- Baneful Plant Petals (Use with Caution) symbolize the threshold between life and death. Handle with gloves on and never ingest. Dried black or deep-purple petals work best.

- Lavender Sprigs add purification, calm, and gentle healing to balance the potent darkness of nightshade.

- Rose Hips embody life force and rebirth; they nourish the cord's magic with restorative energy.

Step-by-Step Binding Ritual

1. Light a white or black candle and cast a protective circle clockwise

2. Lay out the black cord on an altar or flat surface. Place small piles of baneful petals, lavender, and rose hips along its length at roughly equal intervals.

3. Knot magic channels intention through the simple act of tying. For grief, each knot becomes a vessel carrying a specific sorrow, binding it with purpose until you're ready to release. Use 7 knots to include the expanded 7 stages of grief

    1. Shock/Disbelief – Knot 1
    2. Denial – Knot 2
    3. Anger – Knot 3
    4. Bargaining – Knot 4
    5. Depression – Knot 5
    6. Renewal/Hope – Knot 6
    7. Closure/Transformation – Knot 7

    Total knots: 7

4. As you tie each knot:

5. Speak its focus aloud ("With this knot I seal my anger.")

6. Press in a pinch of baneful petals into the knot.

7. After every two or three knots, weave in a single lavender sprig and a few rose hips. This alternation ensures the cord balances dark and light energies, preventing stagnation.

8. Hold the finished cord between your palms and visualize a white or violet light flowing through it. Speak a final blessing: "By death's door and life's return, this cord holds fast the endings I burn."

9. Burying the Cord: Choose a spot beneath a memorial tree, at the base of a Garden of the Dead altar, or alongside a freshly planted remembrance flower.

   • Dig a hole deep enough that the cord is fully covered but accessible if you later choose to renew or reverse the spell.
   • As you lower the cord, say: "Into earth's embrace, these bindings rest. Let endings be honored and transformations blessed."

10. At each new moon or quarter Sabbat, return to the burial site. Whisper thanks or adjust knots if you feel new endings need sealing. Natural fibers will degrade over time. If the cord frays beyond recognition, you can exhume and rebury it in a new binding ritual.

Reversal Protocol: To release what you've bound—say, if grief has eased— dig up the cord and untie each knot widdershins, speaking words of freedom as you go. Bury or burn the remains respectfully.

Remember that the garden you cultivate is more than a collection of herbs, plants, and flowers—it's a living grimoire. Every seed sown, every plant tended, every flower harvested is potent magick. Use with care.

Conclusion

Now our journey has come to an end. We have traveled together through funerals and flowers, the Victorian era, seances, spirit communication, flowers for the dead, gardens for the dead, gardens literally made of the dead, garden care and design, macabre and morbid accessories, death witchcraft, spellwork, and the magick and power contained in the plants and herbs we grow.

As you stand at the threshold of your own *Garden of the Dead*, you'll notice it's more than just soil, plants, and stones—it's a living artwork of memory and renewal. Every carefully placed blossom, every weathered marker, and every whispered ritual you've woven into the landscape speaks volumes about love, loss, and the endless cycle that binds us all. In tending this space, you've carved out a sanctuary where grief finds gentle refuge, ancestral voices rustle through the leaves, and hope takes root beneath the surface.

Ground your practice in respect—of the dead, of the living, of yourself, and of the land itself—and you will find the *Garden of the Dead* transforming beneath your hands. May this *Garden of the Dead* continue to grow as a place of comfort, reflection, healing, and quiet celebration—proof that even in the face of final farewells, life persists in the most beautiful, unexpected ways. Thank you for allowing me to guide you on this journey of death and rebirth. Our grief is fertilizer for new life. Until we meet again…

The cycle of life and death unfolds in every season.

Journal Questions for Creating a Garden for a Ghost

Reflect on Personal Memories:

1. What is your fondest memory of your loved one in nature or a garden setting?
2. Which qualities of theirs—kindness, humor, resilience—do you most want to honor here?
3. How did they find comfort or joy outdoors, and how can that guide your garden's atmosphere?
4. Describe a moment when their presence felt especially nurturing or uplifting.
5. What scents, colors, or textures remind you most vividly of them?
6. If your loved one were a plant or flower, which would they be, and why?
7. What symbolic elements (earth, air, water, fire) resonate with their spirit?
8. How can you capture their element (ex: windchimes for air, stones for earth, bird bath for water, torches/lanterns for fire)?
9. Which cultural or family traditions might you weave into garden details or rituals?
10. How can seasonal changes reflect your ongoing relationship with their memory?
11. What inscriptions, quotes, songs, or poems capture their essence?
12. Where in your yard (or another special spot) feels most fitting for this tribute?
13. How large should the garden be to both honor them and feel manageable for you?
14. Which color palette feels aligned with their personality?

15. What types of pathways (stone, gravel, wood chips) invite reflection and ease of access?

16. How will you incorporate seating or gathering spaces for quiet contemplation or visits with others?

17. Which plants bloom around significant dates—birthdays, anniversaries, milestones?

18. Are there native or low-maintenance species that reflect their nature?

19. Which flowers or plants have scents that trigger happy memories?

20. How can you layer heights (groundcover, perennials, herbs, small trees) to symbolize life stages?

21. What time of day will you enjoy the garden most, and which plants thrive then?

22. What weekly or monthly garden ritual (watering, pruning, lighting a candle) will keep you connected?

23. How will you mark key anniversaries—planting bulbs, adding a new marker, holding a small gathering?

24. What journaling practice can you pair with garden visits to capture fresh insights or emotions?

25. How might you involve family or friends in garden upkeep as a shared remembrance?

26. What celebrations or ceremonies could you host here to honor milestones?

27. One year from now, what do you hope the garden looks and feels like?

28. How will you record the garden's evolution—photos, sketches, notes on growth?

29. In winter, when the garden rests, what elements (evergreens, stones, ornaments) will stand out?

30. How can you adapt the space annually to reflect both your healing and the garden's maturity?

31. What final words would you inscribe on a plaque or marker to capture your enduring love?

32. Anything else that is important to you?

33. Now visualize and imagine your loved one sitting in your garden…

Verus amor numquam moritur. Amor est aeterna rei.
Verus amor numquam moritur.

Love is eternal. True love never dies.

References

Phytognomonica – Giambattista della Porta (1588)

The Signature of All Things – Jakob Böhme (1621)

Complete Herbal – Nicholas Culpeper (mid-17th century)

A Modern Herbal – Maud Grieve (1931)

Stirpium Adversaria Nova – Rembert Dodoens (1583)

Handbook of Medicinal Herbs – Jim Duke (1985)

A Modern Herbal – Maud Grieve (1931)

The English Physician – Nicholas Culpeper (1653)

Native American Ethnobotany – Daniel Moerman (1998)

Folk-Medicine Field Studies – Ronald Buffin (various dates)

Rodale's Illustrated Encyclopedia of Perennials – Rodale Press (2000)

Folklore of Flowers – Raven Faery and Ivy (2014)

Blooms of Remembrance – *BloomsyBox Editorial Team*

The History and Traditions Behind Funeral Flowers – *My Funky Funeral*

The Use of Flowers in Funerals: Symbolism and Meaning – *Farewelling Editorial Team*

The Proto-Neolithic Cemetery in Shanidar Cave. Smithsonian Contributions to Anthropology, No. 9. Washington, D.C.: Smithsonian Institution Press, 1972. By Ralph S. Solecki

Victorian People – Asa Briggs

Victorian People and Ideas: A Companion for the Modern Reader – Richard D. Altick

Victorian England: Portrait of an Age – G. M. Young

The Victorians: A New History – A. N. Wilson

The Victorian City: Everyday Life in Dickens' London – Judith Flanders

Badass Ancestors: Finding Your Power with Ancestral Guides – Patti Wigington

Buckland's Book of Spirit Communications – Raymond Buckland

Morbid Magic: Death Spirituality and Culture from Around the World – Tomás Prower

Victorian Gardens – Caroline Holmes

The Victorian Flower Garden – Jane Loudon

The Victorian Garden – Christopher Thacker

The Victorian Kitchen Garden – Alan Davidson

Cultivating Paradise: A History of British Gardening – Roger Turner

The Doctrine of Signatures: A Defense of Theory in Medicine – Scott Milross

Mythology: Timeless Tales of Gods and Heroes – Edith Hamilton

The Power of Myth – Joseph Campbell

The World's Religions – Huston Smith

Drawing Down the Moon – Margot Adler

The Spiral Dance by Starhawk

Paganism: An Introduction to Earth-Centered Religions by Joyce and River Higginbotham

The Pagan Religions of the Ancient British Isles by Ronald Hutton

The Elements of Ritual by Maggie Hyde and Judy Grahn

Power of the Witch by Laurie Cabot

Living Wicca by Raymond Buckland

Theogony by Hesiod

The Iliad by Homer

The Odyssey by Homer

The Greek Myths by Robert Graves

Myths of Greece and Rome by E. M. Berens

The Library of Greek Mythology by Apollodorus (translated by Robin Hard)

Celtic Myths and Legends by Peter Berresford Ellis

Irish Fairy Tales by W. B. Yeats

Celtic Mythology by John Arnott MacCulloch

Day of the Dead: Día de los Muertos by Diane Hoyt-Goldsmith

The Skeleton at the Feast: The Day of the Dead in Mexico by Elizabeth Carmichael and Chloë Sayer

Mexican Day of the Dead: A Coast to Coast Celebration of la Muerte by Edward H. Spencer

Celebrate the Day of the Dead: Stories, Art, and Poetry by Diane Hoyt-Goldsmith

Death's Holiday: Celebrations of the Dead in the Americas by Jack Santino Calaveras

Treasury Of Egyptian Mythology: Classic Stories Of Gods, Goddesses, Monsters and Mortals – Donna Jo Napoli

Egyptian Mythology – Dale Hansen

Orishas: The Ultimate Guide To African Orisha Deities And Their Presence in Yoruba, Santeria, Voodoo, and Hoodoo, Along with an Explanation of Diloggun Divination – by Primasta

Hindu Mythology: An Illustrated Book Of Gods, Goddesses, And Sacred Stories Of India – Leo North

The Element Encyclopedia of Witchcraft by Judika Illes

Encyclopedia of Spirits: The Ultimate Guide to the Magic of Fairies, Genies, Demons, Ghosts, Gods and Goddesses by Judika Illes

The Curious World of Carnivorous Plants: A Comprehensive Guide to Their Biology and Cultivation by Wilhelm Barthlott, Stefan Porembski, Rudiger Seine, and Inge Theisen

The Savage Garden by Peter D'Amato

Growing Carnivorous Plants by Barry Rice

Pitcher Plants of the Americas by Stewart McPherson and Margaret Douglas

Pitcher Plants of the Old World Volume 1 by Stewart McPherson

Pitcher Plants of the Old World Volume 2 by Stewart McPherson

Kew – Rare Plants: The World's Unusual and Endangered Plants by Ed Ikin and Royal Botanic Gardens, Kew

Rare Plants: The Story of 40 of the World's Most Unusual and Endangered Plants by Ed Ikin

Botanical Stinkers: Foul-Smelling Plants by Karen Bradshaw

Pee-Yew!: The Stinkiest, Smelliest Animals, Insects, and Plants on Earth! by Mike Artell

Gothic Gardening: A Step-by-Step Guide to Cultivating a Mysterious, Elegant, and Darkly Beautiful Garden by Raven Blackthorne

The Goth Garden: The Mystery, Beauty, and Lore of Dark Gardening by Felicia Feaster

Evil Roots: Killer Tales of the Botanical Gothic by Daisy Butcher

Heirloom Plants: A Complete Compendium Of Heritage Vegetables, Fruits, Herbs and Flowers – Thomas Etty

Seeds of Deception: Exposing Industry and Government Lies About the Safety of the Genetically Engineered Foods You're Eating – Jeffrey M. Smith

Nature-Friendly Gardens: Native Plant Gardening For Birds, Bees and Butterflies: Lower Midwest – Jaret C. Daniel

A Guide to Deadly Herbs by Julie Gomez, Julie A Gomez, et al.

Botanical Curses and Poisons: The Shadow-Lives of Plants by Fez Inkwright

Death in the Garden: Poisonous Plants and Their Use Throughout History by Michael Brown |

Entering Hekate's Garden: The Magick, Medicine and Mystery of Plant Spirit Witchcraft by Cyndi Brannen

The Green Mysteries: An Occult Herbarium by Daniel A Schulke and Benjamin A Vierling

Pharmako Gnosis: Plant Teachers and the Poison Path by Dale Pendell

Plants of the Devil By Corinne Boyer (Three Hands Press, 2017)

Plants That Kill: A Natural History of the World's Most Poisonous Plants by Elizabeth A. Dauncey and Sonny Larsson

Plants That Can Kill: 101 Toxic Species to Make You Think Twice by Stacy Tornio

Poison: The History of Potions, Powders and Murderous Practitioners by Ben Hubbard and Sophie Hannah

The Book of Killer Plants: A Field Guide to Nature's Deadliest Creations by Dr. Kit Carlson

The Drunken Botanist by Amy Stewart

The Garden Crypt: Exploring the Other Side of Gardening by Nikki S. Phipps

The Language of Plants: A Guide to the Doctrine of Signatures by Julia Graves and Matthew Wood

The Poison Path Herbal: Baneful Herbs, Medicinal Nightshades, and Ritual Entheogens by Coby Michael

The Poison Garden by A. J. Banner

The Solanaceae: foods and poisons by M R Lee

The Witches' Ointment: The Secret History of Psychedelic Magic by Thomas Hatsis

Thirteen Pathways of Occult Herbalism by Daniel A Schulke

Veneficium: Magic, Witchcraft and the Poison Path by Daniel A. Schulke

Wicked Plants: The A-Z of Plants that Kill, Maim, Intoxicate and Otherwise Offend by Amy Stewart

Wild Witchcraft: Folk Herbalism, Garden Magic, and Foraging for Spells, Rituals, and Remedies

Death Walkers: Shamanic Psychopomps, Earthbound Ghosts, and Helping Spirits in the Afterlife Realm— by David Kowalewski

Dying and Death: Getting Rightly Prepared for the Inevitable by Beeke Joel and Christopher Bogosh

The Elisabeth Kübler-Ross Foundation https://www.ekrfoundation.org/elisabeth-kubler-ross/

Hospice Foundation of America. A Caregiver's Guide to the Dying Process.

Shamanic Guide to Death and Dying— by Kristin Madden

Marie Curie Foundation. Final Moments of Life.

The Pagan Book of Living and Dying by Starhawk and M. Macha

Entering the Summerland by Edain McCoy

All the Living and the Dead by Campbell, Hayley

Death Nesting: The Heart-Centered Practices of a Death Doula (Sacred Planet) Sacred Planet The Heart-Centered Practices of a Death Doula by Keppel, Anne-Marie and Wyatt, Karen

The Grief Deck: Rituals, Meditations, and Tools for Moving through Loss

The Beloved Dead: An Oracle for Divining Ancestral Wisdom by Paris, Carrie

The Egyptian Book of the Dead

Spiritual Perspectives on Death and Dying by Bernice Hill

Death and Dying, Life and Living by Charles A. Corr, Donna M. Corr, et al.

Death and Dying: A Sociological Introduction by Glennys Howarth

Your Guide to Cemetery Research by Sharon DeBartolo Carmack

Death by Shelley Kagan

Greening Death: Reclaiming Burial Practices and Restoring Our Tie to the Earth by Suzanne Kelly

The American Resting Place: Four Hundred Years of History through Our Cemeteries and Burial Grounds by Marilyn Yalom and Reid S. Yalom

Changing Landscapes: Exploring the growth of ethical, compassionate, and environmentally sustainable green funeral practices by Lee Webster

Prehistoric Stone Circles by Aubrey Burl

Death, Mourning, and Burial: A Cross-Cultural Reader by Antonius C. G. M. Robben

The Archaeology of Death and Burial (Volume 3) (Texas A&M University Anthropology Series) by Mike Parker Pearson

Being with the Dead: Burial, Ancestral Politics, and the Roots of Historical Consciousness by Hans Ruin

The Burial of the Dead by W. H. F. Basevi

Spirits, Seers and Séances: Victorian Spiritualism, Magic and the Supernatural by Steele Alexandra Douris

The Seance: Healing Messages from Beyond (Former Title: Seance: A Guide for the Living) by Suzane Northrop

Psychic Development for Beginners: A Practical Guide to Developing Your Intuition and Psychic Gifts by Emily Stroia

Psychic Witch: A Metaphysical Guide to Meditation, Magick and Manifestation by Mat Auryn and Devin Hunter

The History of Spiritualism by Sir Arthur Conan Doyle

The complete guide to the Ouija board: History, Theory, Practice, Psychology by Eleonora Zaupa and Sarah Costalunga

Necromancy, Ouija Boards and Spiritualism: Beginner's Guide by E.M. Fairchilde

Reunions: Visionary Encounters with Departed Loved Ones by Raymond Moody

The Prose Edda by Snorri Sturluson

The Poetic Edda translated by Lee M. Hollander

The Norse Myths by Kevin Crossley-Holland

Norse Mythology by Neil Gaiman

The Viking Spirit: An Introduction to Norse Mythology and Religion by Daniel

Norse Mythology: A Guide to Norse History, Gods, and Mythology by Finn D. Moore Blends archaeological context with colorful retellings. Moore covers the Nine Worlds, the Æsir and Vanir deities

Green Witchcraft: Folk Magic, Herb Craft, and Rituals by Ann Moura

Herbal Folk Lore by Margaret Roberts

Pagan Portals – Plant Spirit Healing by Paul Beyerl

Plant Folklore: 120 Stories by Connie L. Taylor

Enchanted Plants: A Treasury of Botanical Folklore and Magic by Varla Ventura

Floral Folklore: The Forgotten Tales Behind Nature's Most Enchanting Plants by Alison Davies

Folklore and Symbolism of Flowers, Plants and Trees by Ernst Lehner and Johanna Lehner

About the Author

Christina Wilke-Burbach, PhD, is a Spiritual/Transpersonal Psychologist, Anthropologist, Death Witch, Death Doula, Deathwalker, Psychopomp, Psychic, Poisoner, Occultist, Cemeterian, and works full-time in the Deathcare Industry. She is a High Priestess with The New York City Wiccan Family Temple, an ordained minister, and a Reiki Master Teacher.

Her specialty is working with the dead. She works exclusively with chthonic and Underworld Deities. Her ministry and craft focus on death and dying, guiding souls to the otherworld, facilitating communication and messages between the dead and the living as a medium, leading seances, paranormal investigations and clearings, facilitating death rites and funerals, helping people with their death wishes and death plans, placing the dead in their final resting space, writing obituaries, funeral flower arrangements and designing gardens for the dead.

Christina is also a Master Gardener, Herbalist, Certified Aromatherapist, Gardening Instructor, Botanical Artist, and Natural Perfumer, specializing in Poison Gardens, Heirloom Gardening, Gothic Gardening, Graveyard Gardening, Carnivorous Plants, and Gardening for the Dead. Christina has three decades of higher education and experience in psychology, spirituality, magick, the occult, and metaphysics. She holds a PhD in Health Psychology, a master's degree in Clinical Psychology, a bachelor's degree in Psychology, a bachelor's degree in Anthropology, and a minor in Sociology. She is also trained in Transpersonal Psychology, having studied with Stanislav Grof, MD, PhD—the founder of the field.

Her business is Mind, Soul, and Self LLC, based in the Midwestern United States. She offers individual appointments, readings, and consultations and specializes in shadow work, psychic development, death/dying, and mystical experiences. She teaches classes on a wide variety of topics, including gardening, herbalism, psychic development, divination, shadow work, energy work, the chakras, meditation, death and dying, dreamwork, witchcraft, astrology, and spirituality. She is the host of the podcast, *Garden Goth*, a show inspired by the Victorian era and the rise of Spiritualism, Seances, and the Occult. She is the host of the Radio show, *The Happy Death Show with Christina*, a death-positive show focusing on anything and everything that falls under the umbrella of death, dying, spirits, the afterlife, and beyond (on News for the Soul Broadcasting). She is also an author for THE GRAY paranormal magazine.

Visit Christina Wilke-Burbach online: linktr.ee/christina.wilke.burbach

www.ingramcontent.com/pod-product-compliance
Lightning Source LLC
Chambersburg PA
CBHW070548130626
46556CB00001B/65